Minute Book

COURT OF PLEAS AND QUARTER SESSIONS

LAWRENCE COUNTY, TENNESSEE

1818 - 1822

Compiled by:
Polly C. Warren

Southern Historical Press, Inc.
Greenville, South Carolina

This volume was reproduced
from a personal copy located in
the Publishers private library

All rights reserved. No part of this publication may be reproduced,
stored in a retrieval system, transmitted in any form, posted
on the web in any form or by any means without the
prior written permission of the publisher.

Please direct all correspondence and book orders to:
**SOUTHERN HISTORICAL PRESS, Inc.
1071 Park West Blvd.
Greenville, SC 29611**

Originally Published Columbia, TN 1981
ISBN #978-1-63914-695-6
Printed in the United States of America

INTRODUCTION

Becasue of my close association with Lawrence County, Tennessee, both from the standpoint of doing genealogical research and from personal family connections it is a pleasure for me to be able to reprint a book that I feel is a valuable aid to you, the researcher.

This book was first published in October, 1977 by two industrious ladies, Mrs. Marymaud Carter and Mrs. Viola Carpenter. It was printed at that time in a very limited quantity, and therefore was out of print in just a short while. I have recently acquired the reprint rights (along with their best wishes, I might add) to be able to offer this publication for sale on a little larger scale.

Following this introduction, you will find the original foreword and the explanations you will need to get the full benefit from this publication. Also included in this reprint that was not included in the original is a picture of the "Davy Crockett Courthouse" which stood in the city of Lawrenceburg from 1821 until 1905.

This and other publications concerning Lawrence County, Tennessee are available from me at the address below. Please feel free to write for a listing of the books that are available on this area.

                        Mrs. Polly C. Warren
                        Route 7, Box 264
                        Columbia, Tennessee 38401

FOREWORD

A private Act of the Tennessee General Assembly(1817) created the County of Lawrence. It was taken from territory South of Maury and Hickman and West of Giles Counties.

Sec.7 of said Act states "Be it enacted, that it shall, and may be lawful for any justice of the Peace of Giles County, to attend at the place appointed by law, for holding Court in Lawrence County, at the FIRST Court of pleas and quarter sessions, appointed to be holden for said County, for the purpose of administering to the Justices of said County the necessary oaths. Passed Oct.21,1817.

The next reference in the Acts of Tennessee to Lawrence County was not until Nov.of 1819. At that time they appointed five Commissioners to fix on a place for the permanent seat of Justice for Lawrence County.

The records herein were compiled from micro-film at the Lawrence County Public Library. The ORIGINAL book is NOT now at the Courthouse. At one time it was carried to the State Library and Archives. They laminated the pages, and fortunately for us made a micro-film copy of same.

The first 12 pages are missing, both from the ORIGINAL book and the micro-film copy. HOW WE WOULD HAVE LOVED TO HAVE FOUND THOSE 12 MISSING PAGES!!!! Had it not been for an alert County official all of this book would have been lost. Many old books and papers were burned when the 1905 Courthouse was built. He retrieved this one from the bonfire.

We have seen the ORIGINAL book and shall describe it here. It is a rather large, thick book about 7x16, brown in color. Written on the front cover is "Minute Book", on the back side M.H.B. On the back cover "M.H.Buchanan; A.W.Bumpass; Nathan; Minutes of the County Court; A.W.B; A.B.; A.W.Bumpass; A.W.B; M.H.Buchanan,Clerk; A.W.B.

There are several blank pages at the front of the book and on these someone has written in pencil the following: Page 93,Town lots; Page 65,Courthouse; Page 207,James K. Polk license to practice law,J.B.G. 1902; Page 291 Deed of gift; Pages 100,172,177,188, David Crockett signature; Page 193 David Crockett resigns.

In the left hand margin of each page is listed the business contained in that paragraph. Page 191 of the original is the page from which David Crockett's signature has been cut out. The spine of the book is missing. All the pages, therefore, as well as the Front and Back covers are "loose". The last numbered page was 335 (April 15,1821). There was no index.

The page we have copied as the last page appeared thusly on the micro-film copy. However, in the original book it was the first page. We suggest one of two reasons for this. Either the micro-filmer copied it out of sequence,OR, when the pages became loose, someone changed it. This page is not numbered.

At one time the late Mr. John F. Morrison, Jr., made a copy of "exerpts" from the original for a bulletin for the Lawrence County Historical Society. To our knowledge never, until now, has this book been copied in its entirety.

We have tried to copy exactly as on the micr0-film copy. Misspelled words, little punctuation, and various spellings of the same name appeared on the same page. Sometimes we did put (sic) after a word that we felt the reader might think a typographical error. Most of the time, however we just copied as written.

We appreciate being allowed by the person in whose custody the ORIGINAL book now rests for allowing us to examine the book. By so doing, we were able to describe for you, the reader, the appearance of the ORIGINAL.

Incidently, this book is reffered to locally as the "David Crockett Docket".

The county seat of Lawrence County, Tennessee was moved from Jonesboro to Lawrenceburg in 1821, and this is a view of the courthouse built in Lawrenceburg at that time. It was a brick, two-story structure, 25 foot square, and was known as the "Davy Crockett Courthouse". This building was dismantled in 1905, and was replaced by a large brick building with cupola, which stood on the square in Lawrenceburg until its repalcement in 1974.

MINUTE BOOK OF
THE COURT OF PLEAS AND QUARTER SESSIONS OF LAWRENCE COUNTY,
TENNESSEE, FROM MAY 1818 TO APRIL 1822.

At a court of Pleas and quarter Sessions held for the County of Lawrence at the house of Doctor Joseph Farmer, now occupied by Josephus Irvine, on the first Monday in May, 1818, (being May 4th) present the Worshipful Duncan McIntyre, Joseph Guest,(sic), James Forbes, John Hillhouse and Henson Day,Esquires, Justices. Maximilian H. Buchanan, Clerk and Bracewell Farmer, Sheriff.

It being suggested to the court that the Tavern rates on the retailing of foreign spirits heretofore laid were two low, and the court agreeing thereto,ordered the rates of the same in future to be fifty cents on each half pint.

Ordered that the County Tax for this County be one hundred per cent upon the State Tax for this year and that the Clerk proceed to make a list for the collection of the same.

William McCann came into court and prayed and obtained a license to keep a house of public entertainment at his dwelling house, which was granted for one year from and after this date, who gave bond and security agreeable to law and was qualified agreeable to a late Act of Assembly passed for the purpose to suppress gaming (tavern license).

Ordered that in future William McCann a citizen of this County be exempt from the payment of white pole tax.

The sheriff of this County returned into court upon the venire facias to him directed a list of the following named persons as Jurors of this term, to-wit, Henry Ross(sic), Gabriel Bumpass, Daniel Mathews, James, McConnel, Jesse Helton, James Broadstreet, George Rogers, Robert Chaffin, James Helton, Alexander Miller, Andrew Alison, Thomas Keyes, John Anthony, Andrew Choat Sr., Issac Pennington, Arthur M. Alexander, John Voss, George Vandiver,John Brandon, James Welch, of which the following persons were drawn as Grand Jurors, to-wit, Henry Rose(sic), Gabriel Bumpass, Daniel Mathews, James McConnel, Jesse Helton, James Broadstreet, George Rogers,Robert Chaffin, James Helton, Alexander Miller, Andrew Alison, Thomas Keyes, and John Anthony, of whom Henry Ross(sic) was appointed foreman, who were qualified, charged and retired to consider of their presentments under John Wisdom, a constable sworn to attend them.

At least a majority of the acting Justices being present, to-wit, Duncan McIntyre, James Forbes, Pollard Wisdom, Joseph Gist, John Hillhouse, DAVID CROCKETT, Henson Day, Genry Sharp, it is ordered by the court that the following named persons be apointed a jury of view to examine the road from this place to the Maury County line, which runs by John Hunters, to wit, Thomas Welch, George Vandiver, William Voss, Thomas Parkes, Nathaniel Mason, John Voss and John Hail, or any five of them and view the same whether or not the said road should be properly established as a public road, and make report to the next court.

At least five Justices being present, to-wit, Duncan McIntyre James Forbes, John Hillhouse, David Crocket, Joseph Gist, Henson Day and Pollard Wisdom, Esquires, Justices. George Rogers brought into court two wolf scalps over four months old which were ordered to be certified accordingly.

It is ordered by this Court that the second day of this and each succeeding term be set apart for the trial of State's business

John Burns brought into court one wolf scalp over five months old which was ordered to be certified accordingly.

Ordered that James Helton be fined in the sum of one dollar and fifty cents for contempt of the Court and for profane swearing and that he remain in the custody of the sheriff until he pay the same.

A majority of the Justices being present, to-wit, Duncan McIntire(sic), James Forbes, John Hillhouse, Pollard Wisdom, Joseph Gist, Henson Day, David Crocket, and Henry Sharp, Esquires. Ordered that John Adkinson, Thomas Spencer, James Brooks, James Haralson, Daniel McIntire, Henry Brewer and Barney Gabriel, or any five of them be appointed a Jury of review, to view and mark out a road the nearest and best way, beginning on the Federal road about two miles below Clacks, and from thence to the County line n a direction to the head of Cypress and that they make report to next Court. Ordered that Jacob Pennycuff, Elijah Cooper, Richard Bassham, Bradley Fifer(Fisher?), and Andrew McWhorton be appointed a jury of review to view and mark out a road beginning at the Giles County line near the third fork of Sugar Creek, thence the nearest and best way in the direction of Campbells Ferry until it intersects the road to said ferry and that they make report to next Court.

Ordered that John Simonton be appointed overseer of the road leading by his house agreeable to a late Jury of review and from his house to the Maury County line, and that he have all the hands under his direction at least eight miles East and West of that part of said road on which he works and that he keep the same in repair.

Josiah Wallace brought into Court three wolf scalps over 4 months of age which were ordered to be certified accordinly.

John Lockard who was bound over to this court in a case of bastardly came into cpirt and gave bond and security for payment of $25 to be paid quarterly to Polly Billingsley the mother of the said bastard child for the maintenance of same and also a bond generally to keep the county clear of any and all costs in consequence of the same.

The Grand Jurors returned into Court the following bills of presentment, to-wit, The State vs John Alsup and William Tippett for an affray; the same vs Jacob Mattis and James Welch for an affray; the same vs Liles Welch and Samuel Graham for an affray; the same vs Mathaniel Mason and John Smith for an affray- severly with the foreman's name and twelve of their own body assigned thereto.(The minutes of this day;s business, after an adjournment till tomorrow morning at nine O'clock, were signed by H. Day, Joseph Gist and John Hillhouse,J.P's.,editors)

MINUTES OF TUESDAY,5th May,1818

Present, Henson Day, Joseph Gist, John Hillhouse,Esquires.

Daniel Beeler who came and commenced a suit against John Welch in this court by writ returnable to this term, came into open court together with John Welch the defendant in their proper persons and they mutually agreed to refer the said matter of litigation between them be refered to inquire into and determine the same, and they jointly agreed to nominate and appoint David Crocket and William White for that purpose and they the said Daniel Beeler and John Welch do mutually agree to abide by the decision and award of said referees who after an examination of the evidence in this case and mature deliberation had their own will make report to this court.

Duncan McIntire,Esqauire, presented to this court an account of services by him rendered in surveying and marking out this County,whereupon the Court ordered that the County trustee of this County pay to Duncan McIntire the sum of thirty-five dollars out of any monies not otherwise approp.

Daniel Cutbirth who was bound over to make his personal appearance at this court then and there to answer to a case of bastardy who gave bond and security for the security of the payment of forty dollars unto the hands of Pollard Wisdom,Esquire, of the sureties of this County for the use of Stacy Choate, the mother of two bastard children by him begotten of her body,to be by the said Wisdom so paid over to the said Stacy as to him shall appear proper for her support and that of her children and also a bond generally in the sum of one hundred and fifty dollars conditioned that he will not suffer said bastard children to become chargeable to this County.

James Forbes Esquire who was appointed to take a list of taxables,property and polls at the last term within this County made returnable thereof.

John Hillhouse, Esquire, who was appointed to take a list of taxables, property and polls at the last term within this County, made returnable thereof.

George Hanks, Esquire, who was appointed to take a list of taxables, property and polls at the last term within this County made returnable thereof.

Andrew Pickens, Esquire, who was appointed to take a list of taxables, property and polls at the last term within this County made returnable thereof.

William Davis vs Abner Taylor, Matthew F. Montgomery and Benjamin Cuthbert-Original Attachment.
This day came the plaintiff by his attorney and thereupon came John Montgomery, Garnishee in his proper person, who being sworn upon the holy Evangelists of Almighty God the truth to speak according to the Act of Assembly relative to garnishees and sayeth that he hath within his hands the following property belonging to Abner Taylor, to-wit, one old wagon and some harness, one feather bed, one weeding hoe, one grindstone, one small box, one barrel, thirty-nine head of hogs, ten dollars in cash, one rifle gun and caztrage box, whereupon the Court ordered that judgement be rendered against the said John Montgomery for the sum of ten dollars declared to be in his hands and also for the amount of property belonging to the said Abner Taylor in his possession, and the defendant be in mercy &c.

Josephus Irvin, deputy Sheriff came into Court and was duly qualified to act as such.

At least five justices being present to-wit, Duncan McIntyre, James Forbes, John Hillhouse, Pollard Wisdom, John Rhea, William Cook produced in open court two wolf scalps over four months old which were ordered to be certified accordingly.

Joseph Gist, Esquire, who was appointed to take a list of taxables, properties and polls at the last term within this County made returnable thereto.

John Rhea, Esquire, who was appointed to take a list of taxables, properties and polls at the last term within this County made returnable thereof.

The State vs William Clack. On motion of the Solicitor, it was suggested that this case was one over which this Court has no jurisdiction, it is therefore ordered by this Court that a noli proseqaui be entered.

The State vs Thomas Taylor in charge of bastardy the defendent being solemnly called came not. It is therefore ordered by the court that judgement be entered ni-li on his recocnizance, and that a Fire Fasceous issued accordingly.

Same vs Thomas Taylor in charge of bastardy. John Shirley one of the defendants securities though he be solemnly called to come into court and bring with him the body of Thomas Taylor the defendant in this case came not. It is therefore ordered by the court that the judgement be entered Ni Li on his recognizance Lire Fasceous issued accordingly.

Same vs Thomas Taylor in charge of bastardy. Lewis Mathews one of the defendents securities though he be solemnly called to come into court and bring with him the body ofThomas Taylor the defendant in this case came not. It is therefore ordered by the court that the judgement be entered Ni Li on his recognizance Lire Fasceous issued accordingly.

Same vs Thomas Taylor in charge of Bastardy. Aaron Choate one of the defendants securities though he be solemnly called to come into court and bring with him the body of Thomas Taylor the defendant in this case came not. It is therefore ordered by the court that the judgement be entered Ni Li on his recognizance Lire Faseous issued accordingly.

State vs Ezekiel Farmer for Assault and Battery. Henry Sharp, prosecutor in this case came into court and acknowledged himself bound in sum of $100 to be levied of his goos, chattels, lands and tenements to be void on condition that he appear here on 2nd day of next term to prosecute and give evidence in behalf of the state in this case and that he depart not without leave of the court.

State vs Joel Warren, indictment for assault and battery. Henry Sharp, prosecutor in this casecame into court and acknowledged himself justly indebted to the state of Tennessee in the sum of $100 to be levied of his goods and chattels, lands and tenements to be void on condition that he appear here on the 2nd day of next term then and there to prosecute and give evidence in behalf of the state and not depart threupon without leave of the court.

Ordered by the court the following persons be appointed as Jurors to the Circuit Court to be held at the house of Joseph Farmer on the 4th Monday in August next, to-wit, John Simonton, Thomas Forkes, Thomas Welch, George Lucas, John Millhouse, Polard Wisdom, Henson Day, Andrew Pickens, David Crocket, Joseph Gist, Malcolm McIntire, John Haris, Nicholas Welch, James McConnel, James Forbes, Nathaniel Mason, Henry Sharp, George Hanks, William Wisdom, James Brooks, Joshua Wharton, William Straughn, Reubin Tripp, Richard Mabry, Thomas Holland, Johnathan Johnson, and that they do not depart without leave of the Co.

Ordered by the Court that the following persons be appointed as Jurors to the County Court to be held at Doctor Joseph Farmers on the first Monday in Aug.next, to-wit, Samuel Price, William Welch, Sr., John Hail, Casu(sic)Hays, James McMillian, Nathaniel Fuefason(sic), Nathan Jobe, Stephen H.Mote, Jessee Needham, James Smith, Thomas Bird, Andrew Johnson, John Bird, Hugh Sinclear, John Phillips, Charles Hays, Thomas Ethridge, James Strickling, Geo.Isom, Daniel Hughs, Merit Mitchell, Joseph Smith, Thomas Allsup, John Millner, Levi Levis,

Jeremiah Jackson and that they do not depart without leave of the Court.

Malcom McIntire, a citizen of this county came into court prayed and obtained a license to keep a house of ordinary in this County, who gave bond and security and was qualified according to Act of Assembly.

David Crockett and William White, referees to whom were refered the matter of litigation between Daniel Beeler and John Welch on conformity of an order of this court came into court and returned their verdict and say that the defendant in this case pay the plaintiff $5.40 the value of 108 pounds of pork at the rate of $5 per hundred and that the parties each pay one half of the cost accured in the case. It is therefore ordered to be made the judgement and decree of the court in this case.

Nicholas Welch came into Court and prayed and obtained Letters of administration on the estate of Margaret Whitley, dec'd, who gave bond and security agreeable to law.

William Strawn vs James Paine--Appeal

This day came the parties by their attonreys and thereupon came a jury of good and lawful men, to-wit, Henry Ross, Gabriel Bumpass, Daniel Mttthews, Samuel McConnel, Jesse Helton, James Broadstreet, George Rogers, James Holton, Robert Chaffin, Andrew Atkison, Thomas Keyes, and John Anthony who being elected, tried and sworn, well and truly to try this matter of dispute, upon their oaths do say, that the defendant do owe the plaintiff the sum of forty-five dollars. Whereupon it is ordered by the Court that the defendant pay the plaintiff the sum of $45 his debt aforesaid and his cost by him about his suit in this behalf expended and it is further ordered coment(sic) of the parties that no exception issued for the term of 3 months and the defendant in mercy &c.

Duncan McIntire vs Daniel Pearce-Appeal

This day came the parties by their attorneys and thereupon came a jury of good and lawful men, to-wit, Issac Pennington, Arthur M. Alexander, John Voss, George Vandiver, James Welch, Eramus Tracy, John Simonton, John Montgomery, Mason McIntire, Simeon Edwards, John Phillips, and Hugh Sinclear who being elected tryed and sworn well and truly to try this matter of dispute upon their oaths do say, that the defendant doth owe to the plaintiff the sum of $25 besides costs. It is therefore considered by the Court that the plaintiff recover of the defendant the sum of $25 his debt aforesaid and his costs as well before the justices below as in this court as in this behalf expended from which judgement the defendant prayed an appeal to the honorable the Circuit Court to be held in and for the County of Lawrence, he having given bond and security according to law the same is granted him.

The State vs Jacob Lathews-Presentment for an affray
This day came the defendants in his proper person and ack-

nowledged himself guilty of this charge whereupon the Court ordered that the defendant be fined in the sum of $1 and that he pay the cost of this prosecution and that the defendant be in mercy &c.

The State vs James Welch-Presentment for an affray

This day came the defendant in his proper person and acknowledged that his is guilty of the charge in this case. Whereupon the court ordered that the defendant make his fine to the amount of $1 and that he pay the cost of this prosecution and that the defendant be in mercy & c.

Ordered that Daniel Cutbirth and John Lockard who are bound over in this court for a case of bastardy pay severally the cost incurred in each case.

Ordered that Warron Mason and Thomas Spencer be appointed as constables to attend the next court of this County.

Ordered that the Jurors of this County be allowed the sum of fifty cents for each days attendance at this and each succeeding term.

Dun McIntire one of the Justices of this County returned into court his list of taxables property and polls by him taken and ordered that court be adjourned until court in course. Duncan McIntire,J.P.,James Forbes,J.P.,John Hillhouse,J.P.

MINUTES OF MONDAY, AUGUST 3rd, 1818

At a Court of Pleas and Quarter Sessions begun and held for the County of Lawrence at the house of Josephus Irvine, formerly the house of Doctor Joseph Farmer, the present place of holding Court in and for the said County the 3rd day of August 1818. Present Duncan McIntyre, Henson Day,Joseph Gist, Henry Sharp, Esquires.

William Stoddert, Madison Caruthers and John Mayes,Esqs. Having produced their license as attornies, were qualified and admitted to practice in this Court.

Ordered that an ordinary License be granted to John Bull, Jr., for one year from date hereof and no longer to be having given bond and securities and qualified according to law.

A jury of view appointed by order of last County Court to exmine the road from this place to the Maury Co. line which runs by John Hunters, made their return as follows. We, the jurors of view have this day examined the road according to order and do consider it not to be established, this the 6th of June ,1818. Thomas Welch, Geo. Vandiver, William Voss, John Voss, and John Haile.

Ordered that Henry Sharp,Geo. Hanks, Henson Day,Daniel Becler, John McDonald and Wm. White or any five of them be appointed a jury of review to view and mark out a road if found convenient as an addition to the Military road to begin at the most convenient point near Raccon Branch, then to intersect said road at the most convenient point below and that they make report to this Court.

Ordered that Richard Strawn who has heretofore been appointed overseer of that part of the Military road which lies betwixt his house and Raccon Branch in addition to said order have the following named hands to work thereon and keep he same in repairs. To-wit, Samuel McConnel, Nathan Jobe, James McConnell,Jr, John W.Tally, Arthur M. Alexander, Melton H.Jack,John Burns, Levi Blackard, Branch Blackard, Solomon Asbill, Sterling Lindsey,Daniel Lindsey, Issac Brown, Amus Kilburn, Solomon Kilburn, Joseph McGee, Loid Byrne, Daniel Hughs, Stephen M. Moore, Josiah Wallace,Bennett Wallace, Mannole Keltner, Thomas Musgrave, Joseph Baldwin, William Green, Samuel Armstrong,Samuel Issac, James McKew, Charles McKew, John McKew,Stephen Roland, Dempsey Barnes, Samuel Sullivan, Phillip Null, William Wisdom, John Bolds, William Wharton and all others resding in the bounds of said former order.

Ordered that John Simonton be appointed overseer of that part of the road which lies betwixt this place and the ford of Buffalo which leads by said Simonton's and that he have the following hands to work thereon,to-wit, Nicholas Welch,Hugh Revnolds,Moses Pennington, William Counts, Issac Pennington,David Flatt,David Pennington, and slave, John Wisdom, John Lockhart,AustenKendrick, John Farmer, Liles Welch,James Farchman, Bloomer Ashmore,James Ashmore, Abraham Helton, Jesse Helton, James Melton, Hugh Sinclear, Thomas A. Harias, William P. Harris, James Broadstreet, John Phillips,Joel Phillips,Samuel Trice, Hamilton Stinson, John Stinson, Adam Ross, James Haile, John Haile, Simeon Edwards,Shadrick Alvis, Nathaniel Mason, John Voras, Abraham Henry,Bailey Alford, Robert Chaffin, Robert Mason, Malcolm McIntyre, Martin Gaither, Gilbreath Simonton, Henry Ross, Duncan McIntyre, John Crisp, Samuel Grayham, Thomas Welch, James Webb,and all others residing within said bounds.

Ordered that George Sherley,Jr., be appointed overseer of the road from Buffalow to the Maury Co., line which runs by Simonton's and that he have under his direction the following named hands to keep the same in repair. To-wit,William Duck, Aaron Bryan, Nicholas Welch, Joel Warren, Hyram Howard, James McMillon, James Strickland, Obadiah Kendrick, James Kendrick, William Burris, John Voss,William Voss, Nathaniel Ferguson,John Anthony, James Foster, William Welch, George Vandiver, Thomas Parkes,Levi Laughlin, Sawyers Ashmore and all others residing within said bounds.

Ordered that John Mull(Null), be continued overseer of that part of the road which lies between Clacks old place and Richard Straughan,and that he have under his direction the following named hands to keep the same in repair,to-wit, Joshua Wharton, John Wharton, James Mayberry, John Inman, James M. Merley,Willaim Tucker, and his slave,James Welch, Jesse Needham, David Choate, William Austin, Merrit Mitchell, Wm. Wynn,Thomas Archer,George Archer, Wm Story, Elick Smith, Wm Smith,SilasRackley,Daniel Harrison, Wm Brashears, John and Jessee Brashears, and all other hands within said bounds.

Ordered that William White have leave to list with the clerk his taxable property for 1818, to-wit, 1 free poll and one slave and that he be exempt from a double tax on same.

Ordered that Thomas Welch be allowed to enter his list of taxable property and polls with the clerk for the year 1818 and that he be exempt from paying double tax on same.

At least five justices being present, Solomon Asbell produced in opne Court two wolf scalps over four months old which were ordered to be burnt and certified accordingly.

Ordered that George Gresham who is overseer of the Military road from this place to Raccoon branch have the following handsto open and keep the same in repairs, to-wit, Thomas Keys, Richard Bauley, Luke Grimes, M.H. Buchanan, John McDonald, Lewis Franks, Solomon Gresham, William Gresham, George Jones, John Nelson, Robert Montgomery, Jessee Parchman, John Alsup, Melcher Duncan, Robert Haynes, William White, Ezer Evans, Simeon Higgs, Daniel Becler, Christopher Thompkins, Humphrey Tompkins, Rubin Hanks, James Boid, Josephus Irvine, John Guin, Daniel Guin, ---Adams, John Thompson, John Shirley, Luke Arp, John Polly, Thomas Trantham(sic), Ebenezer Thompson, Nathan McClendon, John Edmondson, James Edmondson, Bradley Halford, Abner Burgin, Gabriel Bumpass, Jonathon Jobe, Richard Choate, Thomas Choate, Aaron Choate, George Lucas, John H. Hamilton, Daniel Mathews and hands, William Tippet, James Stockard, William Ragsdale, Michael Bailey, Allen Prewet, John King, William H. Cowen, James Bumpass, William Dillingham, John Kilbreath, Jacob Adair, and all other hands within said bounds.

Ordered that John Smith be appointed Constable for this County, who gave bond and was qualified agreeable to law.

Om application of William F. Cunningham, agent for Henry Phenix, an ordinary license was granted him to keep a house of entertainment at the present dwelling house of William Strawn for the term of three months from this date, who gave bond and security according to law.

Larken Baker, at the request of the High Sheriff of this County came into Court and was qualified to act as Deputy Sheriff for this County.

Ordered that Cornelius Goforth and John Smith two of the Constables for this County be summoned to attend on the next Circuit Court.

Ordered that Lazarous Stewart and William White -two of the Constables for this County be summoned to attend the next County Court.

Ordered that the Sheriff be directed to summon the following persons to attend at the next Court of Pleas and Quarter Sessions to be holden for this County on the first

Monday in November next then and there to serve as Jurors, to-wit, Adam Ross, Thomas Price, Thomas Keyes, John Welch, Daniel Beeler, Humphrey Tompkins, Ezer Evans, Sterling Lindsey, John Lockhart, Ezekiel Farmer, John Farmer, Hosea Straughan, William Morrow, James McConnel, Jr., John W. Tally, Milton H. Jack, Josiah Wallace, Gabriel Bumpass, James Edmondson, James Bumpass, James Stockhart, Samuel Graham, John Crisp, James Hail, Shadrick Alvis and Joshua Ashmore.

At least five justices being present, Jeremiah Jackson produced in court one wolf scalp over 4 months old which was ordered to be burnt and certified accordingly.

Court adjourned until tomorrow morning. Duncan McIntyre, James Forbes, John Hillhouse and John Ray, esquires, Justices.

MINUTES OF TUESDAY, AUGUST 4th, 1818

Court met according to adjournment. Present, Duncan McIntyre, James Forbes, John Hillhouse and John Ray, Esquires, Justices.

The following persons were elected and sworn as a Grand Jury of Inquest for the body of this County, to-wit, John Hail, foreman Hugh Sinclear, Levi Lewis, John Phillips, William Welch, Sr., Charles Hayes, John Bird, Joseph Smith, Samuel Price, James Smith, Andrew Johnston, Thomas Etherage, Stephen H. Moore who having received their charge withdrew to consider of their presentments.

Thomas Spencer. a Constable of this County, was sworn to attend the Grand Jury during the present term of this Court.

The Grand Jury returning into Court the following Bills of indictment, to-wit, The State vs Bailey Brooks--a ture bill
" " " Daniel McIntyre--prosecutor
" " " Bailey Brooks-a true bill
" " " Solomon Grisham-prosecutor

John P. Irwin & Co., plaintiffs vs William P. Harris, defendant

This day came the parties by their attorneys and thereupon came a jury of good and lawful men, to-wit, Nathaniel Fergusson, Jeremiah Jackson, Nathan Jobe, James McMillan, Humphrey Tomkins, Solomon Asbell, Aaron Anglin, Lewis Matthews, Shadrack Alvis, Simon Higgs, William Cottle, Aaron Choate who being elected, tried and sworn the truth to speak upon the issue ore joined upon their oathsdo say that the defendant had not paid the debt on the writing obligatory in the plaintiffs declaration mentioned as in pleadingshe hath alledged and they do assess the plaintiff damages by reason of the detention thereof to $20 besides costs. It is therefore considered by the Court here that the plaintiff recoverof the defendant the sum of $250 their debt aforesaid together withtheir damages aforcasaid in form aforesaid assessed and their costs by them about their suit in this behalf expended and the defendant in mercy & c.

The State, plaintiff vs Jonathon Jobe, defendant

Whereupon came here into Court George Lucas and Aaron Choate who were bound for the appearance of the said Jonathon Jobe to this term and surrendered him to court whereupon they are exhonerated and discharged from their obligation aforesaid and thereupin came Nathan Jobe and Lewis Matthews who being considered good and sufficient bail by the Court and entered into recogniance in the sum of $200 each and that if the said Jonath n should make his personal appearance at this term and not depart without leave of the court.

Joseph Farmer, plaintiff vs William Welch, Sr., defendant

This day came the parties by their attorneys and thereupon came a jury of good and lawful men, to-wit, Nathaniel Ferguson, Jeremiah Jackson, Nathan Jobe, James McMillan, Humphrey Tompkins, Solomon Aswell, Aaron Anglin, Lewis Matthews, Shadrack Allvice,, Simon Higgs, William Cottle, Aaron Choate who being elected, tried and sworn the truth to speak upon the issues joinedm upon their oaths do say that the defendant is NOT guilty in manner and form as in the plaintiff's declaration against him hath alleged. It is therefore considered by the Court that the defendant depart hence without day(sic) and recover of the plaintiff his costs by him about his defense in this behalf expended and from which judgement the plaintiff prays an appeal to the Circuit Court to be holden for the County of Lawrence, he having given bond and security according to law, the same is granted him.

Daniel McIntyre, plaintiff vs Joseph Gist, Sr. & Joseph Gist, Jr. defendants

This day came the parties by their attorneys and thereupon came a jury of good and lawful men, to-wit; (Same list of Jurors as listed in case cited above) who being elected, tried and sworn the truth to tell, upon the issue joined and having heard the evidence it is ordered by the Court that the jury have leave to dispense until tomorrow morning at 8 o'clock. Duncan McIntyre, James Forbes, John Ray

WEDNESDAY AUGUST 5th 1818

Court met according to adjournment-present Duncan McIntyre, James Forbes, John Ray, Esquires, Justices.

Daniel McIntyre, plaintiff vs Joseph Gist, Sr. and Jr., Defs.

This day came the parties by their attoneys and there upon came a jury of good and lawful men, to-wit(Same jurors as listed above) who being joined upon their oaths do say that the defendants is guilty of the troven(sic) and conversion in the plaintiff's declaration mentioned and they do assess the plaintiff damage by reason thereof to $30 besides costs. It is therefor considered by the Court that the plaintiff recover of the defendants his damages aforesaid in form aforesaid by the jurors aforesaid assessed and the said defendant in mercy & c from which judgement the defendants prayed and appealed to the Honorable the Circuit Court to be holden of the County of Lawrence.

The State, plaintiff
vs
Samuel Grayham, defendant

Upon a presentment for an affray with Liles Welch

This day came as well the council for the State as the defendant in his proper person and the said defendant pleads guilty in manner and form as he is charged in the bill of presentment and agrees to put himself upon the justice and mercy of the Court. It is therefore considered by the court that the defendant make his fine with the state in the amount of $1 and that the cost of this prosecution, and the defendant may be taken & c.

The State, plaintiff
vs
Jonathon Jobe, defendant

Upon a presentment for an affray

This day came as well the council for the State as the defendant in proper person and the said defendant pleads guilty in manner and form as he is charged in the bill of presentment and agrees to put himself upon the justice and mercy of the court. Thereforeit is considered by the court that the defendant make his fine with the State in the amount of $1 and he pays the cost of this prosecution and that the defendant may be taken & c.

The State, plaintiff
vs
Liles Welch, defendant

Upon a presentment of an affray with Samuel Grayham

This day came the Solicitor General as well as the defendant in his proper person who being arraigned upon his arraignment pleaded not guilty and for his trial puts himself upon the Country and the Solicitor General, the state licenses. Thereupon came a jury of good and lawful men, to-wit; William Clack, Nathaniel Mason, Daniel McIntyre, Daniel Beeler, Malcohm McIntyre, William Hanks, Lewis Franks, Samuel Sullivan, Richard Bailey, John Shurkly, Lemuel Blythe, James Bumpass who being elected, tried and sworn the truth to speak upon this issue of traverse upon their oaths do say that the defendant is guilty of the affray as he is charged in the bill of presentment. It is therefore considered by the Court that he make his fine with the State to the amount of $1 and that he pay the cost of this prosecution and he may be taken & c.

The Grand Jury returned into court the following bills of indictment, to-wit;
  The State vs Daniel Matthews -Not a true bill
  The State vs John Alsup- A true bill

Ordered that William Wiley be fined in the sum of $2 for getting drunk and that he remain in custody of the sheriff until said fine be paid plus costs.

On the petition of Robert Mason exhibited and sworn to in

open court it is ordered that writs of certeorari and sup-
ucedias issue to remove all proceedings into this Court on
a judgement rendered in Maury County before Tyree Dollams,
Esq., in the case of wherein Bailey Brooks is plaintiff and
the said Robert Mason the defendant which was granted him
who gave bond and security according to law.

It is ordered that letters of Adm., on the estate of
Margaret Whitley,dec'd be granted to Daniel Cooch(sic) in
the room of Nicholas Welch former Adm., who willingly resigns the same. The said Daniel Cooch having given bond
and security was qualified accordingly to law.

Daniel Cooch,Administrator to the estate of Margaret
Whitley,dec'd, returns into court an inventory of said estate which was received and ordered to be recorded.

Ordered that an order of sale issued to Daniel Cooch
Adm., to the estate of Margaret Whitley,dec'd, commanded
him to sale(sic) said estate and make return thereof according to law.

It is ordered by this court that the sum of $5 be
assessed as a county tax on each license which may be
granted to peddlers and hawkers of this County.

The State,plaintiff
vs Upon a presentment of an affray
John Allsup,defendant with William Tippett

This day came as well the counsel for the State as
the defendant in his proper person and the defendant being
arraigned upon his arraignment pleaded not guilty. His
trial puts himself upon the Country and the Solicitor of
the State likewise and thereupon came a jury of good and
lawful men,to-wit, John Wisdom,William McCann, William
Higgs, Thomas Bird,Aaron Choate, John Polly,Abner Burgin,
John McCann,Ezekiel Farmer,John Welch, Geo. W. Jones,and
Bryan McClendon, who being elected tried and sworn the
truth to speak upon this issue of traverse and having
heard the evidence in this case it is ordered by the Court
by and with the consent as well of the counsel for the State
as the attorney for the defendant that the jury have leave
to depart until tomorrow morning at 9 o'clock.

The State, plaintiff
vs Upon a presentment for an affray with
Liles Welch,defendant Samuel Graham

The defendant in this case dissatisfied with the judgement of the court prays an appeal to the Honorable the Circuit Court to be holden for the County of Lawrence on his
entering into the following recognance the same is granted
him.

The State,plaintiff
vs Upon a presentment for an affray
Liles ? , defendant

This day came the defendant in his proper person and

withdraws his motion for an appeal in this case it is therefore commended by the court that the Judgement heretofore rendered in this case be in all respects affirmed.

THURSDAY AUGUST 6th 1818

Court met according to adjournment, present, Duncan McIntyre James Forbes, John Hillhouse, John Ray, esquires, justices.

John Allsup, plaintiff
vs
George Bankhead, defendant

In case on motion of the defendant by his attorney it is ordered that he have commission to take the deposition of John Bankhead, Jr., in Franklin County, Allibama Territory by giving the plaintiff ten days previous notice of time and place of taking same.

The State, plaintiff   Upon a presentment of an affray with
vs   William Tippett
John Allsup, defendant

The jury in this case were suffered to dispense by consent pf the court and with the assent of the Attorney General in behalf of the State as well as the defendants counsel having returned into court who after fully hearing the arguments in this case upon their oaths do say that the defendant is not guilty of the affray in manner and form as he is charged in the bill of presentment. It is therefore considered by the court that the defendant be acquitted and discharged from the affray aforesaid and that he go forth without day(sic).

The State, plaintiff   For an affray with John Allsup
vs
William Tippett, defendant

This day came the Solicitor General as well as the defendant in proper person and the defendant being arraigned upon his arraignment pleaded not guilty and for his trial puts himself upon his County and the Solicitor General in behalf of the state, likewise, and thereupon came a jury of good and lawful men, to-wit, Nathan Jobe, James McMillen, James Bumpass, Aaron Choate, Ezer Evans, James Parchment, Joel Warren, George Rogers, Jonathon Jobe, Nicholas Welch, Simon Higgs and Daniel McIntyre, who being elected and sworn the truth to speak upon this issue of traverse upon their oaths do say that the defendant is guilty in manner and form as is charged in the bill of presentment. It is therefore considered by the court that the defendant make his fine with the state to the amount of $1 and that he pay the cost of this prosecution and that he be taken & c from which judgement the defendant prays and obtained an appeal to the Honorable Circuit Court to be holden for the County of Lawrence on his entering into the following recognance to-wit; William Tippett, George Rogers, Nathan Jobe, comes into court and acknowledges themselves severally indebted to the State of Tennessee in the sum of following, to-wit, William Tippett in sum of $200; George Rogers and Nathan Jobe each the sum of $100 to be levied of their goods and chattel lands and tenements to be void on conditions that the said William Tippett appears before

the Honorable the Judge of our 6th Judical Circuit Court to
be holden for this County at the house of Josephus Irvine,
formerly the house of Doctor Joseph Farmer on the 4th Monday in this month then and there to answer the state upon a
charge for an affray with John Allsup and that he do not depart therefrom without leave of the court.

The State,plaintiff   Upon a presentment of an affray
vs
Ezekiel Farmer,defendant
    This day came as well the Solicitor General for the
State as the defendant in his proper person and the defendant being arraigned and upon his arrignment pleaded guilty
in manner and form as he is charged in the bill of presentment and puts himself upon the justice and mercy of the Court
it is therefore considered by the court that the defendant make
his fine with the state in the amount of $1 and that he pay
the cost of this prosecution and that the defendant may be
taken.

The State, plaintiff   Upon an indictment for assault and
vs   battery upon the body of Abner Bergin
John Allsup,defendant
    This day came as well the Solicitor General for the
State as the defendant in his proper person and the defendant being arraigned upon his arraignment pleaded NOT guilty
in manner and form as he is charged in the bill of indictment and puts himself upon the justice and mercy of the
court and therefore it is considered by the Court that the
defendant make his fine with the state in the amount of $1
and to pay the cost of this prosecution and that the defendant may be taken & c.

The State, plaintiff
vs   On a charge of bastardy
Thomas Taylor,defendant
    This day came as well the Solicitor General for the
State as well as the defendant in his proper person and the
defendant pleads guilty as he is charged in his recognance.
It is therefore considered by the court that the defendant
enter into bond and security in the sum of $200 which was
done accordingly-conditioned that he will keep this court
free from all charges and consequences of said bastardy and
thazt he will pay the cost of this suit and that the defendant may be taken & c.

The State, plaintiff   On the indictment of an affray
vs
Abner Burgin,defendant
    This day came as well the Solicitor General for the
State as well as the defendant in proper person and the
defendant being arrained upon his arrainment pleads NOT
guilty-whereupon came a jury of good and lawful men,to-wit,
James McMillian,James Bumpass,Aaron Choate,Joel Warren,
Johnathon Jobe,Nicholas Welch,Simon Higgs,Daniel McIntyre,
James Broadstreet,William McCann,Lewis Mathews,Nathaniel
McClendon, who being elected,tried and sworn the truth to

speak upon the issue brought upon their oaths, do say, that the defendant is not guilty in manner and form as he is charged in the bill of indictment. It is therefore considered by the court that he be acquited and discharged from the affray aforesaid and that the defendant depart hence without.....

The State, plaintiff
vs   An indictment for an affray with
Joel Warren, defendant   Jonathon Jobe

    This day came as well the Solicitor General for the State, and as the defeendant in proper person, the defendant being arraigned for his arraignment pleaded NOT guilty and for his trial puts himself upon the Country and the State and the Solicitor General for the State likewise, whereupon came a jury of good and lawful men, to-wit, Nathaniel Ferguson, John Thompson, John McCann, Malcom McIntyre, John Welch, Bryan McClendon, Ezekiel Farmer, John Wisdom, Luke Arp, Thomas Keyes, James Parchman, Moses Holloway, who being elected tried and sworn well and truly to try this issue of traverce upon their oaths do say that the defendant is NOT guilty in manner and form as he is charged in the bill of presentment. It is therefore considered by the court that the defendant be acquitted and discharged from the affray aforesaid, and that the defendant depart hence without delay--

The State, plaintiff
vs   Upon a recognuance for assault and
Bailey Brooks, defendant   battery upon the body of Daniel McIntyre

    This day came the Solicitor General for the State and the defendant though solemnly called came not but made default-it is therefore considered by the Court that the judgement NI S I for the sum of $100 according to the tenor of his recognuance and that the Scire Facias issued accordingly be returnable to the next term of this court.

The State, plaintiff
vs   Upon the recognuance of an Assault up-
Bailey Brooks, defendant   on the body of Daniel McIntyre

    Jacob Blythe who was bound in the recognuance for the appearance of said Bailey Brooks who solemnly called came not, neither did he produce the body of the said Bailey Brooks-that made default. Therefore it is considered by the court that a judgement Ni Si be entered up against the said Jacob Blythe for the sum of $100 according to the tenor of his recognuance and that Scere Facias issued accordingly, returnable to the next term of this court.

State of Tennessee, plaintiff
vs   Upon the recognuance of an assault upon the body of Daniel
Bailey Brooks, defendant   McIntyre

    Francis Wisdom who was bound in the recognuance for theappearance of said Bailey Brooks who solemnly called came not, neither did he produce the body of the said Bailey Brooks-that made default-therefore considered by the court that a judgement Ni Si be entered up against the said Francis Wisdom for the sum of $100 according to the tenor of his recognuance and that Scere Facias issued accordingly returnable to next term.

State, plaintiff
vs
John Alsup

On a presentment of an affray with William Tippett

The defendant in this case being acquitted and the trial of the merit of this case by a jury it is considered by the court that judgement be entered up in favor of all those entitled for costs in behalf of the State and that the clerk certify the same to the County Trustee of this court for payment.

Bailey Brooks, plaintiff
vs
Daniel McIntyre, defendant

Appeal

This day came the defendant by his attorney and the plaintiff the solicitor called and prosecute his said appeal came not but made default. It is therefore considered by the court that the defendant go hence without day and recover of the plaintiff as well the cost before the magistraite as in this court in this behalf expended.

John L. Campbell, plaintiff
vs
John Lockhart, defendant

In Trover

This day came the plaintiff by his attorney and thereupon came the jury of good and lawful men, to-wit, John Haile, Hugh Sinclear, Levi Lewis, John Phillips, William Welch, Sr., Charles Hayes, John Bird, Joseph Smith, Samuel Brace, James Smith, Thomas Ethridge, Stephen H. Moore, who being elected, tried and sworn the truth to tell upon the issue joined upon their oaths do say that the defendant is NOT guilty of the trover and conviction in the declaration mentioned in the pleadings he hath alledged. It is therefore considered by the court that the plaintiff take nothing by his bill but for his fals clamons be immerced & c and that the said defendant go hence without day and recover of the plaintiff his costs by him about this suit in this behalf expended from which judgement the plaintiff prayed an appeal to the Honorable Circuit Court to be holden for this County at the house of Josephus Irvine formerly the house of Doctor Joseph Farmer he being biven bond and security according to law the same is granted to him.

State, plaintiff
vs
Andrew Frigate, defendant

Upon a charge of Bastardy

This day came as well the Solicitor General in behalf of the State as the defendant in his proper person and the defendant pleads guilty in manner and form as charged in the bill of recognuance. It is therefore considered by the court by and with the assent of the counsel for the State that the defendant be acquitted from the aforesaid charge by the payment of all costs as well incurred before the magristrate as in this court in this behalf expended and the defendant may be taken & c.

The State, plaintiff   Idictment for an affray
vs
William Clack, defendant

    This day came the Solicitor General in behalf of the State as well as the defendant in proper person and the defendant being arraigned upon his arraignment pleads NOT guilty and for his trial puts himself upon the Court and the Solicior General for the State likewise, whereupon came a jury of good and lawful men to-wit, James McMillan, James Bumpass, Aaron Choate, Joel Warren, Johnathon Jobe, Nicholas Welch, Simon Higgs, Duncan McIntyre, James Broadstreet, William McCann, Levi Mathews, Nathan McClendon, who being elected, tried and sworn well and truly to try this issue of traverse upon their oaths do say the defendant is guilty in the manner and form as charged in the bill of indictment thereupon considered by the court that the defendant make fine with the state in the amount of $1 and he pay the costs of prosecution and the defendant be taken & c.

The State, plaintiff
vs   Upon a procurement for an affray with
Nathaniel Mason,   John Smith

    Daniel Beeler, James Broadstreet acknowledges themselves severally indebted to the State of Tennessee the said defendant in the sum of $100 and the said Daniel Beeler and JAMES Broadstreet each in the sum of $50 to be levied of their goos and chattel lands and tenements to be void if the said Nathaniel Mason appears at the next term of this court on the first day of Novemeber next there and then to answer the State on the charge of an affray with John Smith and not depart therefrom without leave of the court.

    John Smith, Nicholas Welch, Joel Warren came into Court and acknowledged themselves indebted to the state of Tennessee. John Smith in the sum of $100 and said Nicholas Welch and Joel Warren each in the sum of _?_ to be levied of their goods and chattel lands and tenements to be void as conditioned that said John Smith appear here at the first day of the November term of this court on the first Monday in Nov., then and there to answer the State upon a charge of an affray with Nathaniel Mason ____ thereupon without leave of this court.

    Daniel McIntyre and Malcohm McIntyre came into court and acknowledged themselves _?_ to the State of Tennessee $100 to be levied of their goods and chattel lands and tenements to be void on condition that Malcohm McIntyre appear here upon the first day of the next term of this court on the first Monday in Nov., next, then and there to prosecute and give evidence in behalf of the state against Bailey Brooks for an assault and battery on the body of Malcohm McIntyre and depart not herefrom without leave of this court.

State of Tenn., plaintiff
vs   Upon an indictment for an affray
Abner Burgin, defendant   with William Clack

    The defendant being acquitted by a jury of men as the merits of this case it is therefore considered by the court that judgement be entered in favor of all those entitled for costs in behalf of the State and that the clerk certify the same to the County Trustee of the County for payment.

State, plaintiff
vs   On presentment of an affray with
Joel Warren   Jonathon Jobe

    The defendant being acquitted by a jury of men as the merits of this case -it is therefore considered by the court that judgement be entered in favor of all those entitled to costs in behalf of the State and that the clerk certify the same to the County Trustee of the County for payment.

State, plaintiff
vs   Indictment
Daniel Matthews

    The defendant being acquitted by a jury of men as the merits of this case it is therefore considered by the court that judgement be entered in favor of all those entitled for costs in behalf of the State and that the clerk certify the same to the County Trustee of the County for payment.

State, plaintiff
vs   Upon a Ccire Fasias on motion to quash
Thomas Taylor

    An argument on the motion entered in this behalf being tried and fully understood by the Court, it is considered by the Court that the motion be overruled whereupon on motion by the defendant his counsel leave is given him to plead to the Sicre Facias so that a trial may be had in this case and cause at the next term of court.

The State, plaintiff
vs   On motion to be discharged on
George Sherly, defendant   Special bond

    This day came into court John Thompson, Special Bail of the defendant in this cause and suggested to the Court that since the time of his coming special bail for the said defendant in this cause, the said defendant has been removed from this County to the County of Giles for safekeeping, and is at this time confined in the Jail of the said County of Giles under a mittimus from a Justice of the Peace for this County on a charge of Counterfeiting bank notes in this County, all which being made appear to the Court the said John Thompson by his attorney moved the Court to order and direct that the said defendant be retained in the jail of the said County of Giles and that he, the said John Thompson be discharged from all further liability as the Special Bail of the said defendant, which motion was overrooled(sic) by the court and the order refused, from which opinion and judgement of the Court the said John prays an appeal in the nature of a writ of error to the next Circuit Court to be held for this County, which is allowed by the Court by his giving bond and security according to law.

    Ordered that Josephus Irvine be appointed to build a temporary COURTHOUSE for this County on such spot of ground as he may think proper, to be twenty feet square, and that he wait the future generosity of the Court for compensation for the same, to which said Irvine agreed.

Frederick Stricklin appeared in open Court and upon his application was admitted together with Zachariah Stricklin to make affidavit that he, Frederick Stricklin was a private soldier in the regular service in the United States in the Revolutionary War, it is therefore ordered by the Court that the affadavits of the said Frederick and Zachariah Stricklin be entered of record and that a certified copy thereof be sent to the War office of the United States to entitle him to a pension, which affadavits are in the following words and figures, Lawrence County Court, August Term, 1818.

Frederick Stricklin makes oath that sometime about the year 1782 or 1783, it being the last year of the war, he enlisted in the North Carolina line of the Continentals under Captain Winn Dickson, one Dixon being Colonel, his first name not recollected and Nathaniel Green being Commanding General of the Division, that he was enlisted for twelve months, that he was mustered into service at Hillsborough in North Carolina and served his said time of twelve months in the States of North and South Carolina, that at the time of the expiration of his term he was discharged by one Colonel Armstrong, but that said discharge has long been lost or destroyed. This affiant further states that he is in indigent circumstances and that he needs the assistance and support of his Country, and that he knows of no person by whom he can prove the aforesaid facts. That he has never received a pention(sic) of the United States or any accounts, and that he doth hereby release all right to or interest in any or all penon(sic) or penons that he heretofore has or hereafter may have except the present. Signed and sworn to in open Court, this 5th day of August, 1818.   Frederick X(his mark) Stricklin
Test: M.H. Buchanan, Clerk.

State of Tennessee, Lawrence County Court, Aug. term, 1818. Zacharah Stricklin makes oath that the facts set forth in the annexed affidavit of Frederick Stricklin are unknown to him except the fact of his being at the time in the army and service of the Revolution and annexed to the North Carolina line of Continentals, and that he was absent from home in said service about the time mentioned in said affidavit and that from the time he left home it was about thirteen months before his return. Signed and sworn to in open court---Zachariah X(his mark)Stricklin
Test: M.H.Buchanan, Clerk.

Adjournment to Court in course, minutes signed by Duncan Mc-Intyre, James Forbes, John Hillhouse, John Ray, Justices, Esquires.

MINUTES OF NOVEMBER TERM, 1818, MONDAY NOV. 2nd.

At a Court of Pleas and quarter Sessions begun and held for the County of Lawrence at the house of Josephus Irvine, formerly the house of Doctor Joseph Farmer, the present place of holding Courts, in and for said County the 2nd day of Nov., 1818, present, Duncan McIntyre, Henson Day, Joseph Gist, David CROCKETT, John Ray, Esquires, Justices.

Ordered that the money collected or to be collected from

21

John Lockard for the support of a bastard child by him begotten on the body of____(name withheld) be paid to David Crockett,Esq., for the use of said child and that his receipt be good for the same.

At least five Justices being present, Jacob Adair produces in open court one wolf scalp over 4 months old which was ordered burnt and certified accordingly.

At the request of M.H. Buchanan, Clerk of this Court, Ezer Evans came into Court and was qualified to act as Asst., Clerk of said Court.

Nathaniel Casey having produced in this Court his license as practicing attorney was qualified accordingly, agreeable to law.

It is ordered that each individual who have or may make application to this court to be exempted from the payment of a double tax for this year shall be exempted from the same on all property and poles(sic) for which they are bound to pay tax within this County.

Ordered that the Sheriff be directed to summon the following named persons to attend as jurors at the next Circuit Court to be holden for this County on the 4th Monday in Feb., next at the place of holding courts that is to say, to-wit, Robert Chaffin, Henry Ross, Duncan McIntyre, Ezekiel Downs, Robert Brashears, John Smallwood, John Brandon, Jacob Turnbow, Barney Gable, Spencer Pearce, Daniel Mathews, Jacob Mathews, George W. Jones, John Nelson, Henry Sharp, Martin Gaither, Edward Higgs, James Bumpass, John King, Mancil Crisp, Erasmus Tracy, John McAnally,Sr., John Rea, Moses Pennington, Isaac Pennington, John Bromley.

Ordered that the Sheriff be directed to summons the following named persons to attend as jurors at the next Court of Pleas and Quarter Session to be held for this County on the first Monday in February next at the place of holding court George Vandover, Thomas Welch, James Broadstreet, Thomas Bird, Sr., John Bird, ___Woolsey, Charles Hayes, Daniel Pearce, Benjamin May, Elijah Melton, Jacob Blythe, George Archer, William Moton, Simon Higgs, Stephen Roland, Samuel Sullivan, Henry Phoenix, Richard T. Bailey, Levi Blackard,William McNally, Solomon Stone,Jr., George Jones, Phillip Chronister, David Adkins, Wiley Duckworth, John Edminston, .

Moses Pennington came into court prayed and obtained a license to keep a house of ordinary which was granted him who gave bond and security and was qualified according to law.

Daniel Mathews came into court prayed and obtained a license to keep a house of ordinary which was granted him who gabe bond and security and qualifed according to law.

Richard T. Bailey came into Court prayed and obtained a license to keep a house of ordinary, which was granted him who gave bond and security according to law.

Ordered that Henry Sharp, George Hanks, Henson Day, Daniel Beeler, John McDonald and Simon Higgs, or any five of them, be appointed a Jury of review and mark out a road, if found most convenient, as an addition to the Military Road to begin at the most convenient point near Raccoon Branch then to intersect said road at the most convenient point below, and that they make report to this Court.

Ordered that M.H. Buchanan, Clerk of the County Court of this County be allowed the sum of Eighty dollars and twenty-five cents for books by him purchased for said office.

Luke Grimes a minor of this County came into Court and suggested his wish that Richard T. Bailey should be appointed his guardian and appearing expedient to the court it is ordered that the said Richazrd T. Bailey be thus appointed who gave bond and security according to law.

Ordered that the Sheriff be directed to bring into Court at the next term, to-wit, on the first Monday in February next, the following orphan children, those of Polly McGee, those of the widow Dobs on the head of Buffalow, and Joseph Farmer living with Jacob Adair.

Daniel Beeler
vs   Trespassing
Reuben Rollins& Drury Cole

This came into court the defendant in his proper person and saith he will not prosecute his suit farther and the defendant assumes upon himself the payment of all costs in this case. It is therefore ordered by the court that the defendant pay the plaintiff his cost by him about his suit in this behalf expended and that the defendant be in mercy & c.

It appearing to the satisfaction of the Court that Bracewell Farmer, former sheriff of this County is no longer a citizen of this State, but is now a citizen of the Alabama Territory, it is considered by this Court that the appointment of Sheriff is vacant, it is therefore ordered by the Court that the Chairman be directed to advertise at the courthouse door that a new election for Sheriff will take place on tomorrow to fill said vacancy, which was done accordingly.

On petition of Peter Mosely and others for a jury of view to examine the premises specified in said petition for the purpose of erecting Iron Works according to Act of Assembly in such case made and provided. It is ordered by the Court that the following persons be appointed a jury of view for that purpose, to-wit, James Bumpass, Adam Ross, George Lucas, Daniel McIntyre, Daniel Beeler, Thomas Keese, William White, Jacob Blythe, Silas Rackley, Joseph Guest, David Crockett, Henry Phoenix, John Edmonston, William Wisdom, John Hillhouse, and James Forbes, or any twelve of them, and that they make report to next court.

It is ordered that the court be adjourned until tomorrow at nine o'clock. Duncan McIntyre, James Forbes, Henry Sharp, and David Crockett, Justices of the Peace.

MINUTES OF TUESDAY NOVEMBER 3rd, 1818

Court met pursuant to adjournment, present, Duncan McIntyre, James Forbes, John Hillhouse, John Rea, Pollard Wisdom, Henry Sharp, Henson Day, George Hanks, Andrew Pickens, Joseph Gist, and David Crockett, Esquires, Justices.

The Court having made proclamation that the Election for Sheriff was about to take place according to the resolution on yesterday, proceeded to ballot for the same, which on counting out the votes it was found that Bradley Halford was duly and constitutionally elected, who gave bond and security according to law.

The sheriff returned into court the following venire Facias to-wit, Adam Ross, Thomas Price, John Welch, Daniel Beeler, Humphrey Tompkins, Ezer Evans, Sterling Lindsey, John Lockhart, Ezekiel Farmer, Hosea Strawn, William Morrow, James McConnell, Jr., Gabriel Bumpass, of whom the following were drawn as Grand Jurors, to-wit, James Bumpaa, Foreman, James Edminston, Gabriel Bumpass, John Crisp, Samuel Graham, Thomas Price, James Hale, Hosea Strawn, James McConnell, John W. Tally, Milton H. Jack, Shadrack Alvis, Joshua Ashmore who were qualified and after having received their charge retired to consider of their presentments.

Drury Alsup & William Maples
vs   In case
Joseph Farmer

This day came the plaintiff by his attorney and thereupon came a jury of good and lawful men, to-wit, Adam Ross, Daniel Beeler, Sterling Lindsey, John Welch, Stephen H. Moore, Richard Strawn, John Sherley, Hugh Sinclair, Francis Wisdom, John Null, Richard Bailey and Phillip Null who being elected, tried and sworn the truth to speak upon the issue joined on their oaths do say that the defendant is guilty in manner and form as the plaintiff against him hath declared and they therefore do assess the plaintiff damages by reason thereof $216.50 whereupon it is considered by the Court that the plaintiff recover of the defendant his damages upon said___ by the jury aforesaid as well as his costs by him about his suit in this behalf expended and that he be in mercy & c., from which judgement of the court the defendant prays an appeal to the next Circuit Court to be holden for the County of Lawrence and he having entered in the bond to double the amount of said judgement with Geo. Gresham and William White his securities and having filed his reasons said appeal is granted.

Ordered that the County Trustee of this County pay to Alexander Miller the sum of $27.75 for building a temporary jail for this County according to the letting of the Commissioners appointed for that purpose, out of any monies not otherwise appropriated.

Ordered by the Court that John Hillhouse and James Forbes be appointed commissioners to settle with the County Trustee and Sheriff of this County according to Act of Assembly in such cases made and provided.

Ordered by the court that the third day of this and each succeeding term be set apart for the transaction of States business.

Joseph Spears appeared in open Court and upon his application was admitted to make affidavit and that the same should be entered of record that he was a regular soldier in the Revolutionary War of the United States, which affidavit in words and figures following, to-wit, Joseph Spears makes oath that he is now about sixty years old, that he belonged to the North Carolina line of Continental soldiers, that he enlisted at Salsbury in North Carolina under Capt. Alexander Purvard for one year;s service, that his Colonel was one Col. Dixon and that he was under the command of General Green, that he served out onorably the full period of one year and was discharged at Charlestown; he further states that he was in the battle of Utaw(sic) Springs which circumstances this affiant must refer to as fixing the year that he served in as the year has escaped from his memory. This affiant states that his discharge has been lost as he believes and cannot be procured, that he is from age and bodily infirmity unable to support himself without the assistance of his Country, that he has never received from his Country any pension whatsoever, and he is hereby releasing all pensions now allowed or hereafter to be for said service, except the present, that the above facts he is unable to prove by any other person and can only prove them by his own oath. He therefore prays the assistance of his Country as granted by a late provision of the Congress & c....

Signed and sworn to in open Court
              his
            Joseph X Spears
              mark

Phillip Parchman came into Court, prayed and obtained a license to keep a house of Ordinary, which was granted to him who gave bond and security and was qualified according to law.

Bennett Smith
vs   In debt
Josephus Irvine

This day came the plaintiff by his attorney and the defendant comes in his proper person and withdraws the plea by him before plead in his behalf and says that he cannot gainsay that he justly owes the plaintiff $103.60 and confessed the plaintiff has sustained damages by detention thereof to $8.50 whereupon it is casidered by the court that the $\frac{1}{2}$laintiff recover of the defendant $103.60 his debt and $8..50 damage with the cost above about his suit in this damage expended and that the defendant be in mercy & c....

MINUTES OF NOVEMBER 3rd, 1818

Ordered that the court be adjourned until tomorrow at 9 o'clock. John Hillhouse, John Ray, Daniel McIntrye and James Forbes, Justices of the Peace.

MINUTES OF NOVEMBER 4th, 1818

Wednesday morning 9 o'clock, Nov. 4,1818. Court met according to adjournment, present, John Hillhouse, John Rea, Daniel McIntyre, andJAMES Forbes, Esquires, Justices.

It is ordered that Cornelius Goforth be introduced as Constable to attend this Court.

Jacob Blythe who was bound over for the appearance of Bailey Brooks to answer the State of a case of Assault and Battery came into Court and surrendered the said Bailey Brooks in discharge of himself who was prayed into the custody of the Sheriff according to law.

State
vs   Presentment for an Affray
Nathaniel Mason

This day came as well the Solicitor General in behalf of the State as well as the defendant in his proper person and the defendant being arraigned upon his arraignment pleaded guilty in manner and form as he is charged in the bill of presentment and for his trial agrees to put himself upon the jury and mercy of the court. Whereupon it is considered by the court that the defendant make his fine with the court in the sum of $1 and that he pay the cost of prosecution and that the defendant be taken & c...

State
vs   Assault and Battery upon the body of
Bailey Brooks   Daniel McIntyre

This day came the defendant in his proper person as well as the Solicitor General in behalf of the State which case was continued until the next term of this Court on affadavit of the defendant.

State
vs   Assault and battery upon the body of
Bailey Brooks   Solomon Grisham

This day came as well the defendant in his proper person and the Solicitor General in behalf of the State and it being signified to the court that the state is not prepared for trial in consequence ofthe prosecutor being absence it is ordered that his cause be passes over until the next term of this court.

State
vs   Upon a Sci Fa
Thomas Taylor

This day came the defendant by his attorney as well as the Solicitor General in behalf of the State and the defendant by his counsel withdraws his plea of payment heretofore pleaded and relied a lone(sic) upon the plea of dulbill record which being fully tried and well understood by the court it is therefore considered by the court that the said plea be overruled and it is further considered by the court that the judgement Ni Ci heretofore taken against the defendant be set aside and the defendant pay the costs of the prosecution and that the defendant be taken & c-from which judgement the defendant by his counsel prayed an appeal to the next Circuit court of this County who having given bond and security and having filed his reasons the same is granted him.

The Grand Jury returned the following bills of presentment:
State against Noble Stone, Manuel Keltner, a true bill
The same against James Holton- a true bill
The same against John Hamilton- a true bill

The State
vs   Indictment for retailing spiritous
Moses & Isaac Pennington   liquors without license

Came this day the defendants in proper person as well as the Solicitor General in behalf of the State and the defendant being arraigned upon his arraignment plead guilty in manner and form as charged in the bill of indictment and for their trial put themselves upon the judgement and mercy of the court whereupon it is considered by the court that the defendant make their fine with the State to the amount of $5 and that they pay the cost of this prosecution and that they be taken...

Henry Sharp, Henson Day, George Hanks, Simon Higgs, and John McDonald jurys of view appointed to make a review in addition to the Military Road returnable to this court made the following report, to-wit, Beginning at a point near old Mr. McCann's house, thence by way of the old road till said road intersects the Military Road with such little amendments as the Overseer shall think proper to make so as to straighten in some bends in said old road. In testimony whereof we have hereunto set our hands, this 4th of November, 1818.
Henry Sharp, George Hanks, Henson Day, Simon Higgs John McDonald.

State
vs   Recogniance
John Sherly

This day came the defendant in his proper person as well as the Solicitor General in behalf of the State. George Hanks, the complainant in this cause comes into Court and saith that he is not willing to prosecute this suit furhter and the defendant assumes upon himself the payment of the cost whereby it is considered by the court that the defendant pay the cost aforesaid and that he be taken---

State
vs   Affray with George Grisham
John Alsup

This day came the defendant in his proper person as well as the Solicitor General in behalf of the State and the defendant being arraigned upon his arraignment pleaded guilty in manner and form as he is charged in the bill of presentment and for his trial puts himself upon the judgement and mercy of the court, wherefore it is considered by the Court that the defendant make his fine with the State in the sum of $2 and that he pay the costs of this prosecution and that he be taken....

State
vs   Affray with John Alsup
George Grisham

    This day came the defendant in his proper person as well as the Solicitor General in behalf of the State and the defendant being arraigned upon his arraignment plead guilty in manner and form as he is charged in the bill of presentment and for his trial puts himself upon the judgement and mercy of the Court, whereupon it is considered by the Court that the defendant make his fine with the State in the sum of $2 and that he pay the cost of this prosecution and that he be taken...

State of Tennessee   Assault and Battery upon the body of
vs   Solomon Grisham
Bailey Brooks

    This day came the defendant into Court and acknowledged himself justly indebted to the State of Tennessee in the sum of $200 to be levied of his goods and chattel lands and tenements to the use of the State to be void on condition that he appear here on the 3rd day of the next term of this court commencing on the 1st Monday in Feb., next, then and there to answer the State upon the above charge and not depart thereupon without leave of the court.

    James Thomas and Christopher Pilburn (sic) came into Court and acknowledged themselves severally indebted to the State of Tennessee in the sum of $100 each to levy of their goods and chattel lands and tenements for the use of the State to be void on condition that Bailey Brooks appears here on the 3rd day of the next term of this court to commence on the 1st day (Monday) in Feb., next -then and there to answer the above charge of assault and battery committed upon the body of Solomon Grisham and that he do not depart therefrom without leave of this Court.

State   Assault and battery upon the body of
vs   Malcom McIntyre
Bailey Brooks

    This day came the defendant in his proper person as well as the Solicitor General in behalf of the State and the defendant makes affadavit that he is not ready for trial upon which this cause is continued until the next term of this court.

State
vs   Affray
John Smith

    This day came the defendant by his counsel as well as the Solicitor General in behalf of the State and it being suggested to the court that the said defendant is DEAD, it is considered by the court that the judgement be entered upon against tis Court for all those entitled costs in behalf of the State.

State
vs   Case of bastardy
Reuben Rowlins

  Came this day in the proper person as well as the Solicitor General in behalf of the state and it being suggested to the court by the defendant Counsel that the proceedings in this case were illegal and thereupon moved to quash the proceedings in this case and the court having heard the arguments fully thereon it was ordered by the court that the defendant motion by his counsel be sustained and that the defendant shall not be further bound in this case but that he go hence without delay.

  Bailey Brooks came into court and acknowledged himself justly endebted to the State of Tennessee in the sum of $200 to be levied of his goods, chattwl lands and tenements to the use of the State to be void on condition that he appear here on the 3rd day of the next term of this court to convene on the 1st Monday in Feb., next then and there to answer the State upon a charge of assault and battery committed upon the body of Solomon Thornton and that he do not depart therefrrom without the leave of the Court.

  Malcohm McIntyre and Duncan McIntyre came into Court and acknowledged themselves severally endebted to the State of Tenn., Malcohm McIntyre in the sum of $200 and Duncan McIntyre in the sum of $100, each to be levied of their goods, chattel lands and tenements to the use of the State to be void on condition that Malcohm McIntyre appear here on the 3rd day of the next court to begin on the 1st Monday February next then and there to prosecute and give evidence in behalf of the State against Bailey Brooks for charges with having committed assault and battery on the body of Malcohm McIntyre and that he do not depart therefrom witjout leave of this Court.

The State
vs   Upon a Sci Fa
Aaron Choat

  This day came the defendant by his Counsel as well as the Solicitor General in behalf of the State and the defendant by his counsel withdraws his plea of payment heretofore pleaded and and relies a one upon the plea of the Nultell record which being fully heard and well understood by the Court it is therefore understood by the Court that the said plea be overooled and it is further considered by the C urt that the judgement Ni Ci heretofore taken against the defendant be set aside and that the defendant pay the cost of this prosecution and that the defendant be taken from which judgement the defendant prayed an appeal to the next Circuit court to be holden for this County and to abide the Di(sic) and it is agreed by the Counsel on behalf of the State as well as the defendants Counsel by the permission of the Court that this suit abide by the decision of the case of the State against Thomas Taylor entered of record at this term upon Scia Facia and taken by appeal to Circuit Court.

State of Tennessee
vs   Upon a Scri-facia
John Sherley

     This day came the defendant by his attorney as well as the Solicitor General in behalf of the State and whereas a rule of Court has been made at the last term of this Court that this cause should abide the decision of the case of the State against Thomas Taylor upon a Scire facias and judgement final being rendered against said Taylor for the cost whereupon it is considered by the court that the judgement Ni Sci be set aside but that the defendant pay the cost of the suit in this behalf expended and that the defendant be taken&c.

State
vs   Upon a Sci Facias
Lewis Mathews

     This day came the defendant by his attorney as well as the Solicitor General in behalf of the State whereas a rule of court had been entered of record at the last term of this court that this cause should abide the decision of that case of the State against Thomas Taylor upon a scirefacias and judgement final being rendered against said Taylor for the cost whereupon it is considered by the court that the judgement Ni Si be sett aside but that the defendant pay the cost of suit in this behalf expended and that the defendant be taken & c.

State
vs   Upon a Sc Fa
Francis Wisdom

     This day came the Solicitor General on behalf of the State and suggested to the Court that he is unwilling to prosecute this suit farther. It is therefore considered by the Court that the judgement ni si heretofore rendered in this case be altogether set aside and nis fas (sic) then considered by the court that judgement be entered up against the County in favor of all those entitled to costs in behalf of the State.

State
vs
John Counce

     The plaintiff comes into court prays and obtains a commission to take the deposition of Henry Allen and Allen Macy, Edward Macy and Sally Macy in the Alabama Territory by giving the defendant 20 days notice and c.

     Ordered that the court be adjourned until tomorrow 9 o'clock. James Forbes, John Ray, Pollard Wisdom and John Hillhouse, J.P.'s.

THURSDAY NOVEMBER 5th, 1818   12:00 o'clock

     Court met according to adjournment: Present, James Forbes, John Ray, Pollard Wisdom, John Hillhouse, Esquires, Justices.

Abner Bergin
vs   For debt
Daniel Mathis

This day came the defendant by his attorney and the defendant being solemnly called came not but made default. It is therefore considered by the Court that the plaintiff recover of the defendant the sum of $94 together with the sum of $5.40 damages for the detention thereof together with his costs by him the said plaintiff expended in his behalf and the defendant in mercy & c.

A majority of the acting Justices being present, to-wit, John Ray, James Forbes, John Hillhouse, Pollard Wisdom, David Crockett George Hanks, Henry Sharp, it is ordered that the following named persons, to-wit, John Burns, Nathan Jobe, Sterling Lindsey, John Nelson, George W. Jones, George Rogers, Gabriel Bumpass and James Bumpass, or any five of them, be appointed a jury of view to begin at the most convenient point on the Giles County line nearly in the direction from this to Pulaski, thence to view a road the nearest and best way somewhat in the western direction to the Wayne County line towards the neighborhood of the Young Factors on the Natchez Trace and that they make report to next Court.

It is ordered that the following named Magistrates be appointed to take a list of Taxable property and polls within the following Captains Districts, and to take the census according to Act of Assembly, to-wit, Joseph Guest in Capt. Brandon's Company, Henson Day in Capt. Parchman's do, Andrew Pickens in Capt. Cooper's do, John Hillhouse in Capt. Wharton's do, James Forbes in Capt. Wisdom's do, David Crockett in Capt. Matthew's do, John Ray in Capt. Seahorn's do, Duncan McIntyre in Capt. Hail's do, and that they make report to next Court.

Ordered that Court be adjourned till court in course. James Forbes, John Hillhouse, Pollard Wisdom, and John Ray, J.P.'s.

MONDAY FEBY, 1st, 1819

At a court of Pleas and quarter Sessions began and held at the house of Josephus Irvine, formerly the house of Doctor Joseph Farmer, the present place of holding Courts in and for said County, the 1st day of Feby, 1819, present, Pollard Wisdom, David Crockett, Duncan McIntire, Joseph Guest, George Hanks, Henry Sharp, Esq. J.P's.

Ordered that John Davis a minor of this County be bound unto John McIntire until he arrives to lawful age and that the said McIntire be bound to educate said minor reading, writing and arithmetic as far as the rule of three, who gave bond and security according to law.

Ordered by the Court that William R. Davis, Jailor of Giles County be allowed the sum of $17.50 out of any monies not otherwise appropriated in the hands of the Trustee of this County for board and care of John Dixon, confined in said jail

Joseph Gist, Henson Day, John Rhea, Duncan McInture, Esquires who were appointed to take a list of taxable property and polls returnable to this court made returns severally according to law.

Ordered that M.H. Buchanan, Clerk of this court be allowed the sum of $35 to be paid out of any monies in the hands of the County Trustee of this county not otherwise appropriated for his service as Ex Officio for 12 months past and for furnishing the Treasurer of West Tennessee with the copy of the list of taxable property and polls for the year 1818, which appeared by the Treasurers receipt according to Act of Assembly in such case made and provided.

Ordered that Robert L. Cobb, Solicitor of this County be allowed the sum of $35 for his services rendered for 12 months past to be paid out of any monies in the hands of the County Trustee of this County, not otherwise appropriated.

Ordered that William H. Gardner be allowed the sum of $2 for having advertised in the public papers the intention of petitioning the Legislature for laying out the County of Lawrence to be paid out of any monies in the hands of the County Trustee of this County not otherwise appropriated.

Ordered that the tavern rates of this County be as follows: Each meals victuals 37½ cents, Forage for horse one night 50¢, for whiskey per ½ pint 12½ ¢, for do of foreign spirits 25 ¢.

Ordered that the sheriff of this County be allowed the sum of $15 for his ex officio service for 12 months past to be paid out of any monies in the hands of the County Trustee of this County not otherwise appropriated.

William Henderson came into court, prayed and obtained a license to keep a house of ordinary at his own house in the County for a term of 12 months, which was granted him, who gave bond and security and was qualified according to law.

Maxmilian H. Buchanan came into Court, prayed and obtained a license to keep a house of ordinary at his own house in this county for a term of 12 months, which was granted him who gave bond and security and was qualified according to law.

Ordered that Richard T. Bailey, James Broadstreet and Nathan Jobe be appointed Constables in and for this county who severally gave bond and security and were qualified according to Act of Assembly more effectually to prevent dueling.

Ordered that Richard T. Bailey be appointed overseer of the Military road in the room of George Grisham, former overseer and that he have the same hands and keep the same in repair, who were alloted to said Grisham.

Ordered that Stephen Rowland be appointed overseer of the Military road in the room of Richard Strawn, and that he have the same hands to keep the same in repair, which were under the direction of said Strawn for that purpose.

At least five Justices being present, Reuben Tripp presented in Court one wof scalp over 4 months old which was directed to be burnt and ordered that the clerk should certify the same accordingly.

At least 5 justices being present, William Holland produced in court one wolf scalp over 4 months old which was directed to be burnt and ordered that the clerk certify the same accordingly.

The Court proceeded to select from among their own body as aCourt of Quorum for the trial of all jury cases, causes, by ballot, and upon counting the votes it was found that Duncan McIntyre, Pollardz Wisdom, David Crockett, Henry Phoenix and Henson Day were duly selected for the purpose aforesaid, according to Act of Assembly.

Ordered that the sheriff be directed to summon the following named persons to attend as jurors at the next County Court of this county, to-wit, Malcom McIntire, Robert Mason, Bailey Allford, Thomas Keyes, Alexander Miller, Etheldred Thomas, John VOries, Andrew, Alison, James McConnel, Jr., Issac W. Brown, Milton H. Jack, Arthur M. Alexander, Solomon Asbell, Levi Blackard, Sterling Lindsey, William Wisdom, Sr., Elijah Melton, Thomas Ethredge, Lemuel Blythe, Spencer Pierce, John Adkison, Joseph Tease, George Isom, Isaac Pennington, William Seahorn, John Lockard.

William H. Buchanan, Clerk of the Court produced in court the receipts of Thomas Crutcher, Treasurer of West Tennessee for having returned the amount of taxable property and polls and made return of state monies according to Act of Assembly in such cases made and provided.

Ordered that court be adjourned until tomorrow, 9 o'clock, Duncan McInitire, David Crockett, Henry Sharp, J.P.'s.

TUESDAY FEBRUARY 2nd 1819

Tuesday morning 9 o'clock, court met according to adjournment. Present, Duncan McIntire, David Crockett, Henry Sharp, Justices, Esquires.

At least five justices being present, to-wit, Duncan McIntire, David Crockett, Henry Sharp, Pollard Wisdom, and Henson Day. Andrew McWhorter produced in court one wolf scalp over 4 months old which was ordered to be burnt and ordered that the clerk should certify accordingly.

Ordered that Joseph Farmer a minor of this County be bound unto James Edmondson until he arrives to full age and that said Edmondson be bound to educate said boy reading, writing and arithmetic to the rule of three, which said bond was given accordingly.

The sheriff returned into court the following veneri facias, to-wit, George Vandover, Thomas Welch, James Broadstreet,

Thomas Bird,Sr., John Bird, Charles Hays, Daniel Pierce, Benjamin May, Elijah Melton, Jacob Blythe, George, Archer, William Wooten, Simon Higgs, Stephen Rowland, Samuel Sullivan, Henry Phoenix, Richard T. Bailey, Levi Blackard, William McAnnally, Solomon Stone, Philip Chronister, David Adkins, Wiley I. Duckworth of whom the following named persons were drawn as Grand Jurors, to-wit, Henry Phoenix,foreman, Philip Chronister, William McAnnally, Benjamin May, Solomon Stone,Jr, Simon Higgs, Samuel Sullivan, Richard T. Bailey,Levi Blackard, Elijah Melton, George Vandover, John Bird, Thomas Welch who after being duly qualified and having received their charge withdrew to consider of their presentments under the direction of William White, constable qualified for this purpose.

Andrew Pickens and John Hillhouse,Esquires who were appointed to take a list of taxable property and polls returnable to this court made return thereof according to law.

Joseph Baldwin
vs   In case
James Holcomb
    This day came the parties by their attorneys and thereupon came a jury of good and lawful men,to-wit, William Wooten, Stephen Roland, William McAnnally, Nathan McClendon, William Voss, John Alsup, Melcher Duncan, John Welch,Sr., James Helton, George Grisham, Malcom McIntire, Daniel Mathews, who being elected, tried and sworn well and truly to try this issue of traverse upon the oaths do say that the defendant is guilty in manner and form as in the plaintiff's declaration mentioned and they do assess the plaintiffs's damage by reason thereof to $45.87½ besides costs. It is therefore considered by this court that the plaintiff recover of the defendant his damages aforesaid in form aforesaid asessed together with his costs by him about his suit in this behalf expended and the defendant in mercy & c.

Peter R. Booker
vs   In debt
George Sherley
    This day came the parties by their attorneys and the defendant moved for the continuance of this cause upon affadavit until the next term of this court which motion being fully argued and well understood it is considered by the court that the defendant's motion be sustained and that the said defendant pay the cost incurred at the present term of this court on said cause by reason of the continuance thereof.

Jesse Evans
vs   Case
Rowland Tankersley & Moses Spencer, Def.
    This day came the plaintiff by his attoneys and the defendant also who filed here his plea of abatement to which the plaintiff_____ and the defendant joined in _____order, the court argument being made sustained the _____ and overruled the plea in abatement, the defendant referring (sic?) to plead the _____by leave of court ordered their rule at last term of plead and try by his attorney came and the defendant, being solemnly called came not but made default ,whereupon

it is considered by the court that the plaintiff recover of the defendants, but being unknown to the court here what damages the plaintiff hath sustained, it is ordered that a jury come in to inquire of the same, whereupon came a jury of good and lawful men, to-wit, George Archer, John McDonald, Jacob Blythe, John HAIL, Adam Ross, Samuel Graham, John McIntyre, John Crisp, Jacob Mathews, James Webb, Thomas Keys, Nathaniel Mason, who being elected, tried and sworn to inquire what damages the plaintiff hath sustained by reason of the premises aforesaid, upon their oaths do say that he hath sustained damages to the amount of $63-whereupon it is considered by the court that the plaintiff recover from said defendant his damages aforesaid in form aforesaid and assessed together with his cost by him about his suit in this behalf expended and the defendant in mercy & c.

Ordered that court be adjourned until tomorrow, 9 o'clock.
Duncan McIntire, David Crockett and Henson Day, J.P's.

WEDNENESDAY, FEBRUARY 3rd, 1819

Wednesday morning, 9 o'clock court met according to adjournment-present, Duncan McIntire, David Crockett, Pollard Wisdom, Henry Sharp, Esquires, Justices.

James Forbes, Esquire, who was appointed to take a list of taxable property and polls returnable to this Court made return according to law.

Henry Phoenix came into court prayed and obtained a license to keep a house of ordinary, which was granted to him, who gave bond and security and was qualified according to law.

Ordered that the County Tax of this County be 100 per cent upon the State Tax, and that the Clerk be directed to issue the Tax list to the Collector of the same accordingly.

State vs Bailey Brooks — Assault and battery committed on the body of Daniel McIntire

This day came the defendant by his attorney as well as the Solicitor General on behalf of the State and the defendant being arraigned upon his arraignment pleaded not guilty and for his trial puts himself upon his Country and the Solicitor General for the State likewise, whereupon came a jury of good and lawful men, to-wit, George Archer, Jacob Blythe, William Higgs, Daniel Beeler, John Lockard, William H. Cowan, James Webb, Aaron Anglin, Philip Null, Andrew Fugate, Nathaniel Mason, and Jacob Mathews, who being elected tried and sworn well and truly to try this issue of traverse upon their oaths do say that the defendant is guilty in manner and form as he is charged in the indictment bill. It is therefore considered by the court that the defendant make his fine with the State to the sum of 50¢ besides costs and that the defendant be taken & c from which judgement the defendant prayed an appeal to the Honorable the Circuit Court to be holden for this

County on the fourth Monday in this month which was granted him who gave bond and security according to law.

State vs Bailey Brooks — Assault and battery committed on the body of Solomon Gresham

This day came the defendant by his attorney as well as the Solicitor General on behalf of the state and the defendant being arraigned upon his arraignment pleaded not guilty and for his trial puts himself upon his Country and the Solicitor General for the State likewise, whereupon came a jury of good and lawful men, to-wit, John Allsup, John Phillips, Ezekiel Farmer, Thomas Keese, Alexander Miller, Campbell Hays, James Parchman, Robert McCann, Charles McHughs, Lemuel Blythe, John Crisp, John Wisdom, who being elected, tried and sworn well and truly to try this issue of traverse upon their oaths do say that the defendant is guilty in manner and form as charged in the bill of indictment. It is considered by the court that the defendant make his fine with the State to the sum of $15.00 besides costs and that the defendant be taken & c. Upon which judgement the defendant prayed an appeal to the Honourable Circuit Court to be holden for this County on the fourth Monday in this month which was granted him who gave bond and security according to law.

State vs Bailey Brooks — Assault and battery on the body of Malcom McIntire

This day came the defendant by his attorney as well as the Solicitor General on hzlf of the State and the defendant pleaded not guilty and for his trial puts himself upon his Country and the Solicitor for the state likewise, whereupon came a jury of good and lawful men, to-wit, George Archer, Jacob Blythe, Daniel Pearce, William Higgs, Daniel Beeler, John Lockard, William H. Cowan, James Webb, Aaron Anglin, Phillip Bull, Andrew Fugate, and Nathaniel Mason, who being elected tried and sworn well and truly to try this issue of traverse upon their oaths do say that the defendant is guilty in manner and form as charged in the bill of indictment. It is therefore considered by this court that the defendant make his fine with the State to the sum of $50.00 besides costs and that the defendant be taken & c. Upon which judgement the defendant prayed an appeal to the Honourabl Circuit Court to be holden for this County on the fourth Monday in this month which was granted him who gave bond and security according to law.

State vs Bailey Brooks — Indictment for an assault and battery committed on the body of Solomon Thornton

This day came the Solicitor General on behalf of the State as well as the defendant in his proper person and the defendant being arraigned upon his arraignment pleaded guilty in manner and form as he is charged in the bill of indictment and for his trial puts himself upon the justice and mercy of the Court, whereupon it is considered by the Court that the defendant make his fine with the State to the amount of $25 and that the defendant pay the cost of this prosecution and that the defendant be taken & c from which judgement the defendant prayed an appeal to the Honourable Circuit Court to be holden for this County at the place of holding court on the fourth Monday in this month which was granted him who gave bond and security according to law.

State
vs   Presentment for an affray
Mobel Stone

  This day came the Solicitor General on behalf of the State as well as the defendant in his proper person and the defendant being arraigned upon his arraignment pleaded not guilty and for his trial puts himself upon his Country and the Solicitor General for the state, likewise. Whereupon came a jury of good and lawful men, to-wit, John Allsup, John Phillips, Ezekiel Farmer, Campbell Hayes, James Parchman, Charles McKew, Lemuel Blythe, John Wisdom, Malcom McIntire, Daniel Pearce, Samuel Grayham, and Jacob Matthews, who being elected tried and sworn well and truly to try this issue f traverse upon their oaths do say that the defendant is not guilty in manner and form as charged in the bill of indictment. It is therefore considered by the court that the defendant in all respects be acquitted from the affray aforesaid and that he depart hence without delay.

State
vs   Indictment for an affray
Manuel Keltner

  Defendant pleaded guilty in manner and form as is charged in the bill of indictment and for his trial puts himself on the justice and mercy of the court. Whereupon it is considered by the court that the defendant make his fine with the State to the sum of $1 and the defendant be taken & c....

State
vs   Indictment for an affray
Manuel Keltner

  Defendant pleaded guilty in manner and form as he is charged in the bill of indictment and for his trial puts himself on the justice and mercy of the Court. Whereupon it is considered by the court that the defendant make his fine with the State to the sum of $1 and the defendant be taken & c...

State
vs   For retailing spirituous liquors without license
James Boguard

  This day came the Solicitor General in behalf of the State as well as the defendant in his proper person and the defendant being arraigned upon his arraignment pleaded not guilty and for his trial puts himself upon his Country and the Solicitor General for the State likewise. Whereupon came a jury of good and lawful men, to-wit, John Allsup, John Phillips, Ezekiel Farmer,

Campbell Hayes, James Parchman, Charles McHughs, Lemuel Blythe, John Wisdom, Malcom McIntire, Daniel Pearce, Samuel Graham, and Jacob Mathews, who being elected tried and sworn well and truly to try this issue of traverse upon their oaths do say that the defendant is not gulty in manner and form as charged in the bill of indictment. It is therefore considered by the court that the defendant go hence without day (sic) and in all respects be acquited from charge aforesaid.

State
vs   For retailing spirituous liquiors without license
John Hamilton

This day came the Solicitor General in behalf of the State as well as the defendant in his proper person and the defendant being arraigned upon his arraignemnt pleaded not guilty and for his trial puts himself upon his Country and the Solicitor General for the State likewise. Whereupon came a jury of good and lawful men, to-wit, George Archer, Jacob Blythe, John Polley, John Farmer, John Lockard, Melcher Duncan, Nathaniel Mason, John Welch, William H. Cowan, Daniel McIntyre, Phillip Null, and Aaron Anglin who being elected, tried and sworn well and truly to try this issue of traverse upon their oaths do say that the defendant is not guilty in manner and form as charged in the bill of indictment. It is therefore considered by the court that the defendant go hence without day and in all respects be acquitted from charge aforesaid.

State
vs   An affray
James Holton

This day came the Solicitor General on behalf of the State as well as the defendant in his proper person and the defendant being arraigned upon his arraignment pleaded guilty and for his trial puts himself upon the mercy and justice of the court. Whereupon it is considered by the court that the defendant make his fine witht ch State to the sum of $1 and that he pay the cost of this prosecution and that the defendant be taken & c.

Hugh Reynolds came into court prayed and obtained a license to keep a house of Ordinary at his own house in this County which was granted him who gave bond and security and was qualified according to law.

James Forbes who was a witness in the case of Joseph Farmer against William Welch- a judgement in which was rendered at the August term of this court in the year 1818 and from which an appeal is taken to the Circuit Court the said witness having failed to prove his attendance until now it is ordered that the said claim be added in the bill of cost in a full and complete as if the said attendance had been proved before the rendation of said judgement.

John Welch
vs
John Counes (sic)   In Case

This cause is continued until the next term of the Court as upon affadavit of the defendant.

State
vs
Bailey Brooks

This day came into Court the defendant in his proper person and acknowledged himself indebted to the State of Tennessee the sum of $200 to be levied of his goods and chattels and tenements to the use of the State to be void on conditions that he appear at the next Circuit Court to be holden for this County on the fourth Monday in this month at the place of holding courts on the second day of this term then and there to answer the State upon a charge of assault and battery committed on the body of Daniel McIntire and not to depart therefrom without leave of the Court.

Absalum McCommac, George Brooks, Felix Goff came into Court and acknowledged themselves severally indebted to the State of Tennessee in the sum of $50 each to be levyed of their goods, chattels and tenements to the use of the State to be void on conditions that Bailey Brooks appears at the next Circuit Court to be holden for this County at the place of holding court on the fourth Monday of this month and on the second day of this term then and there to answer the State upon a charge of assault and battery committed on the body of Daniel McIntire and not depart thereupon without leave of the court.

State
vs
Bailey Brooks

Absalum McCommac, George Brooks, Felix Goff came into Court and acknowledged themselves severally indebted to the State of Tennessee in the sum of $200 each to be levyed of their goods, and chattels and tenements to the use of the State to be void on conditions that Bailey Brooks appears at the next term of the Circuit Court to be holden for this county at the place of holding court on the fourth Monday of this month and on the second day of this term then and there to answer the State upon a charge of Assault and battery on the body of Solomon Gresham and not depart thereupom without leave of the court.

State
vs
Bailey Brooks

Absalum McCommac, George Brooks, Felix Goff came into Court and acknowledged themselves severally indebted to the State of Tennessee in the sum of $200 each to be levied of their goods chattels and tenements to the use of the State to be void on conditions that Bailey Brooks appears at the next term of Circuit Court to be holden for this county at the place of holding court on the fourth Monday of this month and on the second day of this term then and there to answer the State upon a charge of assault and battery on the body of Malcom McIntyre and not depart thereupon without leave of the court.

State
vs
Bailey Brooks

This day came the defendant into court and acknowledged himself to be indebted to the State of Tennessee in the sum of $200 to be levied of his goods, chattel lands and tenements to the use of the State to be void on conditions that he appear here at the Circuit Court to be holden for this County on the fourth Monday of this month and on the second day of this term then and there to answer the state upon a charge of assault and battery committed upon the body of Solomon Thornton and that he depart not without leave of this court.

Absolum McComick, George Brooks, Felix Goff came into court and acknowledged themselves severally indebted to the State of Tennessee in the sum of $200 each to be levyed of their goods, chattel lands and tenements to the use of the State to be voidon conditions that Bailey Brooks appears at the next term of the Circuit Court to be holden for this County at the place of holding court on the fourth Monday of this month and the second day of this term then and there to answer the state upon a charge of assault and battery upon the body of Solomon Thornton and not depart therefrom without leave of the court.

State   For an affray
vs
Noble Stone

Lewis Mathews who was subpoened to appear at this Court to give evidence on behalf of the State although solemnly called came not but made default. It is therefore considered by the court that judgement Mi Si be entered up against him for said failure according to Act of Assembly.

Malcom McIntire came into court and acknowledged himself to be indebt4d to the State of Tennessee in the sum of $200 to be levied of his goods, chattel lands and tenements to the use of the State to be void on conditions that he appear here at the next term of the Circuit Court to be holden for this county on the fourth Monday of this term at this place on the second day of this term then and there to prosecute and give evidence in behalf of the State against Bailey Brooks for an assault and batt4ry committed on himself and not depart therefrom without leave of the Court.

Duncan McIntire came into court and acknowledged himself indebted unto the State of Tennessee in the sum of $200 to be levied of his goods, chattels lands and tenements to the use of the State to be void on conditions that the said Malcom McIntire appear here at the Circuit to be holden for this county the fourth Monday of this month on the second day of said court then and there to prosecute and give evodence on behalf of the State against Bailey Brooks for an assault and battery committed on the body of Malcom McIntire and not depart therefrm without leave of the court.

Solomon Thornton came into court and acknowledged himself to be indebted to the State of Tennessee in the sum of $200 to be levied of his goods, chattels lands and tenements to the use of the State to be void on condition that he appear here at the Circuit Court to be holden for this County on the fourth Monday of this term at this place on the second day of this term then and ther to prosecute and give evidence in behalf of the State against Bailey Brooks for an assault and battery committed on himself and not depart therefrom without leave of the court.

James Forbes, Esq., came into court and acknowledged himself to be indebted to the State of Tennessee in the sum of $200 to be levied of his goods, chattels lands and tenements to the use of the state to be void on condition that Solomon Thornton appear here at the Circuit court to be holden for this County on the fourth Monday of this term at this place on the second day of this term then and there to prosecute and give evidence in behalf of the State against Bailey Brooks for an assault and battery against Solomon Thornton and not depart therefrom without leave of the court.

Solomon Grisham came into court and acknowledged himself to be indebted to the State of Tennessee in the sum of $200 to be levied of his goods, chattels lands and tenements to the use of the State to be void on condition that he appear here at the Circuit Court to be holden for this County on the fourth Monday of this term at this place on th4 second day of this term then and there to prosecute and give evidence in behalf of the State against Bailey Brooks for an assault and battery against himself and not depart therefrom without leave of the court.

George Grisham came into court and acknowledged himself to be indebted to the State of Tennessee in the sum of $200 to be levied of his goods, chattels lands and tenements to the use of the state to be void on condition that Solomon Gresham appears and gives evidence against Bailey Brooks for assault and battery on himself.

Daniel McIntire came into court and acknowledged himself indebted to the State of Tennessee in the sum of $200 tobe levied of his goods, chatells lands and tenements to the use of the State to be void on condition that he appear here at the Circuit court to be holden for this county on the fourth Monday of this term at this place on the second day of this term then and there to prosecute and give evidence in behlaf of the State against Bailey Brooks for an assault and battery against himself and not depart therefrom without leave of the court.

Lemuel Blythe came into court and acknowledged himself indebted to the State of Tennessee in the sum of $200 to be levied of his goos chattel lands and tenements to the use of the state to be void on condition that Daniel McIntire appears here at Circuit Court to be holden for this county on the fourth Monday of this term at this place on the second day of this term then and ther to prosecute and give evidence in behalf of the state against Bailey Brooks for an assault and battery against himself and not depart therefrom without leave of the court.

  Ordered that court be adjourned until tomorrow at 9 o'clock. David Crockett, Henry Sharp, Pollard Wisdom, and Henson Day, J.P.'s.

GHURSDAY MORNING FEB. 4th 1819

  Court met according to adjournment-Duncan McIntyre, David Crockett, Henry Sharp, Pollard Wisdom and Henson Day, Esquires, Justices.

State
vs   For retailing spirits without license
James Boguard

  On motion of the Solicitor General in behalf of the State it is ordered by the court that the defendant in this case be taxed with the cost the court being of opinion that there is a strong grounds to induce the court to believe that the defendant is guilty in manner and form as he is charged in the bill of presentment.

State
vs   For retailing spirits without license
John Hamilton

  On motion of the Solicitor in behalf of the state, it is ordered by the court that the defendant in this case be taxed with the cost the court being of the oppinion that there is a strong grounds to induce the court to believe that the defendant is guilty in manner and form as he is charge in the Bill of presentment.

Samuel Green and wife
vs
Aaron Anglin and wife

  This day came the parties by their attorneys and thereupon came a jury of good and lawful men, to-wit, Stepehn Rowland, Willam Wooten, William McCann, Nathan McClendon, William Voss, John Allsup, Melcher Duncan, Hugh Sincclair, Jesse Holton, George Gresham, Malcom McInitire, Daniel Mathews who being elected tried and sworn to try this issue of traverse upon their oaths do say that the defendant is guilty in manner and form as in the presentment mentioned and they do assess the plaintiffs damage by reason thereof to $45 besides cost. It is therefore ordered by the court that his damages aforesaid in form aforesaid by the jurors aforesaid assessed together with his costs by him about his suit in this behalf expended and the defendant in mercy &c from which judgement prayed an appeal to the Honorable the Circuit court to be holden for the County which was granted him who gave bond and security according to law.

John Hamilton came into court and acknowledged himself indebted to the State of Tennessee in the sum of $200 to be levied of his goods chattel lands and tenements to the use of the State to be void on conditions that he appear here at the next term of Circuit Court to be holden for this County on the 4th Monday of this month and on the second day of the court then and there to answer the state upon a charge of the state against him for having retailed spirituous liquiors consisting of a smaller quanity than a quart & c without license and not depart therefrom without leave of the court.

Jacob Blythe and Elijah Molton came into court and acknowledged themselves to be severally indebted to the state of Tenn., in the sum of $100 each to be levied of their goods, chattel lands and tenements to the use of the state to be void on condition that John Hamilton appear here at the Circuit court to be holden for this County on the fourth Monday of this month and on the second day of the court then and there to answer the state upon a charge for retailing spirituous liquior consisting of a smaller amount than a quart & c without license and not to depart therefrom without leave of the court.

The Grand Jury returned into court the following bills of indictment, to-wit, State against William Macky for petit larceny, a true bill. State against William Null and Jesse Anglin, a true bill, for an affray. State against William Welch, Jr., assault and battery a true bill. State against John Wharton for assault and battery a true bill. State against Willam Gresham and Rubin Hanks, for an affray, a true bill.

John Welch
vs
John Counts

The defendant came into court prays a commission to issue from this court to Franklin County, Alabama Territory, to take the deposition of John Bankhead, Sr., and Mary Bankhead returnable to next term of this court which was granted him by giving the plaintiff ten days previous notice of the time and place of taking the same.

The State
vs   For an affray
Noble Stone

This day came the Solicitor General on behalf of the state and moved the court that judgement in this case should be entered up in favor of all those entitled for cost which was granted and ordered that the clerk should certify accordingly.

William Macky came into court and acknowledged himself indebted to the state of Tennessee in sum of $500 to be levied of his goods, chattel lands and tenements to the use of the State to be void on condition that he appears here at the next term of court of Pleas and quarter session to be holden for this County on the first Wednesday after the first Monday in May next then and there to answer the state upon a charge of Petit Larceny and not depart therefrom without leave of the court.

William Rogers and Joel Coffee came into court and acknowledged themselves indebted to the State of Tennessee in the sum of $250 each to be levied of their goods, chattel lands and tenements to the use of the state to be void on conditions that William Mackey appears here at the next court of Pleas and Quarter Sessions to be holden for the County on the first Wednesday after the first Monday in May next then and there to answer the state on a charge of Petit Larceny and not to depart therefrom without leave of the court.

Gilbert McMillan by his attorney comes into Court and persecuted his petition praying the court that writs of Certeorari and Supersedias should issue to remove all proceedings in tche case wherein Frederick Sherley is plaintiff and said McMillan is defendant unto this court and having given bond and security according to law the same is granted to him.

William Carothers
vs Trespass on the case
Josephus Irvine

This day came the parties by their attorneys and thereupon came a jury of good and lawful men, to-wit, Charles McHughs, Simon Edwards, Andrew Fugate, Jacob Blythe, Daniel Pearce, George Archer, Samuel Price, John Welch, John Wisdom, John Sherley, James Hale, John Phillips, who being elected tried and sworn well and truly to try this issue of traverse upon their oaths do say that the defendant is guilty in manner and form as in the plaintiff's declaration mentioned and they do assess the plaintiff damages by reason thereof to $771 besides costs. It is therefore considered by the court that the plaintiff recover of the defendant his damages aforesaid in form aforesaid by the jurors aforesaid assessed together with his costs by him about his suit in this vehalf expended and that the defendant in mercy and from which judgement the defendant prayed an appeal who having filed his reasons the same is granted him who gave bond and security according to law.

Gilbert McMillan
vs Certioror
George Sherley

The plaintiff came into court and said he is unwilling further to prosecute his said suit against the defendant and assumes upon himself the payment of the cost. It is therefore considered by the court that the defendant recover of the plaintiff his cost by him about his defense in this behalf expended.

John Bankhead
vs In case
John Allsup

This day came the parties by their arttorneys and thereupon came a jury of good and lawful men, to-wit, Henry Phoenix, Phillip Chronister, William McAnally, Benjamin May, Solomon Stone, Jr., Simon Higgs, Richard T. Bailey, Samuel Sullivan,

Levi Blackard, Elijah Melton, George Vandover, John Birdwho being elected tried and sworn well and truly to try this issue of traverse upon their oaths do say that the defendant is guilty in manner and form as is charged in the plaintiff's declaration and they do assess the plaintiff's damage by reason thereof to the sum of $41.53½ damages besides cost. It is therefore considered by the court that the plaintiff recover of the defendant his damages aforesaid in form aforesaid and by the jurors aforesaid assessed together with his costs by him about this suit in his behalf expended and the defendant in mercy & c.

Ordered that court be adjourned until tomorrow, 9 o'clock. Duncan McIntyre, David Crockett and H. Day, J.P's.

FRIDAY MORNING, FEBRUARY 5th, 1819

Court met at 9 o'clock Friday morning Feb. 5th, 1819 according to adjournment. Present, Duncan McIntyre, David Crockett, and Henson Day, Esquires, Justices

Samuel Green
vs
Charles Hays, Aaron Anglin, John Anglin
At the August term of this court the plaintiff in this case came into court and entered on the appearance docket of said term as follows. The plaintiff comes into court by his council and dismisses as his suit the fourth day of August term and as it was ommitted to enter judgement for cost in this case it is ordered by the court that judgement Nun Pro Tem be considered against the plaintiff for all costs that have accured in the case.

James Killen
vs
William McMahan
At the August term of this court 1818 the plaintiff in this case came into court and entered on the appearance docket of said term as follows. Suit dismissed at Plaintiff's order and as it was omitted to enter judgement for cost in this case, it is ordered by the court that judgement Nun Pro Tem be entered against the plaintiff for all costs that have accured in this case.

John Bankhead
vs   An appeal
John Alsup
The defendant came into court and prayed an appeal to the Honourable the Circuit Court of this County which was granted him who gave bond and security according to law.

George Vandover came into court and suggested that he has attended as a witness at the Aug. term of this Court, 1818, in the case of Joseph Farmer against William Welch, three days and that he has omitted to prove his attendance as a witness aforesaid. It is therefore ordered by the court that he be allowed to prove now for then and that the clerk certify accordingly.

45

Ordered that court be adjourned until court in course. Duncan McIntyre, David Crockett, Henry Sharp, H. Day and Pollard Wisdom, J.P.'s.

MONDAY MAY 3, 1819

At a Court of pleas and quarter sessions began and held at the house of Josephus Irvine, formerly the house of Doctor Joseph Farmer, the present place of holding Courts in and for said County the 3rd day of May, 1910, Present, Duncan McIntire, Pollard Wisdom, David Crockett, Henry Sharp, Henson Day, John Hillis, Joseph Gist, Esquires, Justices.

Ordered by the court that John McClish be exempted from the payment of half of the valuation of a certain steer taken up by said McClish proven to be the property of William Sharp.

Ordered by the court that George Hanks, Esquire, George Lucas and Henry Phoenix be appointed Judges of the ensuing election to be held for the County at this place on the first Thursday and Friday in August next for the purpose of electing members to the next Legislature of this State, Member to Congress, etc.

A deed of conveyance from Daniel Hughs to William Richardson for three hundred acres and twenty acres of land was produced in open Court and proved by the oath of Pollard Wisdom and Archilaus Hogg, two of the subscribing witnesses thereto, which was ordered to be certified for registration accordingly.

Ordered by the court that Nathan Casey, Manuel Crisp, and Robert Chaffin be appointed commissioners to settle with the County Trustee and that they make report to the next Court.

Ordered that William White and Warren Mason be appointed constables to attend the next County Court.

Ordered likewise that James Broadstreet and Nathan Jobe be appointed Constables to attend the next Circuit Court.

Ordered that the Sheriff be directed to summon the following named persons to attend as jurors at the next County Court of this County, to-wit, Joshua Ashmore, Phillip Bryant, William Henderson, John McClish, Moses Pennington, Nathaniel Christian, Josiah Hurley, Jonathon Jobe, Aaron Choate, Sr., Jacob Adair, Benjamin Morrow, John Phillips, Jesse Helton, John W. Henry, Simon Edwards, Samuel Thomas, John Adkisson, Barney Gabriel, Thomas Holland, Daniel McIntyre, Jacob Blythe, William Rickman, James Brooks, John McClaren, Arthur M. Alexander, Thomas Keese.

Ordered that the sheriff be directed to summon the following named persons to attend as jurors at the next Circuit Court to be holden for this County on the 4th Monday in August next at the place of holding courts, to-wit,

Daniel A. Flannery, Spencer Alton, William Burris, John Anthony, Miles Birdsong, William Burleson, Gabriel Bumpass, Willis Lucas, Martin Prewitt, John Crisp, Henson Day, Andrew Pickens, Duncan McIntyre,Esq., John Hillhouse,Esq., Edward Selly, Simon Higgs, James Appleton, Hosea Straughn, John Null, William Boguard, Daniel McConnell, George Rogers, Andrew Ellison, Daniel Beeler, Edward Higgs, Robert Hillhouse.

Joseph Gist, Andrew Pickens and John Rea, Esq., who were appointed at Nov. term 1818 of this court to take a list of taxables property and polls and to take a list of voters according to a late Act of Assembly making provisions for taking the census returned into court their several lists of voters according to law.

Ordered that court be adjourned until tomorrow at 9 o'clock. Henry Sharp, Duncan McIntyre, H. Day, Pollard Wisdom , J.P..'s.

TUESDAY MAY 4th, 1819

Tuesday morning May 4, 1819 nine o'clock court met according to adjournment present, Duncan McIntyre, Henry Sharp, Henson Day, and Pollard Wisdom, Esquires, Justices.

The Sheriff returns into court the following Venire Facias to-wit, Malcom McIntyre, Robert Mason, Bailey Alford, Thomas Koese, Alexandr Miller, Etheldred Thomas, John Voories, Andrew Allison, James McConnell,Sr., Issac W. Brown, Milton H. Jack, Arthur M. Alexander, Solomon Asbell, Levi Blackard, Sterling Lindsey, William Wisdom,Sr., Elijah Melton, Thomas Etheridge, Lemuel Blythe, Spencer Pearce, John Adkisson, Joseph Tease, George Isom, Issac Pennington, William Seahorn, John Lockard, of whom the following persons were drawn as Grand Jurors,to-wit, Alexander Miller, Foreman, Milton H. Jack, Arthur M. Alexander, Andrew Allison, Issac W. Brown, Bailey Alford, Solomon ASBELL, Malcom McIntyre, Sterling Lindsey, Thomas Etheridge, John Vories, William Wisdom, Elisha Melton, who after being qualified withdrew to consider of their presentments under the directions of William White, a Constable sworn to attend them.

On motion of Andrew Pickens , County Trustee for this County, who came into court by his attorney and moved for judgement to be rendered against Bracewell Farmer, Sheriff and Collector of this County for the County tax due and unpaid for the year 1818, against his securities, and it appearing to the satisfaction of this court that the said Bracewell Farmer has been legally notified of this motion, it is therefore considered by the court that judgement be rendered against the said Bracewell Farmer, former sheriff and Daniel Mathews, Lundsford M.Bramlet, Josephus Irvine, securities of the said sheriff for the sum of $41.75 according to the Certificate of the Clerk of this Court and in conformity to an Act of Assembly in such case made and provided for.

Ordered that William Gilchrist,Esq., be appointed Solicitor General to fill the vacancy of Robert L. Cobb, who was qualified accordingly.

Ordered that the petition of Peter Mosely and others made at the November term, 1818, of this Court be in all respects revived.

Bailey Brooks   Trespass
vs
Shadrack Alvis, Warren Mason, Marvin Mason
    This cause is continued until the next term of this Court as on affadavit of the defendants.

John Allsup
vs   Case
George Bankhead
    This day came the parties by their attorneys and thereupon came a jury of good and lawful men, to-wit, Ethelred Thomas, Levi Blackard, Thomas Keese, James Bogard, William Dalton, William Voss, Aaron Anglin, George Sherley, Jr., Austin Willis, Daniel Mathews, Daniel McIntyre, John Siminton, who being elected tried and sworn well and truly to try this issue of traverse upon their oaths do say that the defendant is not guilty in manner and form as the plaintiff in his declaration against him hath alledged. It is therefore considered by the court that the defendant go hence without delay and recover of the plaintiff his costs by him about his defense in this behalf expended.

Bailey Brooks
vs   Trespass on case
Solomon Thornton
    This day came the defendant in his proper person into Court and moved the court that this cause be dismissed and assumes upon himself the payments of all costs whereupon it is considered by the court that the defendant recover of the plaintiff his costs aforesaid by him about his defense in this behalf expended.

Solomon Thornton
vs   Trespass
Bailey Brooks
    This day the defendant in his proper person comes into Court and moved the court that this cause be dismissed and assumes upon himself the payment of all costs, whereupon it is considered by the court that the defendant recover of the plaintiff the costs aforesaid by him about his suit in this behalf expended.

    Ordered that the County Trustee of this County pay Josephus Irvine the sum of $12 for furnishing a stray pen out of any monies not otherwise appropriated. Five of the acting Justices being present, to-wit, David Crockett, Henry Sharp, H. Day, Pollard Wisdom and Daniel McIntyre.

    William Seahorn produced in open court one wolf's scalp over four months old which was ordered to be burned and certified accordingly.

Samuel Price produced in open court one wolf scalp over four months old which was ordered to be burned and certified accordingly.

John Welch, Sr.
vs   Trespass
John Counts

    This cause is continued upon affadavit of the plaintiff until the next term of this court and on application of the defendant. It is ordered that an order be revived to take a deposition of _____ in the Alabama Territory in Franklin Co., by giving the plaintiff ten days notice of time and place of taking the same.

Robert Mason
vs   Certiorary
Bailey Brooks

    This cause is continued until the next term of this court by consent of parties.

David Crocket
vs   In debt
Ezekiel Farmer

    Daniel Mathews one of the defendants securities came into court and confessed judgement for the sum of $150 debt together with the sum of $3.25 damages. It is therefore considered by the curt that the plaintiff recover of the said Mathews the sum of $150 debt together with the sum of $3.25 damages besides his costs by him about his suit in this behalf expended.

Bailey Brooks
vs   Trespass on the Case
Daniel McIntyre

    This cause is continued by consent of parties until the next term of this court and upon application of the plaintiff is ordered that a commission issue to take the deposition of Tyree Dollens in the Chickasaw Nation by giving the defendant 20 days previous notice of time and place of taking the same.

    Ordered that Levi Blackard, a juroer to this term be exempt from further attendance this term.

Thomas Ramsey
vs   Debt
Josephus Irvine

    This day came the parties by their attorneys and thereupon came a jury of good and lawful men, to-wit, Ethelred Thomas, Levi Blackard, Thomas Keese, James Bogard, William S. Dalton, William Voss, Aaron Anglin, George Sherley, Sr., Austin Kendrick, Daniel Mathews, Daniel Beeler, John Simonton, who being elected, tried and sworn well and truly to try this issue of traverse, upon their oaths do say, that the defendant hath not paid the debts in the writing obligatory and the plaintiff's declaration mentioned as in pleading he hath alleged and they do assess the plaintiff damage by reason thereof to $18 besides costs. It is therefore considered by the court here that the plaintiff recover of the defendant the sum of $250 the debt aforesaid together with their damages aforesaid and by the Jurors aforesaid asessed together with his costs by him about his suit in this behalf expended and the defendant in mercy & c.

David Crockett
vs   Trespass on the Case
Ezekiel Farmer
    This cause is continued as on affadavit of the plaintiff

Robert Patton
vs   For debt
Josephus Irvine
    This day came the parties by their attorneys and thereupon came a jury of good and lawful men, to-wit, Ethelred Thomas, Levi Blackard, Thomas Keese, James Bogard, William Dalton, William Voss, Aaron Anglin, George Sherley, Jr., Austin Kendrick, Daniel Mathews, Daniel Beeler, John Simonton who being elected tried and sworn well and truly to try this issue of traverse, upon their oaths do say that the Defendant hath not paid the debt in the writing obligatory in the plaintiff's declaration mentioned as in pleading he hath alleged and they do assess the plaintiff damage by reason thereof to $18 besides costs. It is therefore considered by the court here that the plaintiff recover of the defendant the sum of $400 their debt aforesaid together with their damages aforesaid by the jurors aforesaid in form aforesaid assessed together with his costs by him about his suit in this behalf expended from which judgement he prayed an appeal to the Honourable Circuit Court to be holden for this County on the fourth Monday in August next which was granted him who gave bond and security and filled his reasons according to law.

H.J. Bumpass
vs
Thomas Trentham (sic)
    This day came the parties by their attorneys and thereupon came a jury of good and lawful men, to-wit, Ethelred Thomas, Levi Blackard, Thomas Keese, James Bogard, William S. Dalton, William Voss, Aaron Anglin, George Sherley, Sr., Austin Kendrick, Lemuel Mathews, Daniel Beeler, John Simonton who being elected tried and sworn well and truly to try this matter of dispute upon their oaths do say that the plaintiff recover of the defendant the sum of $20 and the plaintiff's declaration mentioned besides costs. It is therefore considered by the court that the plaintiff recover of the defendant the sum of $20 his costs aforesaid and his declaration before the justices as in this court in this behalf expended from which judgement the defendant prays an appeal to the Honourable Circuit Court to be holden for the County of Lawrence-he having given bond and security according to law, the same is granted him and after deliberation the plaintiff comes into court and dismesses his suit and the defendant assumes upon himself the payment of all costs as well before the Justices below as in this court expended.

Maryann Payne came into court and was admitted to make affadavit, which affadavit is in words and figures following, to-wit, State of Tennessee ., Lawrence County. Mary Ann Payne came into open Court in the court of Pleas and quarter Sessions of Lawrence County of May term, 1819, and made oath that she was present at the marriage of Joshua Hunter and Judith, his wife, and saw them lawfully married in Wayne County in the State of Kentucky, and that he died as she is informed in the service of the United States as a soldier who enlisted in the service of the United States as a soldier who enlisted in the service of the United States for five years and left a widow, the above named Judith Hunter, and left Lucinda a daughter about seven years old, and Marian a daughter about 5 years old, and that the said Judith, the relict, of the said Joshua Hunter still continues a widow.   Marian (sic) Payne
Joshua Hunter was enlisted in Kentucky in Capt. James Hackney's Co., and served in General Harrison's Army against Upper Canady. Sworn to in open court....Test, M.H. Buchanan, Clerk.

Court was adjourned until tomorrow, 9 o'clock. H. Day, Henry Sharp, and Duncan McIntyre, J.P.'s.

WEDNESDAY, MAY 5th 1819

Court met Wednesday May 5th, 1819 at 9 o'clock according to adjournment. Present, Duncan McIntyre, Pollard Wisdom. Henson Day, Henry Sharp, David Crockett, Esquires, Justices.

Ordered that Bracewell Farmer, former Sheriff of this County be allowed the sum of four dollars of insolvencies to be deducted out of the County tax for the year 1818.

Ordered that Josephus Irvine be allowed the list (/) his stud horse for taxation for this year, price of same $4.

The State
vs   Assault and battery
William Welch
This day came the Solicitor General in behalf of the State as well as the defendant in his proper person and the defendant being arraigned upon his arraignment pleaded guilty in manner and form as he is charged in the bill of presentment and for his trial puts himself upon the justice and mercy of the Court. Whereupon it is considered by the court that the defendant make his fine with the State to the sum of $1 and that he pay the cost of this prosecution and that the defendant be takn & c.

The State
vs   An Affray
William Null
This day came the Solicitor General in behalf of the State as well as the defendant in his proper person and the defendant moved upon affadavit for the continuance of this cause until the next term of this court which was granted him who entered into a recognance with his securities for his appearance at said term as follows, William Null, John Null, James Bogard

came into court and acknowledged themselves severally indebted to the State of Tennessee. Will in sum of $100 and his securities each in the sum of $50 to be levied severally of their goods, chattel lands and tenements, to the use of the State to be void on conditions that William Null appears at the next County Court to be holden for this County at the place of holding courts on the first Monday in August, next, on the third day of said term, then and there to answer the State upon a charge of an affray and that he do not depart therefrom without leave of the Court.

State
vs   Assault and battery
John Whorton

This day came the Solicitor General in behalf of the State as well as the defendant in his proper person and the defendant being arraigned upon his arraignment pleaded guilty in manner and form as he is charged in the bill of presentment and for his trial puts himself upon the justice and mercy of the court whereupon it is considered by the court that the defendant make his fine with the State to the sum of $10 and that he pay the cost of this prosecution and that the defendant be taken & c.

State
vs
William Kirksey

This day came the Solicitor General in behalf of the State as well as the defendant in his proper person and the defendant being arraigned upon his arraignment pleaded guilty in manner and form as he is charged in the bill of presentment and for his trial puts himself upon the justice and mercy of the court. Whereupon it is considered by the Court that the defendant make his fine with the State to the sum of one dollar and that he pay the cost of this prosecution and that the defendant be taken & c.

State
vs   Indictment for an affray
Shadrack Alvis

This day came the Solicitor General in behalf of the State as well as the defendant in his proper person and the defendant being arraigned upon his arraignment pleaded guilty in manner and form as he is charged in the bill of presentment and for his trial puts himself upon the justice and mercy of the court, whereupon it is considered by the Court that the defendant make his fine with the State in the sum of $1 and that he pay the cost of this prosecution and that the defendant be taken & c.

State   Petit Larceny
vs
William Macky (sic)

This day came the Solicitor General in behalf of the State as well as the defendant in his proper person and the defendant being arraigned upon his arraignment pleaded NOT guilty and for his trial puts himself upon his Country, the Solicitor General for the State, likewise. Whereupon

came a jury of good and lawful men, to-wit, Robert Mason, Thomas
Keese, Ethelred Thomas, Lemuel Blythe, Joshua Worton, Simon
Edwards, Richard Hill, John Guinn, Robert Gray, Joseph Smith,
Nathan McClendon, and Isaac Pennington who being elected, tried
and sworn the truth to speak upon this issue of traverse upon their
oaths do say, that the defendant is NOT guilty in manner and
form as he is charged in the bill of indictment. Whereupon it
is considered by the court that the defendant go hence without
day (sic) but the court being of oponion that there is strong
grounds to induce a belief that the defendant is guilty it is
therefore considered by the court that the defendant pay the cost
of this prosecution as well before the justice as in this court
expended and that he be takne & c.

John P. Ervin & Co.
vs   In debt
William Bo gard

In this case the plaintiff by his attorney comes into court
and dismisses their suit and the defendant assumes the payment
of all costs.

The State
vs
Bailey Brooks

This day came the Solicitor General in behlaf of the State
as well as the defendant in his proper person and the defendant being arraigned upon his arraignment pleaded guilty in man--
ner and form as he is charged in the bill of presentment and for
his trial puts himself upon the justice and mercy of the court.
Whereupon it is considered by the court that the defendant make
his fine with the State to the sum of $1 and that he pay the cost
of this prosecution and that the defendant be taken & c.

State
vs
Jesse Anglin

This day came the Solicitor General in behalf of the State
as well as the defendant in his proper person and the defendant
being arraigned upon his arraignment pleaded guilty in manner
and form as he is charged in the bill of presentment and for his
trial puts himself upon the Justice and mercy of this court.
Whereupon it is considered by the court that the defendant make
his fine with the State to the sum of $1 and that he pay the cost
of this prosecution and that the defendant be taken & c.

The State
vs   For an affray
William Grisham

This day came the Solicitor General on behalf of the State
and it being suggested to court that the defendant was absent
and with the absence of the Solicitor General it is ordered that
this case be continued until the next term of this Court in consequence of George Grisham's entering into the following recognance. George Grisham comes into court and acknowledges himself
justly indebted to the State of Tenn., in sum of $200 to be
levied of his goods, chattel lands and tenements to the use of

the State to be void on conditions that William Grisham appear here on the third day of next term then and there to answer the state upon a charge of an affray and that he do not depart therefrom without leave of the court.

Ordered that Court be adjourned until tomorrow, 9 o'clock. Duncan McIntyre, H. Day, Henry Sharp, and Pollard Wisdom, J.P.'s.

THURSDAY, MAY 6th, 1819

Court met Thursday, MAY ¢TH, L*L(AT NINE O"CLOCK, ACCORDING TO ADJOURNMENT, present, Duncan McIntyre, Henson Day, Henry Sharp, Pollard Wisdom, Justices, Esquires.

State
vs
Nathaniel Mason

This day came the Solicitor General in behalf of the State, as well as the defendant in his proper person and the defendant being arraigned upon his arraigment pleaded guilty in manner and form as he is charged in the bill of presentment and for his trial puts himself upon the justice and mercy of the court. Whereupon it is considered by the court that the defendant make his fine with the State in the sum of $1 and that he pay the cost of this prosecution and that he be taken & c.

John Edmundson
vs   An original Attachment
John Lester

This day came the plaintiff by his attorney and the defendant although solemnly called came not. It is therefore considered by the court that the plaintiff do recover of the defendant the sum of $180 debt in the plaintiffs declaration mentioned together with his costs by him about his suit as well before the Justices as in this court expended and the defendant in mercy & c.

George Cockburn
vs   Trespass on the case
Rowland Tankersly

It being suggested to the court that at the last term of this court that the plaintiff in this case had taken a non suit and the same entered on the trial docket but the same being NOT entered on the minutes of said court it is therefore considered by the court that the same be entered of record at this term nunc-pro-tunc and that the plaintiff pay the cost of this suit aforesaid and that he be in mercy & c.

Ordered that the sheriff of this County, Beasley Halford be allowed the sum of $11.95 for guarding & c William Mackey, charged with pettit Larceny and that this be a part of the bill of cost of said suit according to the final judgement of the court.

James Forbes, Henson Day, David Crockett, and John Hillhouse, Esqrs., who were appointed at the November term, 1818, of this Court, to take a list of Taxable property and polls, and to take a list of voters according to a late Act of Assembly, making provisions for taking the Census, returned into Court their several lists of Voters according to law.

The following is a list of the number and names of the Census returned by James Forbes, Esqr., as above, to-wit,

Andrew Allison	John Hillhouse	Allen Prewitt
Arthur M. Alexander	Daniel Hughs	Henry Phenix
Solomon Asbell	Archelus Hogg	Silas Rackley
Frederick Rackley	Daniel Harrison	Aaron Anglin
Shadrick Rackley	George Archer	Milton Jack
Francis C. Simpson	Isaac W. Brown	Nathan Jobe
Amos Kilburn, Sr.	Joseph Baldwin	Hartin Spears
Amos Kilburn, Jr.	William Bosheers	Joseph Spears
Henry Bosheers	Solomon Kilburn	William Smith
Starlin Lindsey	John Bosheers	William Story
William Straughan	Jesse Bosheers	Hannah Lindsey
James McConnell, Sr.	William Wisdom, Sr.	Branch Blackard
James McConnell, Jr.	Francis Wisdom, Sr.	John Bell
Samuel McConnel	Joseph Wisdom	William Cooke
John Ethridge	Thomas Musgrave	Thomas Wisdom
Thomas Ethridge	Jonas Musgrave	George Wolf
Polla5d Wisdom	James Forbes	Eli Pascal
Joseph Gosnell		

Amounting in the whole to fifty-two.

The following is a list of the number and names of the Census returned by Henson Day, Esqr., to-wit,

M. H. Buchanan	Bryan McClendon	James Helton
Wm. F. Cunningham	Hugh Sinclair	Robert Gray
John W. Talley	Archer Nail	John Nelson
Samuel Sullivan	Abraham Henry	John Welch
Alexander Miller	Alexander Davis	Ezer Evans
Richard T. Bailey	Abraham Helton	Daniel Beeler
Robert Montgomery	Melcher Duncan	Hugh Reynolds
Nathaniel Casey	William Wooten	Henson Day
Needham Futtrell	John McHughs	John Allsup
Nathaniel Armstrong	John Thompson	Simon Higgs
William Higgs	Samuel Askew	Larkin Baker
Charles McHughs	Barrel Gambrell	James Scott
John L. Henson	Groves Sharp	Joel Phillips
Humphrey Tomkins	James McHughs	John Gray
Stepehn Rowland	Olliver Page	Richard Hill
Geo. W. Jones	Robert Haynes	David Dale
Josephus Irvine	Jesse Helton	Samuel Sealy
Silas Mitchell	John Grimes	George Hanks
John McDonald	George Grisham	Henry Sharp
Edward McDonald	Samuel Thomas	Solomon Grisham
John McCann	Spencer Rice	Thomas Keese
William McCann	David Adams	James Smith
Lazarous Stewart	Hamilton Reynolds	Lewis Franks
Nathan McClendon		

The following is a list of the number and names of the Census returned by DAVID CROCKETT, Esqr., to-wit,

Daniel Matthews	William Thomas	Aron Choat
James Broadstreet	Lewis Mathews	James Wise
Moses Holloway	Jacob Mathews	James Bergin
Nicholas Reynolds	Stephen Holloway	Thomas Choat
Emanuel Keltner	Erasmus Tracey	Wm. Reynolds
Aron Choat, Jr.	Drury Chambers	Geo. Rogers
John McAnally, Sr.	Jonathon Jobe	Wm. Wooten
John McAnally, Jr.	Stephen Roland	Richard Choat
William McAnally	George Lucus	John Smith
Patterson Crockett	Samuel Sullivan	Solomon Stone, Sr.
Solomon Stone, Jr.	John McHughs	Abner Burgin
Gabriel Bumpass	Charles McHughs	Wm. Stone
James McHughs	Jacob Adair	Noble Stone
Nathaniel Armstrong	Samuel Graham	John Poley
Lancelot Armstrong	Ebenezer Thompson	John Crisp
Mancel Crisp	George Shirley	Wm. Green
John Edmondson	John Henson	John King
James Edmondson	John W. Talley	Wm. Cowan
James Bumpass	Joseph Halford	Aaron Anglin
William S. Dalton	Old Mr. Green	Willis Lucus
Old Mr. Rolan	Martin Prewitt	John Shirley
Thomas Trentham	William Lucus	Samuel Askew
Benjamin Morrow	Levi Blackard	Hardin Payne
Green Depriest		

Amounting in the whole to 70.

The following is a list of the number and names of the Census returned by John Hillhouse, Esqr., to-wit,

Archibald Alexander	Joseph Smith, Jr.	Wm. Heraldson
Phillip Burrow	James Hughs	Enoch Tucker
William Tucker	Wiley Brewer	John Inman
William Tacker	Michael Inman	Henry Brewer
Wiley M. Jones	James Welch	John Burns
Morrell Mitchell	Simon Walker	James Burns
Zachariah Walker, Sr.	Andrew Brown	Renolds May
Zachariah Walker, Jr.	Samuel McKinney	Benjamin May
James McCarley	Joshua Wharton	Daniel Pearce
William Gogue	John Wharton	John Swain
Caleb Wharton	Daniel Hunt	James Smith
James Heralson	___Bynam, Sr.	John Smith
Joseph Smith, Sr.	___Bynam, Jr.	John Hamilton

Making in the whole 39

The following is a list of the number and names of the Census returned by Duncan McIntyre, Esqr.

Robert Mason	William Kirksey	Adam Ross
Warren Mason	Robert Chaffin	Thomas Price
Nathaniel Mason	Bailey Alford	Samuel Price
Malcom McIntyre	John Phillips	John Voories
John Simonton	Henry Ross	James Haile
Duncan McIntyre	Martin Gaither	John Haile
Thomas Welch	John Campbell	Simon Edwards

Cornelius Goforth
Jonathan Wallace
Wm. Welch, Sr.
Wm. Welch, Jr.
Jesse Williams
John Stricklin
Joshua Ashmore
James Parchman
Gilbreth Simonton
Making in the whole 47

Shadrack Alvis
George Vandiver
James Ashmore
James Striclon
Nicholas Welch
Thomas Woodruff
John Counce
Stephen Busby
George Shirley

Michael Shirley
Hiriam Howard
John Foster
Eliott Lindsey
John Wisdom
James Kendrick
John Morgan
John Sellars

The following is a list of the number and names of the Census returned by John Ray, Esqr., to-wit,

Phillip Chronister
Adam Chronister
Jesse Hutchinson
William Burris
Joseph Reynolds
Equilla Burns
Robert Heralson
John Garrison
John Pritchford
Jacob Pennington
Moses Pennington
David Pennington
Isaac Pennington
Abraham Pennington
Charles Williams
Alexander Shadrack
William Williams
Samuel Williams
Nathaniel Christian
John Hutchinson
William Ssears
Reuben Peoples
Mr. Cunningham
William Burlison
Ezekiel Farmer
John Lockard, Jr.
Coleman Hutchinson
William McBride
Making in the whole 82

William Sehorn
William Voss
John Voss
Daniel Sims
Thomas Mitchell
John Heralson
John Lockard
Leroy Farmer
Thomas Steele
George Isham
John Duckworth
William Long
Joseph Tease
James Tease
John Anthony
William Alton
Spencer Alton
Daniel Flannery
Joseph Lancaster
Isham Christian
Joel Peoples
Mr. Perkins
John Brumley
John Young
Samuel McBride
William McBride
James Chronister

John Burns
John McClish
John Ray
John Jobe
Dalton Smith
James Foster
John Foster
David Steele
John Farmer
Phillip Bryant
Isaac Shipman
Josiah Hurley
Eli Kennedy
Green Williams
John Alton
Miles Birdsong
Binnet Pope
Charles Gorrell
James Pollock
Henry Pollock
Samuel Adkins
John Sellars
David Adkins
John Canida
Young Yewmans
Thomas Cockran
Wm. Pennington

The following is a list of the number and names of the Census returned by Joseph Gist, Esqr., to-wit,

Wade Blasingham
Wm. Heraldson
Robert Hillhouse
Jonathon Johnson
John Mc Intire
Daniel Mc Intire
Lemuel Blythe
Henry Heffington
William Quilling

James Heraldson
John Adkisson
Robert Carr
Thomas Allsup
Joshua Gist
Barney Gabriel
Thomas Holland
William Morrow
Elijah Melton

Aggus Abner
Wm. Bogard
George Archer
Edwin Denton
Henry Brewer
Jacob Blythe
Elisha Melton
James Brooks
Wiley Brewer

Lazarus Stewart
John McClaren
Andrew McClaren
Brittian Ward
Andrew Pickens
Moses Williams
Wm. Jackson, Sr.
Wm. Jackson, Jr.
Abraham Sizemore

John McMillan
William Story
William Smith
Nathan Spears
Thomas Spencer
Hosea Strawn
William Simons
Henry Pritchett

Wm. Rickman
Reuben Tripp
Jacob Tunrbow
John Null
Elijah Walker
Thomas Prior
Spencer Pearce
Smecer Poleer

Making in the whole 52

The following is a list of the number and names of the Census returned by Andrew Pickens, Esqr., to-wit,

James Adams
William Adams
William Sizemore
Joseph Adkissin
Thomas Bird, Sr.
Thomas Bird, Jr.
William Bird
William Carrau
John Bird
Hugh Crumley
Alexander Campbell
Elisha Cooper
Robert Brashears
Walker Brashears
Ezekiel Downs

John Smallwood
Isaac Swafford
Burrell Gambrelle
Mathew Downs
James Moody
Henry Moody
Moses Moody
Thomas Sharp
James Webster
Samuel Poteet
Jacob Pennicuff
Samuel Woolsey
John Allsup, Sr.
Henry Fonland
James Appleton

John Holt
James Green
Joseph Adams
William Green
Michael Hensley
James McFalls
John Oxford
Anderson McWhorter
William Poteet
Thomas Allsup
James Poteet
Moses McRoly
Bradley Fisher
John Fonlin
Jacob Bird

Making in the whole 46

Making an aggregate of the differents of enumeration taken by the different justices of the Peace who were appointed to take the numeration or Census according to Act of Assembly, the number amounting in the whole to 458.

Ordered that court be adjourned until court in course. Duncan McIntyre, H. Day, Henry Sharp, and Pollard Wisdom, J.P.'s.

MONDAY AUGUST 2nd, 1819

At a Court of Pleas and Quarter Sessions began and held at the house of Josephus Irvine, formerly the house of Doctor Joseph Farmer the present place of holding courts in and for said County, the 2nd day of Aug., 1819, present, Duncan McIntyre, Henson Day, Pollard Wisdom, George Hanks, Henry Sharp, Esquires, Justices.

At least five justices being present, to-wit, Duncan McIntyre, Henson Day, Pollard Wisdom, George Hanks, and Henry Sharp. Benjamin Bynum produced in open court 1 wolf scalp over 4 months old and 3 under, which was ordered to be burnt and certified accordingly.

Bennet Wallace produced in open court 2 wolf scalps over 4 months old which were ordered burnt and certified accordingly.

John Smallwood produced in opne court 4 wolf scalps over four months old which were ordered burnt and certified according.

Ordered that the order made heretofore for Peter Mosely and others, relative to iron works be revived and that the following named persons be appointed as Jurors, to-wit, George Hanks, Wm. White, Simon Higgs, Edward Higgs, Melcher Duncan, Thomas Keese, Robert Haynes, Briant McClendon, Henry Sharp, Lewis Franks, John Nelson, George W. Jones, George Grisham, John Thompson, Edward R.Sealey, John Welch, Stephen Roland, George Lucas, James Bumpass, Willis Lucas, Nathan McClendon, Aaron Choate,Jr., Gabriel Bumpass, and Martin Prewitt, and that the sheriff be directed to summon said Jurors or any twelve of them to attend to said business according to Act of Assembly in such cases made and provided and that they make report to next Court.

Ordered that the Sheriff be directed to summon the following named persons to attend as Jurors at the next County Court of this County, to-wit, Martin Gaither, Robert Haynes, Silas Rackley, George Gresham, John Smallwood,,Samuel Sullivan, Abraham Helton, Nathaniel Mason, John Thompson, John Welch, Hamilton Reynolds, Austin Kendrick, John Wisdom, Thomas Allsup, Andrew Johnson, Enoch Tucker, William Tucker, James Welch, Alexander Campbell, Caleb Whorton, Elijah Cooper, Lewis Franks, George W. Jones, Aaron Choate, Elliott Lindsey, Hardin Payne.

Ordered that Lazarous Stewart and Thomas Spencer be appointed constables to attend the next County Court.

Ordered that the County Trustee of this County pay to Nathaniel Casey, Mancel Crisp, and Robert Chaffin the sum of $2 each for services rendered as commissioners in settlement with the County Trustee up to the 31st of Sept., 1819.

John Ray, Esqr., Justice of the Peace in and for said County came into court and made a resignation as Justice aforesaid, and returned his official papers.

Daniel Kutch administrator to the estate of Margaret Whitley, dec'd returned into court the amount of sales of said estate which was received in order to be recorded.

Court adjourned until tomorrow, nine o'clock. Duncan McIntyre, Henry Sharp, Pollard Wisdom, and Henson Day,J.P.'s.

TUESDAY AUGUST 3rd , 1819

Court met according to adjournment, tuesday morning, Aug.3rd, 1819 at nine o'clock. Present, Duncan McIntyre, Henson Day, Henry Sharp, Pollard Wisdom, Esquires, Justices.

The sheriff returned into court the following Venire Facias to-wit, Joshua Ashmore, Philip Bryant, William Henderson, John McClish, Moses Pennington, Nathaniel Christian, Josiah Hurley, Jonathon Jobe, Aaron Choate,Jr., Jacob Adair, Benjamin Morrow, Simon Edwards, Samuel Thomas, John Adkisson, Thomas Holland,

Daniel McIntyre, Jacob Blythe, William Richmond, James Brooks, John McClaren, Arthur M. Alexander and Thomas Keese. Of whom the following were drawn as Grand Jurors, to-wit, Daniel McIntyre, foreman, Simon Edwards, Jesse Holton, Jacob Adair, John Adkisson, Aaron Choate, Jr., Benjamin Morrow, John McClish, Joshua Ashmore, Thomas Keese, Thomas Holland, and Nathaniel Christian, who being sworn and having received their charges withdrew to consider of their presentments under the direction of Warren Mason, constable sworn to attend them as such.

Ordered that Bracewell Farmer, former Sheriff of this County be allowed fifteen dollars in addition to his former allowance for his officio services.

Francis Wisdom
vs   Trespass with force and arms
John Whorton

  This day came the plaintiff in his proper person and withdrew his suit heretofore pleaded and the defendant assumes upon himself the payment of all costs. It is therefore considered by the court that the plaintiff recover of the defendant his costs by him about his suit in this behalf expended and the defendant in mercy & c.

Peter R. Booker
vs   Debt
George Shirley

  This day came the parties by their attorneys and thereupon came a jury of good and lawful men, to-wit, Samuel Thomas, Joel Phillips, John Counce, Melcher Duncan, John Voories, James Parchman, James Helton, John Welch, James Bumpass, Nathaniel Mason, Ebenezer Thompson, and Simon Higgs, who being elected tried and sworn well and truly to try this issue of traverse upon their oaths do say, that the defendant hath not paid the debt as in the plaintiff's declaration mentioned as in pleading he hath alleged and they do assess the plaintiff damages by reason thereof to $1 besides costs. It is therefore considered by the court that the plaintiff recover of the defendant the sum of $45 together with his damages aforesaid by the jurors aforesaid in form aforesaid assessed and his costs by him about his shit in this behalf expended and the defendant in mercy & c.

William Cook
vs   Slander
James Hill

  This day came the plaintiff into court and withdraws his suit heretofore pleaded, and the defendant assumes upon himself the payment of all costs. It is therefore considered by the court that the plaintiff recover of the defendant his cost by him about his suit in this behalf expended, and the defendant in mercy & c.

Bailey Brooks   Trespass
vs
Shadrack Alvis, Warren Mason, Hugh Sinclair

This day came the parties by their attorneys and therefore came a jury of good and lawful men, to-wit, Samuel Thomas, Joel Philips, Jacob Blythe, Melcher Duncan, John Simonton, James Parchman, Simon Higgs, James Kelton, Josiah Herly, James Bumpass, Nathaniel Mason, Ebenezer Thompson, who being elected tried and sworn well and truly to try this issue of traverse upon their oaths do say that the defendants are NOT guilty in manner and form as the plaintiff in the plaintiffs declaration mentioned. It is therefore considered by the court that the defendant go hence without day and recover of the plaintiff his costs by him about his defense in this behalf expended and the plaintiff be in mercy & c from which judgement of the court the plaintiff prayed an appeal to the Honourable the Circuit Court, to be holden for this County which was granted him who gave bond and security according to lay(sic).

Bailey Brooks
vs
Daniel McIntyre

This day came the parties by their attorneys and thereupon came a jury of good and lawful men, towit, Moses Pennington, John W. Henry, Groves Sharp, George Grisham, Solomon Grisham, William Wisdom, Austin Kendrick, John Lockard, Harden Payne, Samuel Price, James Webb, and Nathan McClendon, who being elected tried and sworn the truth to speak upon this issue of traverse, upon their oaths do say that the defendant is NOT guilty in manner and form as in the plaintiff's declaration mentioned. It is therefore considered by the court that the defendant go hence without day and recover of the plaintiff his costs by him about his defense in this behalf expended and the plaintiff in mercy & c., from whence judgement of the court the plaintiff prayed an appeal to the Honourable, the Circuit Court to be holden for this County, which was graznted him, who gave bond and security according to law.

Ordered that Thomas Welch be appointed overseer of the road by John Simonton's in the rume(sic) of the said Simonton, resigned, and that he over look the same part of road under the care of the said Simonton and have the same hands to work thereon.

Phillip Parchman
vs   Case
John Edmondson

This day came the parties by their attorneys and thereuoon came a jury of good and lawful men, to-wit, Moses Pennington, John W. Henry, Groves Sharp, George Grisham, Solomon Gresham, William Wisdom, Austin Kendrick, John Lockard, Hardin Payne, Samuel Price, James Webb, Nathan McClendon, who being elected tried and sworn well and truly to try this issue of traverse upon their oaths do say that the defendant is guilty in manner and form as in the plaintiff's declaration mentioned and they do assess the plaintiff damages by reason thereof to $52 besides cost. It is therefore considered by the court that the plaintiff recover of the defendant his damages aforesaid by the jurors aforesaid in form aforesaid assessed together with his costs by him about his suit in this behalf expended and the defendant in mercy & c.

Bradley Halford came into Court, prayed and obtained a license to keep a house of Ordinary.

Austin Kendrick produced in Court a bill of sale from Thomas Blackbourn for a negro boy about 7 or 8 years of age and proven to be the Act and deed of the said Thomas Blackbourn by the oaths of Josephus Irvine and William G. Irvine, two subscribing witnesses thereto which was ordered to be certified accordingly.

Ordered that court be adjourned until tomorrow, 9 o'clock. H. Day, Duncan McIntyre, Pollard Wisdom, Henry Sharp, and David Crockett, J.P.'s.

AUGUST 4th, WEDNESDAY, 1819

At a court of Pleas and Quarter Sessions for said County, Wednesday morning 9 o'clock, August 4th, court met according to adjournment. Present, Duncan McIntyre, Henson Day, Pollard Wisdom, Henry Sharp, David Crockett, Esquires, Justices.

At least five justices being present, to-wit, Daniel McIntyre, Henson Day, Pollard Wisdom, Henry Sharp, David Crockett.

William McCann came into court, prayed and obtained a license to keep a house of Ordinary, which was granted him who gave bond and securities and was qualified accordingly.

John Null produced in open court one wolfe scalp over 4 months old which was ordered to be burnt and certified accordingly.

Josiah Hurley produced in open court 2 wolf scalps over 4 months old which was ordered to be burnt and certified accordingly.

James R. Plumer
vs   Debt
Josephus Irvine

This day came the parties by their attorneys, thereupon came a jury of good and lawful men, to-wit, John Phillips, John W. Henry, Samuel Thomas, Jacob Blythe, John Allsup, Nathaniel Mason, James Holton, George Grisham, William Higgs, Simon Higgs, Charles Cook, George Mickey who being elected tried and sworn the truth to speak upon this issue joined upon their oaths do say that the defendant hath not paid the debt in the writing obligatory in the plaintiff's declaration mentioned as in pleading he hath alledged and they do assess the plaintiff damages by reason thereof to the sum of $3 besides cost. It is therefore considered by the court that the plaintiff recover of the defendant the sum of $100 debt together with his damages aforesaid by the Jurors aforesaid in form aforesaid assessed together with his costs by him about his suit in this behalf expended and the defendant in mercy & c.

Ordered by the court that Samuel Thomas, a juror, for wilful absence, be fined the sum of 50 cents.

James R. Plumer
vs   Debt
Josephus Irvine

This day came the parties by their attorneys and thereupon came a jury of good and lawful men, to-wit, John Phillips, John Allsup, Nathaniel Mason, James Helton, George Grisham, William Higgs, Simon Higgs, Charles Cook, George Mickey, who being elected, tried and sworn the truth to speak upon this issue joined upon their oaths do say that the defendant hath not paid the debt in the writing obligatory in the plaintiffs declaration mentioned as in pleadings he hath alleged and they do assess the plaintiff damages by reason thereof to the sum of $62 besides costs. It is therefore considered by the court that the plaintiff recover of the defendant the sum of $1,130.75 debt, together with his damages aforesaid by the jurors aforesaid in form aforesaid, assessed together with his costs by him about his suit in this behalf expended and the defendant in mercy & c.

James R. Plumer
vs   Debt
Josephus Irvine

This day came the parties by their attorneys. Thereupon came a jury of good and lawful men, to-wit, John Phillips, John W. Henry, Samuel Thomas, Jacob Blythe, John Allsup, Nathaniel Mason, James Helton, George Grisham, William Higgs, Simon Higgs, Chas. Cook, George Mickey, who being elected tried and sworn the truth to speak upon this issue joined upon their oaths do say that the defendant hath not paid the debt in pleadings he hath alleged and they do assess the plaintiff damages by reason thereof to the sum of $4 besides costs. It is therefore considered by the court that the plaintiff recover of the defendant the sum of $69.60 debt together with his damages aforesaid by the jurors aforesaid in form aforesaid assessed together with his costs by him about his suit in this behalf expended and the defendant in mercy & c.

James & William Bogard
vs   In debt
Moses Spencer

This day came the defendant into court in his proper person and saith that he cannot gainsay the plaintiff's declaration but that he doth owe the defendant the sum of $107.06¼ debt together with the sum of $2.04 damages according to specialty. It is therefore considered by the court that the plaintiff recover of the defendant the sum of $107 his debt aforesaid together with the sum of $2.04½ damages besides his costs by him about his suit in this behalf expended and the defendant in mercy & c.

63

State
vs   Gambling
William Higgs
    This day came the Solicitor General as well as the defendant in his proper person and the defendant being arraigned upon his arraigment pleaded guilty in manner and form as charged in the bill of presentment and for his trial puts himself upon the justice and mercy of the court. Whereupon it is considered by the court that the defendant make his fine with the State to the sum of $5 and that he pay the cost of this prosecution and that the defendant be taken &c.

The State
vs   Presentment -Gambling
Thomas Keese (sic)
    This day came the Solicitor General as well as the defendant in his proper person and the defendant being arraigned, upon his arraignment pleaded guilty on manner and form as charged in the bill of presentment and for his trial puts himself upon the justice and mercy of the court. Whereupon it is considered by the Court that the defendant make his fine with the State to the sum of $5 and that he pay the cost of this prosecution and that the defendant be taken & c.

The State
vs   Presentment-Gambling
David Adams
    This day came the Solicitor General as well as the defendant in his proper person and the defendant being arraigned, upon his arraignment pleaded guilty in manner and form as charged in the bill of presentment and for his trial puts himself upon the justice and mercy of the court, whereupon it is considered by the court that the defendant make his fine with the State to the sum of $5 and that he pay the cost of this prosecution and that the defendant be taken & c.

The State
vs   Presentment of an affray
James Helton
    This day came the Solicitor General as well as the defendant in his proper person and the defendant being arraigned upon his arraignment pleaded guilty and for his trial puts himself upon the justice and mercy of the court. Whereupon it is considered by the court that the defendant make his fine with the State to the sum of $1 and that he pay the cost of this prosecution and that the defendant be taken & c.

The State
vs   Presentment-Gambling
James Helton
    This day came the Solicitor General in behalf of the State as well as the defendant in his proper person and the defendant being arraigned upon his arraignment pleaded guilty and for his trial puts himself upon the mercy and justice of the court, whereupon it is considered by the court that he make his fine with the State to the sum of $5 and that he pay

the cost of this prosecution and that he be taken & c.

The State
vs
William Null   For an affray

  This day came the Solicitor General in behalf of the State as well as the defendant in his proper person and the defendant being arraigned upon his arraignment pleaded not guilty and for his trial puts himself upon his Country and the Solicitor General for the state, likewise. Whereupon came a jury of good and lawful men, to-wit, John Phillips, John W. Henry, Samuel Thomas, Jacob Blythe, John Allsup, Nathaniel Mason, James Helton, George Grisham, William Higgs, Simon Higgs, Charles Cook, George Archer, who being elected, tried and sworn well and truly to try this issue of traverse upon their oaths do say that the defendant is not guilty in manner and form as he is charged in the bill of presentment. Whereupon it is considered by the court that the defendant go hence without day(sic) and the Solicitor General having suggested to the court that the defendant should be taxed with the cost, it is therefore ordered by the court that the defendant should pay the same and the defendant may be taken & c.

  It is ordered by the court that the fines heretofore assessed against William Higgs, Thomas Keese, James Helton, David Adams for gambling be set aside except the sum of 6¼¢ to each.

  Hugh Sinclear, William White, George Grisham came into court and acknowledged themselves indebted each in the sum of $100 to be levied of their goods, Chattel lands and tenements to the use of the State severally, to be void on conditions that Hugh Sinclear appear here on the third day of the next term of this court then and there to answer the state upon the charge of an affray with Henry Welch and that he depart not therefrom without leave of the court.

  William Welch and Thomas Welch came into court and acknowledged themselves indebted each in the sum of $100 to be levied of their goods chattel lands and tenements severally to the use of the State to be void on condition that Thomas Welch appears here at the next term of this court on the third day of said term, then and there to prosecute and give evidence in behalf of the state against Hugh Sinclear for an affray with Henry Welch and that he do not depart therefrom without leave of the court.

  Ordered that an order heretofore made to take the deposition of John Bankhead and wife in the Alabama Territory be revived in the case of John Welch against John Counce and in said case that an order be made to take the deposition of John Choat in the State of Kentucky, Cumberland County.

The State
vs
Moses Pennington   Retailing spirituous liquors without license
  This day came the Solicitor General in behalf of the State

as well as the defendant in his proper person and the defendant being arraigned upon his arraignment pleaded NOT guilty and for his trial puts himself upon his Country and the Solicitor General for the State likewise. Whereupon came a jury of good and lawful men, to-wit, John Phillips John W. Henry, Eli Pashel, Jacob Blythe, John Alsup, Nathaniel Mason, James Helton, Simon Higgs, William Higgs, Josiah Herly, James Bumpass, William Story, who being elected, tried and sworn, well and truly to try this issue of traverse upon their oaths do say that the defendant is NOT guilty in manner and form as he is charged in the bill of presentment. It is therefore considered by the court that the defendant go hence without day(sic) and the Solicitor moves in the Court that the County should be taxed with the cost. It is therefore considered by the court that the Co. Trustee pay the same out of any monies in his hands not otherwise appropriated.

The State
vs   Peace Recognisance
James Parchman & William Welch

It being suggested to the court that the prosecutor in behalf of the state had absconded, it is therefore ordered by the court that the defendant go hence without day and that the Trustee of this County pay to Bradley Halford the sum of $2 his cost in said case.

A bill of sale was produced in open court by Thomas Blackbourn for 4 negroes to Obediah Kendrick and proved to be the act and deed by Nathaniel Mason one of the subscribing witnesses thereto. It is ordered to be certified.

Joshua & Thomas Parker
vs   Debt
William McMahan

This day came the plaintiff by his attorney and withdraws his said suit whereupon it is considered by the court that the defendant recover of the plaintiff his costs by him about his defense expended and the plaintiff in mercy & c.

The State
vs   Presentment for an affray
Reuben Hanks

This day came the Solicitor General in behalf of the State as well as the defendant in his proper person and the defendant being arraigned upon his arraignment pleaded guilty in manner and form as he is charged in the bill of presentment and for his trial puts himself upon the justice and mercy of the court, whereupon it is considered by the court that the defendant make his fine with the state to the sum of $1 and that he pay the cost of this prosecution and that he be taken & c.

Amuel(sic) Atkisson
vs   Debt
James Morphies

It being suggested to the court by the clerk that various writs had been run against the defendant at least as high as a pleas (sic) and that they were all returned not found and that the court officers being desirous that judgement should be entered for costs. It is therefore considered by the court that judgement be rendered by the plaintiff and security for all costs which have accrued in said case and that they be in mercy & c.

Thomas Cash
vs   Debt
Anderson Johnson

It being suggested to the court by the clerk that various writs had been run against the defendant at least as high as a Pherias(sic) and that they were all returned not found and that the court officers being desirous that judgement should be entered for costs. It is therefore considered by the court that judgement be rendered by the plaintiff and security for all costs which have accured in said case and that they be in mercy & c.

State
vs
William Grisham

This day came the Solicitor General as well as the defendant in his proper person and the defendant being charged upon the bill of presentment pleads thereto guilty and for his trial puts himself upon the justice and mercy of the court, whereupon it is considered by the court that the defendant make his fine with the state to the sum of $1 and that he pay the cost of this prosecution and that the defendant be taken & c.

William McClure
vs   Debt
John McClish

This day the defendant comes into court in proper person and says that he cannot gainsay but that he justly owes the plaintiff $100 debt and $33 damages, whereupon it is considered by the court that the plaintiff recover of the defendant the sum of $133.00 and his costs by him about his suit in this behalf expended and the defendant be in mercy & c.

Ordered that Court be adjourned until to-morrow, 9 o'clock. Duncan McIntyre, H. Day, Henry Sharp, David Crockett, Pollard Wisdom, J.P.'s.

THURSDAY, AUGUST 5th, 1819

Court met according to adjournment, Thursday morning 9 o'clock, Aug. 5th 1819. Present, Duncan McInture, Henson Day, Pollard Wisdom, Henry Sharp, Esquires, Justices.

Thomas Woodruff
vs   Trespass
William Welch, Jr.

It being suggested to the court that no pleas have been plead nor declaration filed in this case according to act of Assembly, it is therefore considered by the court that the plaintiff recover of the defendant and his security Samuel Jenkins his cost by him about his defense in this behalf expended and that he be in mercy & c.

Thomas Woodruff
vs   Trespass
William Welch, Jr.

    It being suggested to the court that no pleas have been plead nor declaration filed in this case according to Act of assembly. It is therefore considered by the court that the plaintiff recover of the defendant and his security James E. Haile, his cost by him about his defense in this behalf expended and that they be in mercy & c.

A.B. Mayfield
vs   Debt
Thomas Alsup & Joseph Dickson

    This day Thomas Alsup one of the defendants came into open court and with the assent of the plaintiff says that he cannot gainsay but that he justly owes to the plaintiff the sum of $246 debt and $ 9.25 damages, whereupon it is ordered by the court that plaintiff recover of the defendant the sum of $246.25 and his costs by him about his suit in this behalf expended and the defendant be in mercy & c.

William H. Gardner, Roland Tancerly, Absalum McConnel
    Wheras the parties failed to come forward and prosecute this suit according to law it is ordered by the court that judgement be entered up against the plaintiff for all costs in this case according to law in such cases made and provided.

    John Wisdom produced in open court a bill of sale from George Green to said Wisdom for a certain negro girl about 8 years old, named Mariah, which was proved to be the Act and deed of the said George Green by the oath of William G. Irvine, one of the subscribing witnesses thereto, and was ordered to be certified accordingly.

    Ordered by the court that James Bumpass be appointed one of the Judges of the present election in the room of Henry Phenix.

    Ordered that court be adjourned until Court in Course.
Duncan McIntyre, Pollard Wisdom, H. Day. J.P.'s.

EDITORS NOTE: Below above signatures there has been cut out of the page a portion thereof, about 2 inches in wideth and length, the signature thus cut out is no doubt that of DAVID CROCKETT.

MONDAY NOVEMBER 1st, 1819

    At a Court of Pleas and Quarter Sessions began and held at the house of Josephus Irvine, formerly the house of Doctor Joseph Farmer, the present place of holding courts in and for said County, the 1st day of Nov., 1819, present...........

EDITORS NOTE: Here again the names of the Justices were cut from the page, except the Intyre of the name McIntyre; and the kett of the name Crockett. The names of these Justices were noted on next page of the book.

At least five justices being present, to-wit, Duncan McIntyre, Henson Day, Joseph Gist, Pollard Wisdom, David Crockett.

Duncan Smith produced in open court one wolf scalp over 4 months old which was ordered burnt and certified accordingly.

George Rogers produced in open court one wolf scalp over 4 months old which was ordered burnt and certified accordingly.

Josiah Hurley produced in open court three wolf scalps over 4 months old which was ordered burnt and certified accordingly.

DAVID CROCKETT, WHO WAS AN ACTING JUSTICE OF THE PEACE IN AND FOR SAID COUNTY, CAME INTO COURT AND MADE HIS RESIGNATION AS SUCH IN DUE FORM OF LAW, AND ORDERED TO BE ENTERED OF RECORD.

A power of attorney from William G. Irvine to Josephus Irvine was produced in open court and proved to be the act and deed of said Wm. G. Irvine by the oath of Melcher Duncan, a subscribing witness thereto and ordered to be certified accordingly.

Ordered that James Stricklin be appointed overseer of the Military Road in the room of George Sherley, resigned, and that he have all the hands to work thereon and that he keep the same in repair.

The bond of Mary Tripp and Thomas Pryor to idennify(sic) the County from the costs of a bastard child of the said Mary Tripp was proven in court with the sum of ____ dollars as a fine according to Act of Assembly in such cases made and provided.

It is ordered by the court that the following Certificate of James Hill as defendant in a suit wherein William Cook was plaintiff and the said Hill defendant, in a suit of slander, be entered of record, to-wit, State of Tennessee, Lawrence County, I, the undersigned do hereby certify that some time past, I was very much intoxicated and spoke some words injurious to the character of William Cook, that I did not speak those words out of spite or malice, and did not wish to injure his character, and if I had been sober would not have spoken them as I know nothing of my own knowledge to injure his character.
August 3, 1819___James Hill
Test: N. Casey, George Micky, Josephus Irvine

It is ordered by the court that the sheriff be directed to collect only a single tax of Daniel Pearce for his stud horse in the same manner as if the same had been entered for taxation according to law.

It is ordered by the court that the sheriff be directed to summon the following named persons as jurors to the next County court to be held for this County on the first Monday in Feb., next, to-wit, Richard Hill, John McDonald, Needham Futrell, Daniel Beeler, Groves Sharp, John Simonton, Malcom McIntyre, John Vories, John Foster, Abraham Pennington, Adam Chronister, Miles Birdsong, Paulyer Smelyer, Henry Brewer, William Hickman, Reuben Tripp, Josiah Wallace, Joseph Smith, William Takeer, Jonathon Johnson, Nathan Spears, William Morrow, Andrew Fugate, Levi Lewis, Wilson Wever, Andrew McClaren.

It is ordered by the court that the sheriff be directed to summon the following named persons as jurors to the next Circuit Court to be held for this County on the 4th Monday in February next, to-wit, John Haile, Adam Ross, George Sherley,Jr., Ebenezer Thompson, Green DePriest, John Edmondson, David Crockett, William G. Dalton, Joseph Halford, Alexander Miller, Henry Phenix, William Lucas, John H. Hamilton, William Strawn, John Hillhouse, William F. Cunningham, Daniel Mathews, George Hanks, Edward R. Sealey, Edward McDonald, William Voss, John Voss, John Garrison, Zachariah Strickling, Jonas Musgraves, Pollard Wisdom.

The sheriff returned into court the following list of insolvencies of taxations amounting in the whole to $5.50 State Tax for the present year and the same for County Tax at the rate of 100% according to the order of this court and after being duly sworn saith that he cannot find property on which to distrain (sic) to make the same-it is therefore ordered by the court that Bradley Halford, sheriff aforesaid be allowed the sum aforesaid as a credit in the final settlement according to law.

Ordered by the court that John Hillhouse, George Hanks, and Henry Sharp be appointed commissioners to settle with Daniel Kutch as administrator to Margaret Whitley, deceased, and that they make return to this court.

The Jury who were appointed at last court for the purpose of laying off land for the purpose of Iron Works in conformity to the petition of Peter Mosely & Co., made their report to this court, as follows, to-wit " State of Tennessee, Lawrence County, Oct. 2nd, 1819. We the jury whose names are hereunto annexed, who were appointed, summoned and qualified to examine and lay off several Tracts or parcels of land hereafter to be described, to be condemned for the purpose of establishing Iron Works agreeable to the petition exhibited to the County Court of this County by Peter Mosely & Co., report as follows, to-wit, that we have proceeded to examine and lay off___

The first named tract in said petition beginning at a hickory marked thus M near a spring not far from where James Welch now lives, running South 20 poles to a white oadk, thence West 650 poles to a chestnut and black oak, thence North 480 poles to a stake, thence East 800 poles to a stake, thence South 460 poles to a stake, thence West 860 poles to the beginning, containing 2380 Acres all of which we condemn for the use of the Iron Works as believing it unfit for cultivation, EXCEPT, Forty acres plotted out East and North from the beginning corner and Seventy-eight Acres commencing 100 poles North from the Southwest corner of said tract running East 130 poles, thence South 100 poles to the beginning.

Also the second named tract on FACTOR's FORK, beginning at a sweet gum marked thus M(EDITORS NOTE; this marking is a capital P with a capital M on top of the P) opposite the mouth of a small branch running East 480 poles to a stake, thence South 240 poles to a stake, thence West 480 poles to a white oak, thence North 240 poles to the beginning, containing 720 Acres, all of which is condemned for the use of Iron Works, believing it to be unfit for cultivation, EXCEPT 150 Acres, beginning 80 poles East from the beginning corner running South 240 poles, thence East 100 poles, thence North 240 poles, thence West 100 poles to the beginning.

Also the third named tract beginning at a Spanish Oak on the East bank of Shoal Creek marked thus M at the point of a rocky bluff running South 240 poles to a chestnut and Hickory, West 800 poles to a black oak and poplar, thence North 480 poles to a Hickory, thence East 800 poles to a chestnut and Dogwood on a high ridge, thence South 240 poles to a stake, thence West 20 poles to the beginning. All of which we have condemned for the use of Iron Works, believing it to be unfit for cultivation, EXCEPT, 367 Acres, beginning 145 poles East of the Northwest corner, running West 145 poles, thence South 480 poles, thence East 100 poles, thence South 480 poles, thence East 100 poles, thence North 480 poles to the beginning.

Also the Fourth named TRACT, beginning at a beech on the West bank of Shoal Creek marked thus M near the mouth of a small branch below Samuel____? running East 800 poles to a red oak and gum, thence North 480 poles to a black oak and dogwood at the head of a small hollow, thence West 800 poles to a black oak and chestnut on a ridge, thence South 480 poles to the beginning, containing 2,400 Acres, all of which we condemn for the use of Iron Works believing it to be unfit for cultivation.

Also the FIFTH TRACT, beginning at three chestnuts on the Military Road marked thus M, running West 640 poles to a dogwood in a steep hollow leading into Pond Creek, thence North 640 poles to a chestnut and dogwood on the West side od Crowson's Ford at Edmundson's Mill, thence East 480 poles to a white Oak on the head of a small hollow, thence South 320 poles to a hickory, thence East 106 poles to a black gum and hickory on the East side of Shoal Creek, thence South 320 poles to the beginning, containing 2,240 poles, all of which we condemn for the use of Iron Works, believing the same to be unfit for cultivattion, EXCEPT, 720 Acres, beginning 130 poles North of the Southwest corner, running East 320 poles, thence North 360 poles, thence a straight line so as to strike the North boundary line 40 poles from teh Northwest corner, thence West and South with said line to the beginning.

Also the Sixth TRACT, on Crowson's Fork of Shoal Creek, beginning at two white oaks marked thus M, running West 480 poles to a stake, thence North 400 poles to a stake, thence East 480 poles to a stake, thence South 400 poles to the begining, containing 1,200 Acres, including an iron Ore Bank, all of which we condemn for the use of Iron Works, believing it unfit for cultivation, except, 784 Acres running from the beginning corner North degrees West 210 poles , thence North 55 degrees West to the North boundary line, thence West and South and East with the said line to the beginning.

Also the SEVENTH named Tract on Shoal Creek beginning 160 poles Southeast of John McIntyre dwelling house, on a hic.kory on top of a high ridge running West 166 poles to two ellums in the creek bottom, thence South 200 poles to a stake, thence East 160 poles to a stake, thence North 200 poles to the beginning, all of which we condemn for the use of Iron Works, believing it to be unfit for cultivation. Except, 50 Acres, beginning at the Northwest corner of said tract, thnce East 40 poles, thence South 200 poles, thence West 40 poles, thence North 200 poles to the beginning. It appearing to the jury that the interference of the above tracts together with the land plated out by the jury amounts to 3,070 Acres and 120 poles short of the quanity prayed for which we jave layed for the benefit of the said establishment in the following manner, to-wit,

One tract beginning at a beech marked thus M near the mouth of a small branch below Samuel Sullivants, running East 800 poles to a red oak and gum, thence South 300 poles to a stake, thence West 800 poles to a stake, thence North 300 poles to the beginnning, containing 1,500 Acres. One other Tract adjoining the North Boundary line which included the Block House and beginning at a white oak, northeast corner of said tract, thence with said line 400 poles to a stake, thence North 500 poles to a stake, thence East 400 poles to a stake, thence South 500 poles to the beginning, containing 1,250 Acres. Also another tract containing 321 Acres, beginning at a dogwood in a steep hollow leading into Pond Creek, a Southwest corner of said tract, including said Block House, thence East with the line of said tract 250 poles to a stake, thence South 205 poles to a stake, thence West 250 poles to a stake, thence North 205 poles to the beginning, including 321 Acres, all of which they report to be not fit for cultivation.
Given under our hands the date above. George Hanks, Simon Higgs, Thomas Keese, George W. Jones, Melcher Duncan, James Bumpass, Martin Prewit, Aaron Choate,Jr., Henry Sharp, Gabriel Bumpass, George Grisham and Nathan McClendon.

Ordered that court be adjourned until tomorrow, 9 o'clock. Duncan McIntyre, Pollard Wisdom, Henry Sharp, and H. Day, J.P.'s.

TUESDAY NOVEMBER 2nd, 1819

Court met Tuesday morning Nov. 2nd, 1819, 9 o'clock, according to adjournment, present, Duncan McIntyre, Henry Sharp, Henson Day, Pollard Wisdom, Esquires, Justices.

The sheriff retuned into court the following venire Facias to-wit; Martin Gaither, Robert Haynes, John Wisdom, George Grisham, John Smallwood, Samuel Sullivan, Abraham

Helton, Nathaniel Mason, John Thompson, John Welch, Hamilton Reynolds, Austin Kendrick, Thomas Allsup, Andrew Johnson, Enoch Tucker, William Tucker, James Welch, Caleb Whorton, Elijah Cooper, Lewis Franks, George W. Jones, Aaron Choate, Elliott Lindsey, Harden Paine of whom the following were drawn as jurors, to-wit, Harden Paine, Foreman, Lewis Franks, Samuel Sullivan, Elijah Cooper, Martin Gaither, George Grisham, Austin Kendrick, Enoch Tucker, Nathaniel Mason, George W. Jones, Hamilton Reynolds John Thompson, and Caleb Whorton, who after being sworn and charged withdrew to consider of their presentments.

Samuel Green
vs	Trespass
Aaron Anglin & Others

    This day came the defendant by his attorney and the plaintiff although solemnly called came not but made default. It is therefore considered by the court that the defendant recover of the plaintiff his costs by him about his defense in this behalf expended and that he go hence without day and that the plaintiff in mercy &c.

    James Strawn came into court prayed and obtained a license to keep a house of Ordinary at his dwelling house which was granted him who gave bond and security according to law.

    Josephus Irvine came into court prayed and obtained a license to keep a house of Ordinary at his dwelling house which was granted him who gave bond and security according to law.

Joseph Farmer
vs	Trespass on the case
James Broadstreet

    This day came the parties by their attorneys and thereupon came a jury of good and lawful men, to-wit, Thomas Alsup, Elliott Lindsey, Aaron Choate, Jr., Robert Haynes, Jonas Musgroves, James Moody, Moses Holloway, Thomas Keese, Simon Edwards, James Haile, Daniel McIntyre, Hugh Sinclear, who being elected, tried and sworn, well and truly to try this issue of traverse, upon their oaths do say that the defendant is NOT guilty in manner and form as in the plaintiff's declaration mentioned. It is therefore considered by the court that the defendant go hence without day and recover of the plaintiff his costs by him about his defense in this behalf expended from which judgement the plaintiff prayed an appeal to the Honorable the Circuit Court to be holden for this County which was granted him who gave bond and security according to law.

John Bankhead
vs	Appeal
John Allsup

    This day came the parties by their attorneys and thereupon came a jury of good and lawful men, to-wit, Elliott Lindsey, Aaron Choate, Jr., Robert Haynes, Jonas Musgroves, James Moody, Moses Holloway, Thomas Keese, Simon Edwards, James Hail, Daniel McIntyre, Hugh Sinclear, and Aaron Anglin, who being tried and sworn well and truly to try this issue of traverse upon their oaths do say that the defendant is guilty in manner and form as the plaintiff against him hath alleged and they do assess the plaintiffs damages by reason thereof to $30 besides costs. It is therefore considered by the court that the plaintiff recover of the defendant his damages aforesaid by the jurors aforesaid, in form aforesaid assessed together with his costs by him about his suit in this behalf expended and the defendant in mercy & c.

    John B. Stribling came into court and at the request of M.H.Buchanan, Clerk and with the assent of the court was qualified as a Deputy Clerk, aforesaid.

Aaron Anglin
vs   Qui ? Debt
Samuel Green

    This day came the plaintiff by his attorney and the defendant though solemnly called came not but made default. Whereupon it is considered by the court that the plaintiff have judgement final by default and that he recover for the State as well as for himself of the defendant the sum of $100, the debt in his declaration mentioned also the costs of suit by him in his behalf expended and that the defendant be in mercy & c.

    Ordered that court be adjourned until tomorrow, 9 o'clock. Henry Sharp, Duncan McIntyre, H.Day, Pollard Wisdom, J.P.'s.

WEDNESDAY, NOVEMBER 3rd, 1819

    Court met Wednesday morning, Nov.3rd, 1819 at 9 o'clock, according to adjournment. Present, Duncan McIntyre, Henry Sharp, Henson Day, and Pollard Wisdom, Justices, Esquires.

State
vs
Hugh Sinclear

    This day came the Solicitor General in behalf of the State as well as the defendant in his proper person and the defendant being arraigned upon his arraignment pleaded NOT guilty and for his trial puts himself upon his Country and the Solicitor General for the State likewise. Whereupon came a jury of good and lawful men, to-wit, Robert Haynes, Thomas Allsup, William Tucker, Aaron Choate, Elliott Lindsey, Simon Edwards, Simon Higgs, Moses Holloway, William Burris, Thomas Holland, Asa Jernaken, who being elected, tried and sworn well and truly to try this issue of traverse, upon their oaths do say that the defendant is NOT guilty in manner and form as he is charged in the bill of indictment. Whereupon the Solicitor moved the Court to tax the defendant with the cost and for reasons to the Court which appears sufficiently strong to induce a belief that the defendant is guilty in manner and form as he is charged in the said bill of indictment. It is therefore considered by the court that the defendant pay the cost of this prosecution and that he be taken & c.

The State
vs
William Merady

This day came the Solicitor General in behalf of the State who moved the court that a Nole prosequi should be entered in this case and that a judgement be entered up against the County for costs, it is therefore considered by the court that the same be granted and that the county Solicitor pay all those entitled to cost in behalf of the State out of any monies in his hands not otherwise appropriated.

State
vs
Polly Kirk

On motion of the Solicitor Genral in behalf of the State that a Nole prosequi should be entered in this case and a judgement against the county for costs. It is ordered by the court that the same be entered and that the county pay allthose entitled to costs in behalf of the State out of any moneys in his hands not otherwise appropriated.

A bill of sale from Thomas Blackbourn to Jesse Kendrick for a negro boy was produced in open court and proved to be the act and deed of the said Thomas Blackbourn by the oath of Josephus Irvine a subscribing witness thereto, which was ordered to be certified accordingly.

Ordered by the court that William Seahorn be exempted from the payment of half the valuation of a certain read(sic) cow by him posted.

State
vs
James Moody   Assault and battery

This day came the Solicitor General in behalf of the State as well as the defendant in his proper person and the defendant being charged upon the bill of presentment pleads guilty thereto and for his trial puts himself upon the justice and mercy of the court, whereupon it is considered by the court that the defendant make his fine with the State to the sum of $1 and that he pay the cost of this prosecution and that he be taken & c.

The State
vs
Abraham Pennington   Assault and battery

This day came the Solicitor General in behalf of the State as well as the defendant in his proper person and the Solicitor General moved the court that a Noli prosequi should be entered and that the judgement be entered in favor of those entitled to costs in behalf of the State which was granted, to be paid by the County Trustee out of any monies not otherwise appropriated.

The State
vs
John Barnes   Assault and battery

     This day came the Solicitor General in behalf of the State as well as the defendant in his proper person and the defendant being charged upon the bill of presentment pleads guilty thereto and for his trial puts himself upon the justice and mercy of the court. Whereupon it is consdiered by the court that the defendant make his fine with the State to the sum of $ 1 and that he pay the cost of this prosecution and that he be taken & c.

State
vs
William Sehorn   Retailing spirituous liquiors without license

     This day came the Solicitor General in behalf of the State as well as the defendant in his proper person and the defendant being charged upon the bill of presentment pleads thereto NOT guilty and for his trial puts himself upon his Country and the Solicitor General for the State, likewise. Whereupon came a jury of good and lawful men, to-wit, James Foster, Thomas Welch, John Foster, Groves Sharp, Richard Hill, Adam Ross, John Welch, John A. Hail, Philip Bryon, Hugh Sinclear, James Welch, Phillip Chronister, who being elected tried and sworn well and truly to try this issue of traverse upon their oaths do say that the defendant is NOT guilty in manner and form as he is charged in the bill of presentment, whereupon the Solicitor General moved the court to tax the defendant with the cost and the court being of opinion that there is strong grounds to believe that the defendant is guilty it is therefore ordered by the court that he pay the cost of this prosecution and that he be taken & c.

State
vs
John N. Brown

     This day came the Solicitor General in behalf of the State as well as the defendant in his proper person and the defendant being arraigned upon his arraignement pleaded guilty and for his trial puts himself upon the justice and mercy of the court. Whereupon it is considered by the court that the defendant make his fine with the state to the sum of $1 and that he pay the cost of this prosecution and that he be taken & c.

The State
vs
John Lockard

     This day came the Solicitor General in behalf of the State as well as the defendant in his proper person and the defendant being charged upon the bill of presentment plead thereto guilty and for his trial puts himself upon the justice and mercy of the court. Whereupon it is considered by the court that the defendant make his fine with the State to sum of one dollar and that he pay the cost of this prosecution and that he be taken & c.

The State
vs
Jesse Sims

This day came the Solicitor General in behalf of the State as well as the defendant in his proper person and the defendant being charged upon the bill of presentment pleads NOT guilty and for his trial puts himself upon the justice and mercy of the court and the Solicitor General for the State, likewise, whereupon came a jury of good and lawful men, to-wit, Robert Haynes, Thomas Alsup, William Tucker, Aaron Choat, Eliott Lindsey, Thomas Welch, Simon Edwards, John W. Henry, William Henry, Willia Burris, Wm., Higgs, Thomas Holland and Asa Jernagon, who being elected, tried and sworn well and truly to try this issue of traverse upon their oaths do say that the defendant is NOT guilty in manner and form as he is charged in the bill of presentment and the Solicitor moved that the court should enter judgement up in favor of all those entitled to costs in behalf of the State which was ordered and that the County Trustee pay the same out of any monies in his hands not otherwise appropriated.

The State
vs
Moses Holloway

This day came the Solicitor General in behalf of the State as well as the defendant in his proper person and the defendant being charged upon the bill of presentment pleads NOT guilty and for his trial puts himself upon the justice and mercy of the Court and the Solicitor General for the State, likewise, whereupon came a jury of good and lawful men, to-wit, Robert Haynes, Thomas Allsup, William Tucker, Aaron Choat, Eliott Lindsey, Thomas Welch, Simon Edwards, John W. Henry, William Burris, William Higgs, Thomas Holland and Asa Jernagon, who being elected, tried and sworn well and truly to try this issue of traverse upon their oaths do say that the defendant is NOT guilty in manner and form as he is charged in the bill of presentment and the Solicitor General moved that the court should enter judgement up in favor of all those entitled to costs in behalf of the State which was ordered and that the County Trustee pay the same out of any moneys in his hands not otherwise appropriated.

Ordered that Hugh Reynolds, a Grand Juror be fined the sum of $1.50 for getting drunk in time of session.

Ordered that court be adjourned until Court in Course.
Duncan McIntyre, Henry Sharp, and H. Day, J.P.'s.

MONDAY, FEBRUARY TERM, 1820

At a Court of Pleas and Quarter Sessions begun and held for the County of Lawrence at the house of Josephus Irvine, formerly the house of Doctor Joseph Farmer, the present place of holding Courts for said County, the 7th day of February, 1820. Present, Duncan McIntyre, John Hillhouse, James Forbes, Henson Day,

Pollard Wisdom and Joseph Gist, Esquires, Justices

The following persons who were appointed by the last Legislature of this State, Justices of the Peace in and for this County, to-wit, Samuel Poteet, Thomas Welch, Mancel Crisp, George Lucas, Andrew Brown, William Vance, Robert Chaffin, Jacob Pennycuff and Daniel A. Flannery, came into court and were qualified as such according to law and invited to take a seat.

Ordered that Jesse Needham be exempt from the appraisment of a certain bay filley by him posted as such.

A majority of the Acting Justices of this County being present it is ordered that M.H. Buchanan, Clerk of the Court be allowed the sum of $28 for his ex-officio service for the year 1819 to be paid by the County Trustee of this County out of any monies in his hands not otherwise appropriated and that the clerk certify accordingly.

A majority of the acting Justices being present it is ordered that Bradley Halford, Sheriff be allowed the sum of $36 for his ex-officio services for one year expiring the first of November term, 1819, to be paid by the County Trustee of this County out of any monies in his hands not otherwise appropriated and that the clerk certify accordingly.

A majority of the acting Justices being present, it is ordered that Robert L. Cobb be allowed the sum of $ 32.50 for his ex-officio services for the year past, to be paid out of any monies in the Treasurer's hands not otherwise appropriated, and that the clerk certify accordingly.

At least five of the acting justices of the Peace being present, to-wit, Duncan McIntyre, John Hillhouse, James Forbes, Henson Day, Henry Sharp,-George Roggers came into court and presented one wolf scalp over four months old which was ordered to be burned and certified accordingly.

A majority of the acting Justices being present, to-wit, Duncan McIntyre, John Hillhouse, James Forbes, Henson Day, Henry Sharp,-Nathan Jobe came into court and presented one wolf scalp over four months old which was ordered to be burned and certified accordingly.

Ordered that the following Justices be appointed to take a list of taxable property and polls within the following Captain's Districts in this County, to-wit, William Vories in Captain Seahorn's Company, George Lucas in Captain Prewitt's Do., Pollard Wisdom in Captain Wisdom's Do., Andrew Brown in Captain Horton's Do., Henry Sharp in Captain Grisham's Do., Thomas Welch in Captain Hail's Do., Joseph Gist in Captain McClaren's Do., and Samuel Poteet in Captain Cooper's Do., and that they make report to next court.

Burrell B. Quimby came into Court, prayed and obtained

a license to keep a house of Ordinary at his own house in this County, which was granted, who took the oath to suppress gambling and gave bond and security according to law.

Ordered that Robert Haynes be appointed overseer of the Military Road in room of Richard Bailey, resigned, and that he have the same hands under his direction as were under the direction of said Bailey.

Ordered that the following named persons be appointed as Jurors to attend the next County Court of this County on the first Monday in May, next, to-wit, Willis Lucas, Archer Nail, Harden Paine, David Steel, Eli Kendy, Charles Christian, George Grisham, Henry Pickard, Luke Grimes, James Brooks, John McClaren, John McDonald, William Jackson, John Thompson, Samuel Jenckens, Melcher Duncan, Frederick Rackley, Simon Higgs, Martin Gaither, Michael Hensley, Alexander Campbell, Robert Brashears, Burrel B. Quimby, Austin Kendrick, George Vandover, and that they do not depart therefrom without leave of the Court.

Ordered that Henson Day be appointed Chairman of this Court in the room of Duncan McIntyre, Esquire, resigned.

The Court proceeded to select from among their own body five Justices for the purpose of trying all jury causes or Court of Quorum, when, upon counting the votes, it was found that Henson Day, Henry Sharp, Mansel Crisp, William Vance, and John Hillhouse were elected for the purpose aforesaid.

A majority of the acting Justices being present, it is ordered that the following persons be appointed a Jury of View to view and mark out a road the nearest and best way to commence where the road from Pulaski strikes the Giles County line near the forks of Sugar Creek, thence to the Alabama line in the direction of Florence, to-wit, Thomas Allsup, Robert Brashears, William Poteet, Henry Moody and J. Holt, and that they make report to next Court.

M.H. Buchanan, clerk of this Court produced a receipt from the Treasurer of West Tennessee certifying that the clerk aforesaid had paid over such moneys as had been collected by him which were due the State up to the first of October 1819.

Ordered that William White, Elihu Crisp, John Kenady, William Sisemore and Lazarous Stewart be appointed constables in and for said County who gave bond and security and were qualified according to law.

Ordered that James Bumpass, Martin Prewit, and Wm. F. Cunningham be appointed Commissioners to settle with the late County Trustee of this County and that they make report to the next Court.

A majority of the Acting Justices of the peace being present ordered that William R. Davis, jailor of Giles Co. be allowed the sum of $17 for the keeping, committment and releasement of George Sherley, a prisoner committed to the jail of Giles County, and that the same be paid by the County Trustee of this County out of any monies not otherwise appropriated.

Ordered that William R. Davis, Jaier of Giles Co., be allowed the sum of $ 4 for keeping and bringing before the Judge, David Flatt by writ of habias corpias, that the same be paid by the County Trustee of this County out of any monies not otherwise appropriated.

Ordered that court be adjourned until tomorrow morning, 9 o'clock. Duncan McIntyre, Henry Sharp, H. Day, J.P.'s.

TUESDAY, FEBRUARY TERM, 1820

Tuesday morning, Feb. 8th, 1820- 9 o'clock, court met according to adjournment, present, Duncan McIntyre, Henry Sharp, Henson Day, Esquires, Justices.

The Court being and having advertised on the first day of this term that they should proceed on this day to the election of a County Trustee and Coroner, proceeded to the election of same, whereupon it was found that Thomas Welch was duly elected County Trustee, and William Welch, Sr., Coroner, who were qualified and gave bond and security according to law.

Duncan McIntyre and George Hanks, Justices of the peace in and for this County came into court and resigned their appointments as such, which was ordered to be certified.

Elijah Melton by his attorney came into court and presented a petition praying that writs of Certiorori and Supercedias should issue in this case wherein Barnett is plaintiff and sai Melton ddefendant and the said Melton being qualified to the facts contained in the said petition and said reasons being thought sufficient by the Court the same was granted him who gave bond and security according to law.

Ordered that Elihu Crisp and Lazarous Stewart, two of the Constables in and for said County be appointed to attend as such at the next Circuit Court to be holden for the County on the 4th Monday in this month and that they do not depart therefrom without leave of the court.

A majority of the acting Justices of the peace being present, it is ordered that the Tavern License for this County be as follows, to-wit, for for Horse fead(sic) per night 50¢, for for diet-37½¢ per meal, -for Lodging-12½¢ per night, for whiskey-per half pt., -12½¢, for Foren(sic) spirits-25¢ per half pint.

Ordered that the County Tax of this County be assessed at the rate of 100% on the State Tax. and that the clerk certify the same to the Collector, whose duty it shall be to collect for the same according to law.

Ordered that a Tax be laid for five dollars on each License issued to Peddle and Hawk for one year, and that it be the duty of the clerk to collect the same.

The sheriff returned into court the following venire Facias to -wit, Richard Hill, Needham Futerall, Andrew McLauron, Groves Sharp, William Tacker, Daniel Beeler, Malcom McIntyre, John McDonald, Levi Lewis, Joseph Wallace, William Wever, John Vories, John Foster, Abraham Pennington, Henry Brewer, Adam Chronister, Andrew Fugate, Miles Birdsong, of whom the following persons were drawn as Grand Jurors, Richard Hill, Needham Futrell Andrew McLawren, Groves Sharp, William Tacker, Daniel Beeler, Malcom McIntyre, John McDonald, Levi Lewis, Joseph Wallace, Wilson Wever, John Vories of whom Richard Hill was appointed foreman, who having received their charges and were qualified returned to consider of their presentments.

Ordered by the Court that each case on the records of this Court to which Bailey Brooks is either plaintiff or defendant by motion of his counsel be sett(sic) for trial for the next term of this court.

Ordered that John Wisdom former prosecution bail in the case of John Welch against John Counce be released and that William White be received in his room instead.

Issac Pennington
vs
John McClish   Debt

This day came the defendant, John McClish, in his proper person and says that he cannot gainsay but that he owes the plaintiff 182.50 debt, and $5.40 interest, this being what is due on the notes mentioned in the plaintiff's declaration after deducting the credits thereon given, and the plaintiff agreeing that this is correct. It is therefore considered by the court that the plaintiff recover of the defenant the aforesaid sum of $182.50 debt and $5.40 interest, and also his costs by him about his suit in this behalf expended, and the defendant in mercy & c.

The State
vs
Moses Williams   Malicious Mischief

William Quillen and William McCann came into court and acknowledged themselves indebted to the State of Tennessee, each in the sum of $100 to be levied of their goods, chattel lands and tenements to the use of the State severally to be void on conditions that William Quillen appear at the next term of this Court and on the third day of said term which commences on the first Monday in May next, then and there to prosecute and give evidence in behalf of the State against Moses Williams for malicious mischief and that he nor depart without leave of the court.

Daniel Harrison
vs
Wiley Jones

Silas Rackley and William White came into court and acknowledged themselves to be indebted to the State of Tennessee in the sum of $100 each to be levied of their goods, chattel lands and tenements to be void on condition that Silas Rackley appears here on the third day of the next term of this court to commence on the first Monday in May, next, then and there to prosecute and give evidence in behalf of the State against Wiley Jones.

The Grand Jury returned into open court the following bills of Indictment, indorsed each a true bill, State vs Moses Williams, State vs Daniel Harrison and Wiley Jones, State vs John Allsup.

Ordered by the court that court be adjourned until tomorrow, 9 o'clock. Henson Day, William Voss, Henry Sharp, John Hillhouse, and Mancil Crisp, J.P.'s.

WEDNESDAY, FEBRUARY TERM, 1820

Court met Wednesday, February 9th, 1820 at 9 o'clock according to adjournment, present, H. Day, William Voss, Henry Sharp, John Hillhouse, Mancil Crisp, Esquires, Justices.

Jesse W. Agnew, produced his license as attorney, who was qualified and authorized to practice as such.

John Welch
vs
John Counce   In case

This day came the parties by their attorneys and thereupon came a jury of good and lawful men, to-wit, Henry Brown, Adam Chronister, Andrew Fuget, Edward R. Sealy, George Sherley, Jr., Gabriel Bumpass, Harden Payne, John Hamliton, Simon Higgs, James Bumpass, Thomas Keese, Melcher Duncan, who being elected tried and sworn well and truly to try this issue of traverse and the arguments in this case being fully heard withdrew to consider of their verdict.

State
vs
John Allsup   Indictment for an assault and battery

This day came the Solicitor General in behalf of the State as well as the defendant in his proper person and the defendant being charged upon the bill of Indictment pleaded thereto guilty and puts himself upon the justice and mercy of the court. Whereupon it is considered by the Court that the defendant make his fine with the State to the sum of $5 and that he pay the cost of this prosecution and that he be taken & c.

The State
vs
John Garner   Indictment for an assault and battery

This day came the Solicitor General in behalf of the State as well as the defendant in his proper person and the defendant being charged upon the bill of Indictment pleaded guilty and puts himself upon the justice and mercy of the court. Whereupon it is considered by the court that the defendant make his fine with the state to the sum of $1 and that he pay the cost of this prosecution and that he be takne &c.

State
vs
Solomon Grisham   Indictment for Assault and battery

This day came the Solicitor General in behalf of the State as well as the defendant in his proper person and the defendant being charged upon the bill of indictment pleaded guilty and puts himself upon the justice and mercy of the court. Whereupon it is considered by the court that the defendant make his fine with the state to the sum of $ 1 and that he pay the cost of this prosecution and that he be taken &c.

State
vs
William McAnala(sic)

This day came the Solicitor General in behalf of the State as well as the defendant in his proper person and the defendant being charged upon the bill of presentment pleaded guilty and puts himself upon the justice and mercy of the court. Whereupon it is considered by the court that the defendant make his fine with the State to the sum of $ 1 and that he pay the cost of this presentment and that he be taken &c.

State
vs
Emanuel Keltner

This day came the Solicitor General in behalf of the State as well as the defendant in his proper person and the defendant being charged upon the bill of presentment pleads thereto NOT guilty and for his trial puts himself upon the Country and the Solicitor General for the State, likewise. Whereupon came a jury of good and lawful men, to-wit, William McCan, John Allsup, Hugh Sinclear, Shadrack Alvis, William Pennington, Jesse Helton, James Smith, Wm. F. Cunningham, Charles McHughs, William Higgs, Adam Ross, John Welch, Sr., who being elected tried and sworn well and truly to try this issue of traverse upon their oaths do say that the defendant is NOT guilty in manner and form as he is charged in the bill of indictment. Whereupon it is considered by the court that the defendant go hence without day and in all respects be acquitted from the charge aforesaid.

Jeremiah Jackson who was appointed one of the Justices of the Peace in and for said County at the last Legislature of this State, came into court and was qualified as such according to law.

State
vs
Abraham Henry   Presentment for an affray

The sheriff having returned into Court a writ endorsed thereon NOT FOUND and suggested that he had removed from the County and on motion of the Solicitor General it is ordered by the Court that Noli prosqui entered and judgement against the County in favor of all those entitled to cost in behalf of the State.

The State
vs
John Smith

The sheriff having returned into Court a writ endorsed thereon NOT FOUND and suggested that he had removed out of the County, whereupon motion of the Solicitor General it is ordered that a Noli prosequi be entered and a judgement against the County in favor of all those entitled to cost in behalf of the State.

John McClish
vs
Doughtery, Langley & Co.   Motion as Security for judgement

This day comes the plaintiff on his motion against John Doughtery, George Doughtery and Caleb Langley, merchants and partners trading under the firm and style of Doughtery, Langley and Company, for $187.90, the amount of a judgement recorded in this court against the said John McClish by Issac Pennington on two notes executed by the defendants and the said John McClish, and the said John McClish avers(sic) here before the Court that he is only security in said notes and this not appearing on the face of said notes, on motion of the plaintiff, it is ordered that a jury be empanelled to find whether the said plaintiff is security in said notes or not, and hereupon comes a jury of good and lawful men, to-wit, William McCan, John Alsup, Hugh S. Clain, Shadrack Alvis, Jesse Helton, James Smith, William Pennington, William F. Cunningham, Charles McCue, William Higgs, Adam Ross, and John Welch, Sr., who being elected tried and sworn well and truly to try and a true verdict render accordingly to evidence whether or not the plaintiff is security in said notes, to-wit, one note executed by defendants and plaintiff to Issac Pennington for $112.00 payable 5th of Sept., 1819, and the other executed by the same for $128.00 payable on the same day, upon their oaths do say that the plaintiff John McClish is security for the defendants in said notes and it appearing to the Court of record here that the said Isaac Pennington has recovered judgement on said notes for $187.90 in this Court against said John McClish, it is therefore ordered by the court that the said John McClish recover of the said John Doughtery, George Doughtery and Caleb Langley the sum of $187.90 and his costs by him about his motion in this behalf expended, and that the defendants be in mercy & c.

State
vs   Present Affray
John McCue

This day came the Solicitor General on the part of the State as well as the defendant in his proper person who being charged upon the bill of presentment pleads thereto NOT guilty and for his trial puts himself upon the Country and the Solicitor General on the part of the State, likeswise, whereupon came a jury of good and lawful men, to-wit, Miles Birdson, Abraham Pennington, James Strawn, Alexander Miller, Jchas Musgrove, David Crocket, Warren Mason, George Rogers, Archibald Huston, Silas Rackley, Moses Pennington, who being elected, tried ans sworn well and truly to try and a true verdict to render according to evidence on the issue between the State and the defendant upOn their oaths do say that the defendant is guilty in manner and form as in the bill of presentment he is charged. Whereupon it is considered by the court that he make his fine with the State in the sum of $ 5 and pay the costs of this prosecution and that he be taken & c.

Ordered that Court be adjourned until tomorrow, 9 o'clock. Mansil Crisp, Henry Sharp, William Voss, H. Day and John Hillhouse J.P.'s.

THURSDAY MORNING FEBRUARY 10, 1820

Court met according to adjurnment, Thursday morning 9 o'clock. Present, Henson Day, Henry Sharp, Mansil Crisp, John Hillhouse, William Voss, Esquires, Justices.

John P. Irvine & Co.
vs
William Bogard   In debt

The defendant came into court in his proper person and says that he cannot gainsay but that he does owe the plaintiff a $ 600 debt and $ 33 interest by way of damage. It is therefore considered by the court that the plaintiff recover of the defendant his debt aforesaid together with his damages aforesaid together with his costs by him about his suit in this behalf expended and the defendant in mercy & c.

John C. Hayes
vs
Richard Strawn

This day came the parties by their attorneys and thereupon came a jury of good and lawful men, to-wit, Miles Birdsong, John Foster, Abraham Pennington, William Higgs, Phillip Null, Aaron Anglin, Warren Mason, John Welch, James McConnel, John Wisdom, Nathaniel Mason, William McCann, who being elected, tried ans sworn well and truly to try this issue of traverse, upon their oaths do say that the defendant is guilty as he is charged in the plaintiff's declaration and they do assess the plaintiff damages by reason thereof to $25. It is therefore considered by the court that the plaintiff recover of the defendant his damges aforesaid by the jurors aforesaid, in form aforesaid, assessed together with his costs by him about his suit in this behalf expended and the defendant in mercy & c from which judgement the defendant prays an appeal to the Honourable the Circuit Court to be holden for this County, who having given bond and security and filed his reasons according to law the same is granted him.

State
vs
Abraham Pennington   An Affray

    This day came the Solicitor General in behalf of the State as well as the defendant in his proper person and the defendant being charged upon the bill of presentment pleas thereto guilty and puts himself upon the justice and mercy of the court, whereupon it is considered by the court that the defendant make his fine with the State to the sum of $1 and that he pay the cost of this prosecution and that he be taken &c.

    M.H. Buchanan came into court, prayed and obtained a License to keep a house of Ordinary, who gave bond and security and was qualified according to law.

John Goodman
vs
Bailey Alford   Case

    This day came the plaintiff by his attorney and the defendant though solemnly called came not but made default, whereupon it is considered by the court that the plaintiff recover of the defendant -but it being unknown to the court here what damages the plaintiff has sustained by reason of the premises in the said plaintiff's declaration mentioned, it is therefore ordered by the court that a jury be summoned to appear at the next term of this Court and assess the damages in this case sustained by the plainitiff in order that final judgement may be entered.

John Welch
vs
John Counce

    Ordered by the court that a commission issue to take the depositions of Sally Maxy, Henry Allen, Walter Maxey, Edward Maxey, Edward Maxey, and Allen Maxey in the Alabama State, Lodderal (sic) County in behalf of the plaintiff on giving 20 days notice to the defendant.

    The jury to whom was referred the case of John Welch against John Counce, came into Court and returned that they could not agree on their verdict. Whereupon it is considered by the court that this case be made a Neyes trial and that it be set for trial at the next term of this Court.

    Ordered that Court be adjourned until Court in course, H.Day, Henry Sharp, and John Hillhouse, J.P.'s.

MONDAY , MAY 1st, 1820

    At a Court of Pleas and Quarter Sessions begun and held for the County of Lawrence at the house of Josephus Irvine, the present place of holding Courts for said County, the 1st day of May, 1820, present, a majority of the Acting Justices for this County, to-wit, Pollard Wisdom, Henson Day, George Lucus, Mansel Crisp, Samuel Poteet, William Voss, Henry Sharp

John Hillhouse, Andrew Brown and Joseph Gist.

The following Magistrates returned a list of taxable property and polls by them taken according to an order of the last County Court of this County, to-wit, Pollard Wisdom, George Lucas Samuel Poteet, William Voss and Henry Sharp, which were received accordingly.

The Jury to whom was referred an order to view a road through the souteast corner of this County made report that they had viewed and marked out the same, and it is ordered by the Court that the same be opend accordingly, and James Appleton be appointed overseer to open and keep the same in repairs from the Giles County line to Anderson's Creek, and that he have all the hands to work thereon who live on the waters of Sugar Creek and within the bounds of Capt. Cooper's Company, and it is further ordered that John Bird be appointed overseer to open and keep in repair that part of said road which lies between Anderson;s Creek and the State line, and that he have all the hands to work thereon who live on the waters of Second Creek and within the bounds of Captain Cooper's Company.

Ordered by the Court that William F. Cunningham, Martin Prewitt, James Bumpass be appointed commissioners to settle with Andrew Pickens, late County Trustee of This County according to a late Act of Assembly and that they make report to next Court.

Ordered by the Court that Shadrack Alvis be appointed overseer of the Military Road in room of Stephen Rollin, resigned, and that he have the same hands to work thereon which were under the direction of said Rollin.

Ordered that James McConnel, George W. Jones, Harden Payne, William F. Cunningham, John Hillhouse, James Forbes and Silas Rackley or any five of them be appointed a jury of view to view and mark out a road the nearest and best way from M.H.Buchanan's to the West boundary line of the County in a direction to Waterloo in the State of Alabama, and that they make report to next Court.

Ordered that William Wisdom, Pollard Wisdom, Andrew Brown, Thomas Ethredge, Henry Brashears, John Swain, and John Dalton, or any five of them, be appointed a jury of view and mark out a road beginning at the most convenient point on the review of the intended Waterloo Road, thence the nearest and best way to the southern or western boundary of the County in a direction to Florence, and that they make report to next Court.

At least five acting Justices being present, to-wit, Henry Sharp, Pollard Wisdom, George Lucus, Samuel Poteet, William Voss. Nicholas Reynolds produced in Court one wolf scalp over 4 months which was ordered to be burned and that the clerk certify.

At least five acting justices being present, to-wit, Henry Sharp, Pollard Wisdom, George Lucas, Samuel Poteet, and Wm. Voss.

Levi Lewis produced in open court one wolf scalp over 4 months old which was ordered to be burnt and that the clerk certify it accordingly.

At least five acting Justices being present, to-wit, Pollard Wisdom, George Lucas, Samuel Poteet, William Voss, and Henry Sharp. Thomas Mathews produced in Court one wolf scalp over 4 months old which was ordered burnt and that the clerk certify accordingly.

Ordered that Austin Kendrick be appointed overseer to open and keep in repair that part of the Military Road which lies from Colonel Josephus Irvine's to the Giles Co., line, and that he have all the hands to work thereon who live East of the Simonton Road in this County and north of a line to run East from said Irvine's including Edward R. Sealy, Warren Mason, and Melcher Duncan.

Ordered that Simon Higgs be appointed overseer to open and keep in repair the road according to the markers of a Jury of View which was marked out from the west boundary of Giles County to M.H. Buchanan and that he have all the hands to work thereon who live East of the Military Road and within the bounds of Capt. Gresham's Company, except Edward R. Sealy, Warren Mason and Mecher Duncan.

At least five acting justices being present, to-wit, Pollard Wisdom, George Lucas, Samuel Poteet, William Voss, and Henry Sharp. M.C.McKenday produced in court one wolf scalp over 4 months old which was ordered by the Court to be burnt and that the clerk certify accordingly.

Issac Swafford, James Perrimore and Richard Fondren came into Court and acknowledged themselves severally indebted to the State. Issac Swafford in the sum of $100, James Perrimore and Richard Fondren each in the sum of $50 to be levied of their goods, chattel lands and tenements to the use of the State, to be void on condition that Issac Swafford keep the peace toward all the good citizens of this State, and more particularly toward Mary Parker of this County for the term of three months from this date, and that he pay the costs of this behalf expended.

William Seahon by his attorney came into Court and presented his petition praying that writs of cerciorari and Supersedus should issue to remove all proceedings unto this court in the case wherein a certain Nobles is plaintiff and he is defendant which was granted him upon giving bond and security according to law.

Judith Hunter came into court and prayed that John Smallwood might be appointed guardian of her two children, Lucinda Hunter and Marian Hunter, whihc was granted and the said John Smallwood gave bond and security according to law.

A majority of the acting Justices being present, it is

ordered that M. H. Buchanan clerk of this Court be allowed the sum of $ 6.75 for furnishing the court with certain record books to be paid out of any monies in hands of the County Trustee of this County not otherwise appropriated and that the clerk should certify accordingly.

A majority of the acting justices being present, it is ordered that Alexander Miller, Register of this County be allowed the sum of $2 for record books furnished for the use of his office. And that the County Trustee pay the same out of any monies in his hands not otherwise appropriated and that the clerk certify accordingly.

Ordered that a venire Facias issue to the sheriff of this County commanding him to summon the following persons to attend at the next term of this court to serve as Jurors, to-wit; Willis Lucus, John McAnally, William McAnally, Richard Hill, Solomon Grisham, Groves Sharp, Solomon Asbell, Sterling Lindsey, Levi Blackard, Cornelius Goforth, James Strickland, Nathan Swain, Joseph Smith, William Tacker, John Wharton, Benjamin May, Daniel Hunt, Caleb Wharton, Elijah Melton, George Hanks, Edward Higgs, George Isom, William Seahon, Jesse Lindsey, Robert Newton and Jordon Nipper.

Ordered that the sheriff of this County be directed to summon John Smith, Lazarus Stewart constables of this County to attend the next term of this court and attend on the jury at that time.

Court was adjourned until tomorrow, 9 o'clock. Henry Sharp, William Voss, George Lucus, John Hillhouse, Mancil Crisp, and H. Day, J.P.'s.

TUESDAY , MAY 2nd ,1820

Tuesday morning, 9 o'clock, court met according to adjournment, present, Henry Sharp, William Voss, George Lucus, John Hillhouse , Mancil Crisp, and Henson Day, Esquires, Justices.

Ordered that a Venire Facias issue to the sheriff of this County commanding him to summon the following persons to attend at the next term of the Circuit Court to be held for this County at the place of holding courts on the fourth Monday in August, next, then and there to serve as Jurors to said court, to-wit, Phillip Chronister, Daniel A. Flannery, Moses Pennington, Joseph Gist, Mansil Crisp, Thomas Welch, Henry Sharp, Henson Day, Robert Chaffin, James Forbes, Duncan McIntyre, Samuel Poteet, Jacob Penticuff, George Lucus, Jeremiah Jackson, William Wisdom, Andrew Brown, Henry Phenix, John McCann, Jacob Blythe, Barney Gabels, Joshua Ashmore, G.W.Jones, William Wisdom, and Thomas Ethridge.

Ordered that the sheriff of this County be directed to summons William Sizemore, John Kenedy constables of this County to attend at the next Circuit Court of this County and attend on the jury at that term.

Ordered that Austin Kendrick be appointed overseer of that part of the Military Road which lies betwixt Col. Josephus Irvine and the Giles Co. line.

This day came Bradley Halford, Sheriff of this County into Court amd protested against the sufficiency of the jail of this County which was ordered to be certified of record.

The State
vs   Assault and battery
Phillip Borrow

This day came the Solcitor General in behalf of the State as well as the defendant in his proper person and the defendant being charged upon the bill of indictment pleads guilty and puts himself upon the justice and mercy of the court, whereupon it is considered by the court that the defendant make his fine with the State to the sum of $ 6.50 and that he pay the cost of this prosecution and that the defendant be taken & c.

Mansil Crisp, John Hillhouse and Robert Chaffin, commissioners appointed to settle with Daniel Cooch, Adm., to the estate of Margaret Whitley de'c, came into court and made report of said settlement which was received and ordered to be recorded.

Ordered that Mancil Crisp, John Hillhouse and Robert Chaffin, commissioners appointed to settle with Daniel Kutch(sic), adm., to the estate of Margaret Whitley, dec'd be allowed each the sum of 50¢ to be paid out of said estate.

The Sheriff returned into court the following Venire Facias (Editors, note: The rest of this page was bland?)

At least five of the acting justices being present, to-wit, Mansil Crisp, Henry Sharp, Henson Day, William Voss, John Hillhouse, Thomas Holland produced in court one wolf scalp over 4 months old which was ordered to be burned and that the clerk certify accordingly.

Bailey Brooks
vs   In Case Trespass
Daniel McIntyre and Others

This day came the parties by their attorneys and thereupon came a jury of good and lawful men, to-wit, Michael Hensley, Melcher Duncan, Martin Gaither, William Welch, Jr., Silas Rackley, John Polly, Daniel Harrison, Wm. F. Cunningham, John Wisdom, Elijah Cooper, Stephen Rollen, Archer Nail, who being elected, tried and sworn, well and truly to try this issue of traverse, upon their oaths do say, that the defendants are guilty in manner and form as in the plaintiff's declaration mentioned and that they do assess the plaintiffs damages by reason thereof to $175 besides costs, whereupon it is considered by the court that the plaintiff recover of the defendants his damages aforesaid by the jurors aforesaid in form aforesaid together with his costs by him about his suit in this behalf expended and the defendant in mercy & c from which judgement the defendants prayed an appeal to the Honorable the

Circuit Court to be holden for this County and having given bond and security according to law and having filed their reasons the same is granted them.

The Grand Jurors returned into Court a bill of indictment the State against Ezekiel Farmer-a true bill.

James Broadstreet came into court and acknowledged himself indebted to the State of Tennessee in the sum of $100 to be levied of his goods, chattel lands and tenements to the use of the State to be void on condition that he appear at the place of holding courts for this County on the first Wednesday after the first Monday in August, next, then and there to give evidence in the case of wherein the state is plaintiff and Ezekiel Farmer, Defendant in behalf of the State and that he shall not depart therefrom without leave of the court.

Ordered by the court that Alexander Campbell, a juror to this court, be fined in the sum of $ 5 for getting drunk and for further contempt of the court, and that he remain in the custody of the sheriff until the same be paid.

State
vs   An affray
William Higgs
                    (Recorded in margin"Rec'd of Wm. Higgs,$2)
This day came the Solicitor General in behalf of the State as well as the defendant in his proper person and the defendant being charged upon the bill of presentment pleads thereto guilty and agrees to put himself upon the justice and mercy of the court. Whereupon it is considered by the court that the defendant make his fine with the State to the amount of $1 and that he pay the cost of this prosecution and that the defendant be taken & c.

John P. Erwin & Co.
vs   Garnishee
William Bogard

This day came the plaintiff by his attorney and the sheriff having returned the fine facias that Henry Sharp, Richard T. Bailey, and William White had been guarnished(sic) according to law who on motion of the plaintiff's counsel were examined according to law after being duly sworn and the said Richard T. Bailey saith that at the time of serving said guarnishment there was in his hands belonging to the said William Bogard, about $ 75, said Sharp saith at said time there was in his hands belonging to the said Bogard $ 31.90 said Sharp saith that there was in his hands at said time $ 35.50 together with the sum of $113.50 in notes. It is therefore considered by the court that judgement be rendered in favor of the plaintiff for the respective sums in the hands of the Guarnishees aforesaid and a conditional judgement in favor of the plaintiff for the above sum of notes in the hands of said William White and to stand against the said White for the amount which he may actually collect.

Bailey Brooks
vs   Cerciorari
Robert Mason

This day came the parties by their attornies and thereupon came the plaintiff who moved to dismiss Culiroa and Supersedes in this case which was overooled(sic) by the court, whereupon came a jury of good and lawful men,to-wit, Melcher Duncan, Archer Nail, Martin Prewitt, William Welch,Jr., Silas Rackley, John Polly, Daniel Harrison, Wm.F,Cunningham,John Wisdom, Elijah Cooper, Stephen Roland, Michael Hensley, and John Mcdonald who being elected, tried and sworn well and truly to try this issue of traverse upon their oaths do say, that the defendant does not owe the plaintiff anything as in pleadings he hath alleged. It is therefore considered by the court that the defendant recover of the plaintiff his costs by him about his defense in this behalf expended from which judgement the plaintiff pryaed an appeal to the Honorable the Circuit Court to be holden for this County, who after having filed his reasons and entered into bond according to law the same is granted to him.

Ordered that court be adjourned until tomorrow, 9 o'clock, Henson Day, Henry Sharp, Mancil Crisp, Wm. Voss, John Hillhouse, J.P.'s.

WEDNESDAY , MAY 3rd , 1820

Wednesday morning May 3rd , 1820, court met according to adjournment. Present, Henson Day, Henry Sharp, Mancil Crisp, William Voss and John Hillhouse, Esquires, Justices.

The State
vs   Affray
James McKew

The Solicitor Genrel came into court and moved that in consequence of the Sheriff having returned up the Capias -not found-and that from the best information the defendant has removed out of the County, that a Nole prosequi should be entered. Whereupon it is ordered by the court that the same be done accordingly and that judgement be entered in favor of all those entitled to cost in behalf of the state and that the clerk certify the same accordingly.

The State
vs   Indictment for Assault and Battery
James McKew

The Solicitor Genral came into court and moved that a Capias having been returned into court by the sheriff -not found- and from the best information the defendant has removed out of the County that a Nole prosequi be entered, it is therefore considered by the court that judgement be entered in favor of all those entitled to cost in this case and that the clerk certify the same accordingly.

The State
vs   Assault and battery
Wiley Jones

This day came the Solicitor General in behalf of the State as well as the defendant in his proper person and the defendant being charged upon the bill of indictment pleads thereto guilty and puts himself upon the justice and mercy of the court. Whereupon it is considered by the court that the defendant make his fine with the State to the sum of $ 5 and that he pay the costs of this prosecution and the defendant be taken & c.

The State
vs
Daniel Harrison   Assault and battery

This day came the Solicitor General in behalf of the State as well as the defendant in his proper person and the defendant being charged upon the bill of indictment pleads thereto guilty and puts himself on the justice and mercy of the court, whereupon it is considered by the court that the defendant make his fine with the State to the sum of $ 10 and that he pay the costs of this prosecution and that the defendant be taken & c.

William Quillen comes into court and acknowledges himself indebted to the State of Tennessee in the sum of $ 150 to be levied of his goods chattel lands and tenements to the use of the State to be void on conditions that he appear at the place of holding courts for this County on the first Wednesday after the first Monday in August, next, then and there to prosecute and give evidence in behalf of the State for an indictment _____(?) for malicious mischief and not depart therefrom without leave of court.

The State
vs
Joseph Baldwin   Presentment for an affray

This day came the Solicitor General in behalf of the State as well as the defendant in his proper person and the defendant being charged upon the bill of presentment pleads thereto guilty and puts himself upon the justice and mercy of the court, whereupon it is considered by the court that the defendant make his fine with the state to the sum of $ 1 and that he pay the costs of this prosecution and the defendant be taken & c.

The State
vs
Andrew Fugate   Assault and battery

This day came the Solicitor General in behalf of the State as well as the defendant in his proper person and the defendant being charged upon the bill of indictment pleads thereto NOT guilty and for his trial puts himself upon his Country and whereupon came a jury of good and lawful men, to-wit, Nathaniel Mason, Bailey Alford, James Strawn, Daniel Bently, Simon Edwards, William Burris, John Welch, Isaac Swafford, John Null, Eliot Lindsey, Duncan McDuffy, and Adam Ross who being elect4d tried and sworn well and truly to try this issue of traverse, upon their oaths do say that the defendant is guilty in manner and form as he is charged in the bill of indictment and they do assess the defendants fine to $ 50.25 besides costs. It is therefore consicred by the court that the State recover of the defendant his fine aforesaid together with the costs in this behalf expended and the defendant be taken & c.

James T. Baisey (sic)
vs
George Shirley, Jr.　　　　Case

On motion rendered by the court that each party have commissioners to take depositions in the State of Alabama or Kentucky on given twenty days notice to the adverse party of time and place of taking the same.

Ordered that court be adjourned until court in course. Henson Day, William Voss, John Hillhouse, Mancil Crisp, and Henry Sharp, J.P.'s.

OCTOBER TERM, MONDAY, OCTOBER 2nd, 1820

At a Court of Pleas and Quarter Sessions began and held for the County of Lawrence at the house of Josephus Irvine, the present place of holding Courts for said County, the 2nd day of October, 1820, present, a majority of the acting Justices for said County, to-wit, Henson Day, Mancil Crisp, John Hillhouse, Pollard Wisdom, Daniel A. Flannery, Henry Sharp, George Lucus, Robert Chaffin, Jeremiah Jackson and Andrew Brown.

Richard Hill, who was appointed by the last Legislature of the State a Justice of the Peace in and for said County, who came into Court and was qualified according to law.

John Crostwaite came into court, prayed and obtained a license to keep a House of Ordinary at his own house in this County which was granted, who took the oath to suppress gambling and gave bond and security according to law.

James K. Polk, Esquire, attorney at law, came into court and after being qualified under the direction of the Court as such was allowed to practice law in this County.

At least five of the acting justices being present, to-wit, Henson Day, Mancil Crisp, George Lucus, Robert Chaffin and Henry Sharp, John Smallwood produced in opne court one wolf scalp over 4 months and 5 under 4 months which was ordered to be burned and the clerk certify accordingly.

At least five of the acting justices being present, to-wit, Henson Day, Mancil Crisp, George Lucus, Robert Chaffin and Henry Sharp, Burrelle Gambelle produced in open court 7 wolf scalps under 4 months old which was ordered to be burned and the clerk to certify accordingly.

Ordered by the court that the last will and testement of Thomas Gambrelle, dec'd, be recorded and that John Smallwood and Robert Ross, subscribing witnesses to said will be qualified, whihc was done accordingly, and that letters testamentary issue.

Ordered that John Silers, John Ray and Joshua Ashmore be appointed commissioners to take off one years provisions for the support og Judiah Kendrick, wife of John Kendrick, dec'd, and that they make report to next court.

Ordered by the court that a Commission issue to take the examination of Elizabeth Taylor, wife of John P. Taylor, and Nany Horn, wife of James Horn, tuching (sic) their relinquishment of their right of dowry to 150 Acres of land conveyed by the said John P. Taylor and James Horn to Samuel Poteet and that Henry Sharp and Thomas Welch, Esquires, be appointed to take the examination of the above named women which was done accordingly.

Ordered that John Simonton be appointed overseer of the Military Road from Col. Josephus Irvine's to the creek below Thomas Welch's and that he be allowed the following hands, to-wit, Gilbreth Simonton, Malcom McIntyre, James Williams, Robert Mason, Bailey Alford, John Vorous, Matthew Swan, Simon Edwards, Adam Ross, Nathaniel Mason, John A. Haile, Thomas Williams, Geo. Shirley, Jr., ____ Pevihouse, James Helton, Jesse Helton, and ____ McFalls and that he keep the same in good repair.

Ordered by the Court that John Croswhite(sic) be appointed overseer of the Military Road from the Ford of the creek below Thomas Welch's to his own house, and that he be allowed the following hands, to-wit, Henry Ross, James Parchman, Angus McDuffy, Zachariah Stricklin, Geo. Vandiver, Duncan McDuffy, Martin Gaither, Austin Kendrick, John Campbell, Hamilton Stenson, John Price, Samuel Price, Archibald Huston, James Broadstreet, Alexander Murphy, John Wisdom, John L. Welch, Robert Chaffin, Nathan Clifton, and John Chaffin.

Ordered by the court that Moses Spencer, Sr., pensioner under an Act of Congress provide for certain persons engaged in the land and naval service of the United States in the Revolutionary War to be sworn to the schedule of his property, which was done accordingly.

Ordered by the court that Susa Gambrell, Executrix and Burell Gambrel, Executor, to the will and last testament of Thomas Gambrell, dec'd, be bound with their security, John Smallwood, in the sum of $400 for the performance of their duty, which was done accordingly.

Ordered by the court that Judah Kendrick and William Henderson be appointed Administratrix and Administrator of the estate of John Kendrick, dec'd, and they gave Alexander Miller and William Welch, Jr., securities who were bound in the sum of $1,000 and that letters of Administration issue.

Ordered by the court that Robert Chaffin, Moses Pennington, David Crockett, William Welch, Sr., William Seahorn, John Ray, and George Rogers, or any five of them, be appointed a jury of view to view and mark out a road to begin at a proper point near the head of Big Creek on the east boundary line of the County, thence the nearest and best way to the west boundary of this county near the head of Indian Creek, and that they make report to next court.

Ordered by the court that James Scott be allowed to build a mill across Shoal Creek, near Lawrenceburg,.

Ordered by the court that Douglas H. Stockton be appointed overseer of the Waterloo Road beginning at Buchanan's thence to Esquire Hillhouses and that he have the following hands to work, to-wit, all who live on Shoal Creek and Crowsons Fork from the junction of said creek and west of the Military road.

Ordered by the court that Samuel McKinney be appointed overseer of the Waterloo road from John Hillhouse's to James Forbes, and that he have the following hands, to-wit, all who live on Shoal Creek west of the Military road below the mouth of Crowson Fork as low down as Armstrong's shop, also those who live on Spring and Nob Creek as low as Sterling Lindsey's and below the said road, including Josiah Tippett, and that he keep the same in repair.

Ordered by the court that Daniel Kilburn be appointed overseer of the Waterloo Road beginning at James Forbes thence to where the Waterloo road crosses Aaron's Branch, and that he have the following hands to work thereon, to-wit, to include all on the waters of Knob Creek above said road and those on Chisholm's fork below said road, including John Smith.

Ordered by the Court that John Burns be appointed overseer of the Waterloo Road from Aaron's Branch to the West boundary line of this County and that he have the following hands to work, to-wit, all who live on Chisholm and Factors Fork above the said road to work under the direction of said Burns and keep the same in good repair.

Ordered that Henry Brashears be appointed overseer of a road beginning near Joseph Halfords fence and running to the frame of a house near the meeting house on Nob Creek. And that he have the following hands to work, to-wit, Sterling Linzy(sic) and all of Captain Wisdom's Company below him on Nob and Shoal Creeks.

Ordered that Meshack Inman be appointed overseer of the Florence Road to begin at the frame of a house on Nob Creek near the Nob Creek meeting house and running to the west boundary line of this County in a direction toward Florence, and that he be allowed the following hands, to-wit, to include John Smith and all the hands in Captain Wharton's Company below John Smiths, and keep the same in order.

At least five acting justices of the peace being present, to-wit, Henry Sharp, eorge Lucas, Henson Day, Robert Chaffin, and William Voss. Charles McAnally produced in open court 1 wolf scalp over four months old which was ordered to be burned and the clerk certify accordingly.

At least five acting justices of the peace being present, to-wit, Henry Sharp, Geoge Lucus, Henson Day, Robert Chaffin, & Wm. Voss. Hugh Reynolds produced in open court 1 wolf scalp

Ordered by the Court that Moses Moody, Henry Moody, John Smallwood, Issac Swafford, Michael Hensley, Alexander Campbell, and Robert Brashears, or any five of them be a jury of view to view and mark out a road from the three Forks of Sugar Creek the nearest and best way to the town of Lawrenceburg, and that they make report to next Court.

Ordered by the court that Robert Chaffin, Richard Hill and George Lucus, Esquires, be appointed Commissioners to inquire in to the conditions of Paupers and Poor persons who may make application for support from this County and that they report all such to this Court.

Ordered by the court, a majority of the acting justices being present that John Hillhouse be exempt from paying a double tax and that single tax be taken.

At least five of the acting justices being present, to-wit, Henson Day, Henry Sharp, George Lucus, Robert Chaffin, John Hillhouse. Solomon Asbell produced in open court 1 wolf scalp under four months old which was ordered to be burned and that the clerk certify accordingly.

Ordered by the court that the suit wherein James McConnel vs John Conner be withdrawn and that James McConnel pay all costs.

Ordered by the court that John Smith be and is hereby appointed Constable in and for Capt. Wharton's Company and gave bond and security was then qualified accordingly.

Ordered by the court that Wm. F. Cunningham, James Bumpass, and Martin Prewitt be and they are hereby appointed Commissioners to settle with the Collector of the State and County Taxes and to settle with alos with the County Trustee as the law directs.

Ordered by the court that court be adjourned til tomorrow, 9 o'clock, H. Day, Geo. Lucus, Wm. Voss, Henry Voss, Daniel A. Flannery, and Robert Chaffin, J.P.'s.

TUESDAY OCTOBER 2nd, 1820

Tuesday morning 9 o'clock, Oct. 2nd 1820 court met according to adjournment, present, Henson Day, Mansil Crisp, Henry Sharp, John Hillhouse, Esquires, Justices.

Ordered by the court that Josephus Irvine be allowed the sum of $12 for furnishing a STRAY PEN for the year 1819, and that the County Trustee pay the same out of any monies in his hands not otherwise appropriated, and that the clerk certify accordingly.

Ordered by the court that Josephus Irvine be allowed the sum of $7.30 for furnishing a STRAY PEN for the present year and that the County Trustee pay the same out of any monies not otherwise appropriated and that the clerk certify accordingly.

Ordered by the court that Bradley Halford, Sheriff of this

County be allowed the sum of $ 5.75 for the insolvent free poles tax of this County out of any monies in the hands of the County Trustee not otherwise appropriated and that the clerk certify accordingly.

Ordered that Sally McGee, orphan daughter of Polly McGee be bound to James McConnel until she arrives at the age of eighteen years, and said McConnel enters into bond to the Chairman of the Court with security in the amount of $500, with conditions to have her taught to read and write and to clothe and treat her well and turn her off with decent clothing for a girl of eighteen years of age.

Ordered that John McGee, an orphan boy (son) of Polly McGee, be bound to Archer Nail until he arrives to the age of twenty-one years and said Archer Nail enters into bond to the Chairman of the Court with security in the sum of $ 500 with conditions to have him taught to read and write and sipher as far as the rule of three inclusive, and learn him the Blacksmith's trade to the best of his knowledge and skill, and that he find the said John McGee good and holsome(sic) diate (sic) and decent apparel during his apprenticeship at the expiration of which he the said Nail shall furnish the said John McGee with two full suits of decent clothing.

Ordered by the court that all delinquents living in Capt. McClains Company be exempt from paying a double tax and that single tax be received.

At least five of the acting justices being present, to-wit, Henson Day, Mansel Crisp, Henry Sharp, John Hillhouse and Robert Chaffin. David Pennington produced in open court 1 wolf scalp over 4 months old which was ordered to be burned and the clerk certify accordingly.

Ordered by the court that Samuel Poteet, Andrew Johnson, Thomas Allsup, Lazarous Stewart, William Weaver, James Strawn, John Bird, and Levi Lewis, or any five of them be appointed a Jury of view to view and mark out a road from James Strawn to the County line the nearest and best way in a direction to Lambs Ferry on the Tennessee River and that they make report to next court.

James Maberry
vs   Trespass
John Smith

Ordered by the court on motion of the defendant by his attorney and it appearing to the satisfaction of the court that the security given by the plaintiff for the prosecution of the said suit is insufficent, that the said plaintiff give good and sufficent security by the second day of next term of the court for the costs of said suit or otherwise that the same be dismissed.

Ordered by the court that the Sheriff be directed to summon the following named persons to attend as jurors at the next County Court on the first Monday in January next at the place of holding courts, on the 2nd day of said term, to-wit, William McCann, Alexaner Miller, John McDonald, Abedingo Merryman, William Altum, Henry Ross, John Wisdom, Robert Johnson, Thomas Alsup, Thomas Springer, Sr., William Snodgrass, Reynolds May, Henry Brewer, Benjamin Gosnell, William Brashears, James Edmundson, Joseph Halford, John Edmundson, Josiah Tippett, James McConnel, George Sherley, Jr., Shadrack Rackley, and Geo. Rogers.

Ordered by the court that the sheriff be directed to summon the following named persons to attend as Jurors at the next term of Circuit Court on the 4th Monday in Feb., next at the place of holding courts, to-wit, Richard Hill, Capt. Daniel Beeler, Bryan McClendon, Daniel Steele, John Altum, John Vorees, James Parchman, Levi Lewis, Anderson Johnson, Thomas Springer, Robert Brashears, Robert Hightower, Archibald C.J. Anderson, George Wolf, Jesse Brashears, John Hillhouse, Willis Lucas, William Lucas, John Tjompson, Harden Paine, Martin Prewitt, John H. Hamilton, James Bumpass, Nathaniel Mason, Samuel W. Sullivan and William Wooten.

Ordered by the court tjat James McGee, an orphan child of Polly McGee be bound to John McDonald untilhe arrives to the age of 21 years and said McDonald enters into bond to the Chairman of the Court with security to the amount of $500, with conditions to have him taught to read, write and cypher as far as the rule of three inclusive and learn him the said James McGee how to tan, curry, and dress leather and furnish him the said James McGee with holsum diet and decent apparel during his apprenticeship and at the expiration of this apprenticeship said McDonald shall give him the said James McGee two decent suits of clothing.

Court was adjourned until tomorrow, 9 o'clock. H. Day, John Hillhouse, Mansel Crisp, Henry Sharp, William Voss, J.P.'s.

WEDNESDAY, OCTOBER 4th, 1820

Court met according to adjournment, Wednesday Oct. 4th, 1820 at 9 o'clock. Present, Henson Day, John Hillhouse, and Mancel Crisp, Justices, Esquires.

John Welch, Sr.
vs
John Counce   Trespass on the case

This day came the plaintiff by their attorneys and thereupon came a jury of good and lawful men, to-wit, John Ray, Jordan Nipper, Elijah Melton, William Higgs, Martin Prewitt, John H. Hamilton, Stephen Roland, Isaac Swafford, Aaron P. Cunningham, Thomas Holland, Groves Sharp, and Warren Mason who being elected, tried and sworn well and truly to try this issue of traverse upon their oaths do say that the defendant is guilty in manner and form as in the plaintiff's declaration mentioned and that the plaintiff recover of the defendant the sum of $125 damages together with his costs in this behalf expended and that the defendant in mercy & c.

John Goodman
vs   Case
Bailey Alford

It appearing to the satisfaction of the Court that at the Feb. term of this court a judgement by default was had and at the May term a writ of inquiry was executed and the jury assessed the plaintiff's damages to $25, it is therefore consdiered by the court on motion of the plaintiff by his attorney that judgement be entered, thereupon now for then, whereupon it is ordered by the court that the plaintiff recover against the defendant his damages aforesaid,in form aforesaid, by the jury aforesaid assessed together with his costs by him about his suit in this bhalf expended and the said defendant in mercy & c.

The State
vs   Retailing spirituous Liquors
Burwell B. Quimby

This day came the Solicitor General in behalf of the State as well as the defendant in his proper person and the defendant being arraigned pleaded thereto not guilty and for his trial puts himself uppn his Country and the Solicitor General for the State likewise, whereupon came a jury of good and lawful men , to-wit, John King, James Strawn, John Smallwood, George Sherley,Jr., Luke Grimes, John Wisdom, John Edmundson, James McConnel, Levi Blackard, William Tacker, George Isom, and Wm. Welch,Sr., who being elected, tried and sworn well and truly to try this issue of traverse, upon their oaths do say that the defendant is not guilty in manner and form as he is charged in the bill of presentment. It is therefore considered by the court that the defendant go hence without day and the Solicitor General moving the Court that the County be taxed with the cost. It is therefore considered by the court that the County Trustee pay the same out of any monies in his hands not otherwise appropriated and that the clerk certify accordingly.

State
vs   Indictment Assault and battery
William Matthews
   (Under the above was written-Cancelled by order of the
   (Court, editor note)

The State
vs   Indictment Assault and battery
William Melton

This day came the Solicitor General in behalf of the State as well as the defendant in his proper person and the defendant being arraigned upon his arraignement pleaded thereto guilty and for his trial puts himself upon the justice and mercy of the Court, whereupon it is considered by the court that he make his fine with the State to the amount of $ 1 and that he pay the cost of this prosecution and that the clerk certify accordingly.

The State
vs
Ezekiel Farmer   Recognisance for an assault and battery

This day came the Solicitor General in behalf of the State and the said Ezekiel Farmer who was recognized although solemnly called came not but made default. Whereupon it is considered by the court that the State recover of him $ 500 the amount of his recognizance unless he appears at next term of this court and show cause to the contrary and it is ordered that Sciri Facias issue accordingly.

State
vs
Moses Williams   Indictment Malicious Mischief

This day came the Solicitor General and with the consent of the Court enters Noli Prosiqui and judgement is rendered against the County in behalf of those entitled on behalf of the State and ordered that the clerk certify accordingly.

Ordered by the court that Court be adjourned until tomorrow, 9 o'clock, Henson Day, William Voss, Henry Sharp, Mancil Crisp, J.P!s

THURSDAY, OCTOBER 5, 1820

Thursday morning Oct 5, 1820, court met at 9 o'clock according to adjournment, present Henson Day, Mancil Crisp, and Henry Sharp, Esquires, Justices.

State
vs
James Helton   Assault and battery

This day came the Solicitor General in behalf of the State as well as the defendant in his proper person and the defendant being charged upon the bill of presentment pleaded thereto guilty and for his trial puts himself upon the justice and mercy of the Court, whereupon it is ordered by the court that the defendant make his fine with the State to the sum of $1 and that he pay the cost of this prosecution and that he be taken & c.

William Higgs
vs
Bradley Halford   Garneshee (sic)

(This entry marked through with a large X, editors)

The State
vs
James Adams   Indictment for assault and battery

This day came the Solicitor General in behalf of the State as well as the defendant in his proper person and the defendant being charged upon the bill of indictment pleaded thereto guilty and for his fine puts himself upon the mercy and justice of the court, whereupon it is considered by the court that the defendant make his fine with the State to the sum of $3 and that he pay the cost of this prosecution and gave Jordan Nipper for his security.

The State
vs   Assault and battery
Josephus Irvine

    This day came the Solicitor general in behalf of the State as well as the defendant in his proper person and the defendant being charged upon the bill of indictment pleaded thereto guilty and for his fine puts himself upon the mercy and justice of the court, whereupon it is considered by the court that the defendant make his fine with the State to the sum of $1 and that he pay the cost of this prosecution and that he be taken & c.

    Harden Payne came into court and produced a Bill of Sale from Gabriel Bumpass to himself for a negro girl named Rose, eleven or twelve years of age and acknowledged by Gabriel Bumpass to be his act and deed, ordered to be certified accordingly.

    Erastus Tippet, a pensioner under the Act of the United States, came into court and made application that a schedule of his property might be entered of record which was granted him which is recorded in words and figures following, to-wit, DISTRICT OF WEST TENNESSEE
    On the 5th day of Oct. ,1820 personally appeared in open court being a court of record for the County of Lawrence and State of Tennessee at a court of pleas and quarter sessions for said County, Erastus Tippet, aged 60 years on the 1st day of last August, resident in Lawrence County, who being first sworn according to law doth on his oath declare that he served in the Revolutionary War as follows, to-wit, in Col. James Hogan's Regiment, the 3rd Regiment in Capt. Joseph Mumfords Company in the North Carolina line which he claimed originally on the 5th day of Aug.1819 and has received a pension Certificate No. 13788 and I do solemnly swear that I was a resident citizen of the United States on the 18th day of March 1818 and that I have not since that time by gift, sale or in any manner desposed of my property or any part thereof with interest thereby so to dimish it so as to bring myself within the provisions of this Act of Congress entitled, An Act to provide for certain pensioners engaged in the land and naval service of the United States in the Revolutionary War passed on the 18th day of March,1818 and that I have not nor has any person interest for me any property or securities or contracts or debts due to me nor have I any income other than what is contained in the schedule hereto annexed and by me subscribed.
                              Erasmus Tippet (Seal)
Sworn to an subscribed on the 5th day of Oct.
                              M.H. Buchanan ,Clerk
    A schedule of my property , beds and necessary clothing, except to-wit, 1 cow and calf, 4 sows, 16 choats about 8 months old. My occupation is farmer, seven in family, myself, my wife Judith, sons 3, Ross, James and John, 2 daughters, Jane and Nancy. My youngest son is 12 years old.
    I, M.H. Buchanan, Clerk of the Court of Pleas and Quarter do hereby certify that the foregoing oath and the schedule hereto annexed and truly copied from the record of said court

and I do further certify that it is the opinion of the said court that total amount in value of the property exhibited in the aforesaid schedule is $ 38. In testimony whereof I have hereunto set my hand and affixed the seal of the said court, it being a PRIVATE SEAL , there being no seal of office.
This 5th day of October 1820
(PRIVATE SEAL)   M.H. Buchanan, Clerk of the Court of Pleas and Quarter Sessions for said County.

James Appleton
vs
Isaac Swafford   Appeal

  This day came the defendant by his attorney and the plaintiff though solemnly called came not but made default. It is therefore considered by the court that the defendant recover of the plaintiff his costs by him about his defense in this behalf expended and that he go hence without day and that the plaintiff be in mercy & c.

William Higgs
vs
Bradley Halford   Garneeshee

  This day came the parties by their attornies and the said Bradley Halford, garneeshee under an execution against John Davidson being examined on oath and it appearing to the satisfaction of the court from his examination that he has in his hands $ 51.50 of the money of said Davidson. It is considered that the plaintiff recover of P.B.Halford that sum after deducting from it the amount of this garneesheement and that the cost aforesaid be paid out of said sum of $ 51.50 from which judgement of the court the P.B.Halford prays an appeal to the next Circuit Court for this County and giving bond with security and signing his reasons, certify sufficient it is granted him accordingly.

  Mancil Crisp, Esquire, returned into Court the bond of Elizabeth Stinson with Richard T. Bailey and A.C. Huston, her securities to indemnify the Court from costs and charges of an bastard child, son of said Elizabeth Stinson. Also $12.50 the fine paid and bond gave accordingly.

  Henry Sharp, Esquire, returned into court the bond of Anny Montgomery with Richard T. Bailey and John Thompson her security to indemnify the court from costs and charges of an bastard child, son of said Anny Montgomery. Also paid the fine and gave bond accordingly.

  This day was produced in open court a deed of gift from Doctor Joseph Farmer to his daughter Eliza Farmer for four negroes therein mentioned, and the said Joseph Farmer came into court and acknowledged the execution of the same, whereupon it is ordered by the court that it be certified for registration.

  Ordered by the court that the prison bounds for this County be as follows, Beginning at the most northern part of Jenkins blacksmith shop, thence to the most northern part of the widow Irvine's house, thence to the most northern corner of the old school house near the jail, thence to the Southeast corner of Col. Irvine's plantation, thence with the fence of the same to the beginning, including all said plantation.

Ordered that Court adjourn until Court in Course.
John Hillhouse, Henry Sharp, Henson Day, Mansel Crisp,J.P.'s.

MONDAY, JANUARY TERM , 1821

At a Court of Pleas and Quarter Sessions holden for the County of Lawrence at the house of Josephus Irvine, formerly the house of Josephus Irvine(Editors note: evidently the last Irvine is clerical error, the correct name we think should be Farmer) on this 1st Monday in Jan.,1821, court met according to adjournment, present, Henson Day, Henry Sharp, Mansil Crisp, Thomas Welch, Robert Chaffin, Geo. Lucus, William Voss, Richard Hill, Jeremiah Jackson, and John Hillhouse, Esquires, Justices.

On motion of the Heirs and legatees of Joseph Gist, dec'd and with the consent of the Executor it is ordered by the court that Andrew Brown, Jeremiah Jackson, and Wm. Wisdom be and they are hereby appointed Commissioners to make partition for division of the estate of the said Joseph Gist, dec'd among said Legatees according to the directions and meaning of the last will and testement of the said Gist, dec'd, they having the same laid before them and such division so to be made that the said Commissioners shall make report of the same in writing to the next term of this Court.

The Commissioners who were appointed at the last term of this court for the purpose of seting apart certain property of John Kendrick, dec'd, for the support of the widdow and according to an Act of Assembly made then part in words and figures following, to-wit, State of Tennessee, Lawrence County. Agreement to an order of Court in appointing John Ray, John Sellars, Joshua Ashmore to make an allowance to Judy Kendrick wife of John Kendrick, dec'd for her maintanance for one year have allowed the said Judy Kendrick $140, viz, 1 steer at $10, 2 cows and calves at $19,and 9 barrels of corn at $ 1 per bbl., zmounting in the whole to $ 38, the balance of $102 is the amount that we the said John Ray, John Sellars and Joshua Ashmore have made in allowance to the said Judith Kendrick. Given under our hands this 10th day of Nov., 1820 which we received and ordered to be entered of record which report was assessed by the said John Ray, John Sellars and Joshua Ashmore.

Whereas it is represented to this court that an order which was made at the last court allowing the Administrator of John Kendrick, dec'd, to sell said estate was NOT entered of record, it is therefore ordered by the court that an order as aforesaid be entered now for then.

The Administrator of John Kendrick,dec'd, returned unto Court a bill of sale of said estate which was received and ordered to be recorded accordingly.

Robert Chaffin, Esquire and others, who were appointed at the last term of this court a jury of view to view and mark out a road from the eastern to the western boundary of this County, which was returned to the Court.

At least five of the acting justices being present, to-wit, Henson Day, Thomas Welch, George Lucas, Mansil Crisp, Henry Sharp, John Hillhouse, Jacob Penticuff, Robert Chaffin and Jeremiah Jackson. William Reynolds produced in open court 1 wolf scalp over 4 months old which was ordered to be burned and that the clerk certify accordingly.

A majority of the acting Justices being present it is ordered by the court that Bradley Halford, Sheriff, be allowed the sum of $39.09 for his ex-officio services for the year 1820 to be paid by the County Trustee out of any monies in his hands not otherwise appropriated and that the clerk certify accordingly.

A majority of the acting justices being present it is ordered by the court that M.H. Buchanan, clerk of this Court be allowed the sum of $26.81¼ for his ex-officio services for the year 1820 and that the County Trustee of this County pay the same out of any monies in his hands not otherwise appropriated and that the clerk certify accordingly.

A majority of the acting justices being present it is ordered by the court that M.H. Buchanan be allowed the amount of $19.09 for making out the Tax List for the year 1820 and that the County Trustee of this County pay the same out of any monies in his hands not otherwise appropriated and that the clerk certify accordingly.

Josephus Irvine, Henry Phenix, and M.H. Buchanan, a majority of the Acting Commissioners of the Town of Lawrenceburg having reported to this court that the lands appropriated to the use of said Town was entered according to Act of Assembly in such case made and provided for, and that a Temporary Court House was prepared therein in which Court could be held and the Court having examined maturely the letter and spirit of the law regulating their removal from this place to said Town are of opinion that it is now encumbant on them to make an adjournment from this place, whereupon it is ordered by the court that on the adjournment of this day's business that they adjourn all business relative to this Court to meet on tomorrow at the Temporary Court House in the Town of Lawrenceburg at the hour of ten O'clock in the morning and that the clerk enter the same of record.

A majority of the acting Justices being present, it is ordered by the Court that the Tavern rates of this County be as follows, for each ½ pint of whiskey or peach brandy sold, 12½¢, for each ½ pint of Furen (sic) spirits, 25¢, for each meals victuals 37½¢, for lodging each person per night 12½¢, for each horse feed 25¢, for each horse all night 50¢.

A majority of the acting justices being present, it is ordered that the following named magistrates be appointed to take a list of taxable property and poles in the following Captain's companies, to-wit, Richard Hill in Capt. Grisham's Company, Jeremiah Jackson in Capt. McClary's do, Robert Chaffin in Capt. Welch's do, George Lucas in Capt. Prewitt's do, Jacob Pennticuff in Capt. Sizemore's do, John Hillhouse in Capt. Wisdom's do, Daniel A. Flannery in Capt. Seahorn's do, Joseph Gist in Capt. Wharton's do, and that they make report to next court.

A majority of the acting justices of the Peace being present, it is ordered that the County tax of this County be levied at the rate of 100 per cent on the State tax and that the Clerk render a list of the same to the Collector whose duty it shall be to collect the same accordingly.

Thomas J. Matthews came into court, prayed and obtained a license to keep a house of Ordinary at his own house in this County, which was granted him, who gave bond and security and was qualified according to law.

A majority of the acting justices of the peace being present it is ordered by the Court that Josephus Irvine be allowed the sum of $25 for having furnished the court heretofore with a Court House and Stray pen, to be paid out of any monies in the hands of the County Trustee not otherwise appropriated and that the Clerk certify accordingly.

It is ordered by the court that John McDonald be appointed overseer of the Military Road in the room of Robert Haynes, former overseer.

It is ordered by the court that Joseph Halford who is in Capt. Prewitt's Company be appointed a Constable to fill the vacancy of Elihu C. Crisp, resigned, who gave bond and security and was qualified according to law.

Josephus Irvine, Henry Phenix and M. H. Buchanan, a majority of the acting Commissioners for the Town of Lawrenceburg having reported to this court that David Crockett, a former Commissioner of said town has resigned his said appointment, and the court being of opinion that the vacancy occassioned by the said resignation should be filled, it is therefore ordered by the court that Martin Prewitt be appointed a Commissioner for the Town of Lawrenceburg in the room of David Crockett, resigned as aforesaid, who was qualified and gave bond and security according to law.

The Court proceeded to select from among their own body five Justices as a Court of Quorum for the purpose of trying Jury causes, when, upon counting the votes, it was found the following Justices were selected for the purpose aforesaid, to-wit, Henson Day, Mansel Crisp, John Hillhouse, Robert Chaffin, Andrew Brown, which was ordered to be entered of record and that the Clerk certify accordingly to law.

Court adjourned until tomorro at 10 o'clock to meet in the Town of Lawrenceburg. John Hillhouse, H.Day, Mansil Crisp, Andrew Brown, and Robert Chaffin, J.P.'s

TUESDAY JANUARY 2nd 1821

Tuesday morning 2nd day of Jan. 1821, court met in the Town of Lawrenceburg according to adjournment, at 10 o'clark in the morning. Present Henson Day, Mansil Crisp, John Hillhouse, Robt. Chaffin and Andrew Brown, Esquires, Justices.

At least five of the Acting Justices being present, to-wit. Henson Day, Mansil Crisp, John Hillhouse, Robert Chaffin, and Andrew Brown. Thomas Welch produced in open court 1 wolf scaky over 4 months old which was ordered to be burned and that the clerk certify accordingly.

The sheriff returned into court the Venire Facias returnable to this term containing the following named persons, to-wit. William McCann, Alexander Miller, John McDonald, Abidnego Merryman, William Alton, Henry Ross, John Wisdom, Robert Johnson Thomas Springer, Sr., William Snodgrass, Reynolds May, Henry Brewer,Benjamin Gosnel, William Brashears, James Edmundson, Joseph Halford, John Edmundson, Robert Scales, Jesse Hilton, Ebenezer Thompson, Josiah Tippet,James McConnel, George Shirley, Jr.,Shadrack Rackley, and George Rogers with the following endorsements made by the Sheriff thereon. Executed on 11 but George Rogers by me Bradley Halford, sheriff and upon calling the Venire aforesaid, the following named persons appeared, to-wit, Alexander Miller, John McDonald, John Wisdom, Robert Johnson,Thomas Alsup, Thomas Springer, Jr., James Edmundson, Rob. Scoles, Jesse Holton, Abednigo Merryman, Josiah Tippet, James McConnel, Geo. Shirley, Jr., and Wm. McCann, of whom the following persons were drawn as Grand Jurors to inquire for the body of the Court of Lawrence, to-wit, Alexander Miller, foreman, John McDonald, John Wisdom, Robert Johnson, Thomas Alsup, Thomas Springer, Jr., James Edmundson, Robert Scoles, Jesse Hilton, Ebenezer Thompson, Josiah Tippet, James McConnel, Geo. Shirley, Jr., who were qualified and after having received their charge withdrew to consider of their presentments, under the direction of Joseph Halford, a constable who was sworn to attend them.

William Davis, Esquire, having produced his license as an Attorney was qualified and admitted to practice in this Court as such.

The Court having advertised on the 1st day of this term that on this day they would proceed to the election of a Sheriff to fill the vacancy of Bradley Halford, former Sheriff, whose term has legally expired, and after having made proclamation, proceeded to the election when upon counting out the votes, it was found that Bradley Halford was duly and constitutionally elected, who gave bond and security as Sheriff and Collector of the Publick and County Taxes and was qualified according to law.

Joseph Gist, Jr. Executor to the estate of Joseph Gist., Sr., dec'd, came into court and gave bond and security as such and was qualified according to law.

    M.H. Buchanan, Clerk of this Court produced his receipt from Thomas Crutcher, Treasurer of West Tennessee, certifying that the said clerk had paid over to said Treasurer the State Tax on lawsuits and on licenses issued to merchants, peddlers, to keepers of Houses of Ordinary, shows, etc, which receipt was acknowledged satisfactory and ordered that the same be entered of record.

James Maberry
vs
John Smith   Trespass on the case

    Whereas at the last term of this court the defendant by his councel came into court and suggested that the plaintiff's security was insufficient for the prosecution of said suit and the court after considering the same ordered that the plaintiff appear by the 2nd day of the present term of this court and give good and sufficient security for the prosecution of said suit otherwise the same should be dismissed and the plaintiff failing to appear altho solemnly called but made default it is therefore considered by the court that the defendant go hence without day and recover of the plaintiff his costs by him about his defence in this behalf expended and the plaintiff in mercy & c.

Robert Mason
vs
Bailey Brooks   Trespass with force and arms

    This day came the plaintiff by his attornies and therefore came a jury of good and lawful men, to-wit, Abedingo Merryman, James Adams, James Payne, Martin Prewitt, aaron Choat, Jr., Nathan Mc lendon, Aaron Anglin, David Crockett, Jesse Williams, Charles Cook, Archer Naile, William Burris, who being elected tried and sworn well and truly to try this issue of traverse, upon their oaths do say that the defendant is not guilty in manner and form as the plaintiff in his declaration hath alleged, whereupon the plaintiff by his attorney moved the court for a new trial and leave to amend his declaration which was granted him by paying the cost of this present term and ordered that a new trial be had at the next term of this court.

Nicholas Welch
vs
George Gresham   Appeal

    The plaintiff is this case comes into Court and withdraws his plea heretofore pleaded and suffers a non suit to be entered against him. Whereupon it is considered by the court that the defendant recover of the plaintiff his costs by him about his defense in this behalf expended and the plaintiff in mercy & c.

James T. Bacy (sic)
vs
George Shirley, Jr.   Case

This day came the parties by their attorneys and on motion of the plaintiff's Counsel by and with the consent of the defendant in proper person, it is ordered that the case be dismissed by the defendant paying the cost in this behalf expended. Whereupon it is charged by the court that the plaintiff recover of the defendant his costs by him about his suit in this behalf expended and the defendant in mercy & c.

Charles Cook by his attorney came into court and exhibited his petition praying the court that writs of Certiorari and Supersedus should issue. Defendant removes all proceedings into this Court in the case wherein___ Rollins is plaintiff and said Cook is defendant which was granted him accordingly.

Court adjourned til tomorrow, 10 O'clock. H. Day, Andrew Brown, John Hillhouse, and Mancil Crisp, J.P.'s.

WEDNESDAY, JANUARY 3rd, 1821

Wednesday morning, 10 o'clock, Jan. 3rd, 1821, Court met according to adjournment. Present, Henson Day, John Hillhouse, Mancil Crisp, Andrew Brown, Robert Chaffin, Esquires, Justices.

In the case of Fany Asburn vs John Counts the plaintiff by her attorney moved the court that an order to be made to take the deposition of William Cook in Wayne County in this State by giving the adverse party ten days notice of the time and place of taking the same.

Ezekiel Farmer
vs
George Shirley, Jr.   Debt

This day came the parties by their attornies and thereupon came a jury of good and lawful men, to-wit, Abedingo Merryman, Hartwell J. Bumpass, Thomas Holland, Silas Rackley, Luke Grimes, Samuel Thomas, William Burris, Thomas Howard, Erasmus Tracey, Warren Mason, Robert Haynes, and Aaron Choate, who being elected, tried and sworn well and truly to try this issue of traverse upon their oaths do saythat the defendant hath not paid the debt in writingobligatory in the plaintiff's declaration mentioned as in pleading he hath alleged and they do assess the plaintiff damages by reason of the detention thereof to $ 17.85 besides costs. It is therefore considered by thecourt that the plaintiff recover of the defendant the sum of $244.29 their debt aforesaid together with their damages aforesaid by the jury aforesaid in form aforesaid assessed together with his costs by him about his suit in this behalf expended and the defendant in mercy & c.

McRae & Lanier
vs
John McClish   Debt

It being suggested to this court that the plaintiff is in this case withdrawn his writing obligatory and he having failed to prosecute his suit, it is therefore considered by the court that this cause be dismissed and that the plaintiff recover of the defendat his costs by him about his suit in this behalf expended and the plaintiff in mercy & c.

The State
vs   Indictment for an assault and battery
Calton Tracey

    This day came the Solcitor General in behalf of the State as well as the defendant in his proper person and the defendant being charged upon the bill of indictment pleads thereto guilty whereupon it is considered by the court that the defendant be fined in the sum of 25¢ and that he pay the cost of this prosecution and that the defendant be taken & c.

M.H. Buchanan & Co.
vs   Debt
Bradley Halford

    This day came the plaintiff and withdraws his plea and assumes to pay all costs whereupon it is considered by the court that the defendant recover of the plaintiff his costs by his defense in this behalf expended and the plaintiff in mercy & c.

Joseph Farmer
vs   Case
John Allsup

    This day came the defendant by his counsel and suggested to the court that this cause in law was dismissed from the docket in consequence of the same having been left to the judgement of M.H. Buchanan, a referee mutually agreed on by the parties litigant several terms past, and the same being fully considered by the court, that in consequence of the plaintiff's failing to prosecute his said suit as well before the said referee as in this court that the same be dismissed from the docket and that the defendant recover of the plaintiff his costs by him about his defense in this behalf expended, and the plaintiff in mercy & C.

    Augustine Bumpass at the request of M.H. Buchanan, Clerk by and with the consent of the court came into court and was qualified as a Deputy Clerk of this Court.

    The Grand Jurors, returned into Court with the following Bill of Presentment, to-wit, State vs Shadrack Alvis-true bill.

    On motion of the Solicitor a Noli Prosequi is entered by leave of the court in the following cases, severally.
State vs Robert Montgomery-Indictment for an affray
State vs Charles McCue-Indictment for Assault and Battery
State vs Edmund Reynolds-Bastardy
and that the clerk certify in behalf of those entitled on the part of the State to the Co. Trustee accordingly.

State
vs   Recogn. Bastardy
William Sizemore

    On motion of Solicitor General with consent of the Court it is ordered that this case be dismissed at Defendants cost.

Ordered that court be adjourned until tomorrow, 9 o'clock. H. Day, Andrew Brown, John Hillhouse, Robert Chaffin, Mancil Crisp, J.P.'s.

THURSDAY, JANUARY 4th, 1821

Thursday morning Jan. 4th, 1821, court met at 9 o'clock according to adjournment. (Editors note; Names of Justices not shown in caption of minutes.)

Ordered by the court that Nathan Jobe and Joseph Halford, Constables, be appointed to attend at the next Circuit Court to be holden for this County the 4th Monday in Feb., next to serve said court as such.

William F. Cunningham came into court, prayed and obtained a license to sell spirituous Liquiors, which was granted him who gave bond and security and was qualified according to law.

Nathan McClendon came into court and produced a bill of sale from Bryon McClendon for certain property, to-wit, crops, kitchen and household furniture, etc, which was acknowledged by the said Bryon McClendon to be his own act and deed which was ordered to be recorded and that the clerk certify for registration.

Nathan McClendon came into court, prayed and obtained a license to keep an House of Ordinary, which was granted him, who gave bond and security and was qualified according to law.

Ordered by the court that William Seahorn, Martin Prewitt, James Bumpass, George Isom, David A. Flannery, William Welch, Moses Pennington or any five of them be appointed a jury of view to view and mark out a road beginning at Lawrenceburg to run the nearest and best way to the extreme bounds of this County on a direction on to Vernon in Hickman County, and that they make report to next Court.

Ordered by the Court that a Venire Facias issued to the Sheriff of this county commanding him to summon the following persons to attend the next County Court, to-wit, William Cunningham, Thomas Howard, Luke Grimes, Solomon Grisham, Willis Lucas, Green Depriest, James Bumpass, Benjamin Morrow, Edward Higgs, Samuel Woolsey, Willis Hammonds, Walter Brashears, John Inmon,Sr., John Inman,Jr., James Moore, Simon Walker, Elijah Melton, Robert Haynes, Groves Sharp, Thomas Blythe, Archibald Huston, James E. Hail, William Alton, David Adkins, John Duckworth, Matthew Swan.

Ordered by the court that Douglas H. Stockton have the following hands to work in the Waterloo road from the top of the hill on the West side of Crowson Fork to Esq. Hillhouses, which part he is overseer of, said hands, to-wit, Ebner Burgin, Hartwell Bumpass,_____Roberson, James Wise, Aaron Choat, Richard Choat, David Choat, Jonathan Jobe, Jacob Adair, Ebenezer Thompson and Elihu C. Crisp.

Ordered by the court that M.H. Buchanan be appointed overseer of that part of the Waterloo Road which lies from the Military Road in Lawrenceburg to the top of the ridge on the West side of Crowson Fork and that he have the following hands to work, to-wit, under his direction all who reside on the waters of Crowson Fork as high up as to include Daniel Matthews except those allowed to Douglas H. Stockton, including said Buchanan hands.

Ordered that James Adams be exonerated from the payment of $ 2 so much valuation of 6 head of hogs posted by him which $2 shall be deducted out of the settlement of his account final for said hogs.

Ordered by the court that George Lucas, Richard Hill and Robert Chaffin be appointed Commissioners to let to the lowest bidder, Mary Jones, thus keeping for one year as a pauper at the house of Jacob Adair and that they advertise the same fifteen days beforehand.

Ordered that John McDonald, overseer of Military Road, have the following hands to work under his direction, to-wit, Samuel Linam, Josiah P. Thomas, Robert Haynes, Josephus Irvine and hands, John Montgomery, John Thompson, William Hefley, Solomon Gresham, A.P. Cunningham, Wm. F. Cunningham, Augustine Bumpass, Bryon McClendon, O.T. Stribling, Francis Drennan, Nathan McClendon, Thomas Howard, James Argo, William Davis, Richard T. Bailey, Henry Sharp and hands, James Scott, Needham Futrell, and all others within said bounds not particularly now commanded to other overseers.

Ordered by the court that Simon Higgs, overseer of the Pulaski Road have the following hands to work under his direction, to-wit, H. Reynolds, Isaac Reynolds, Gilbert Prince, Thomas Keese, Henson Day and hands, George Hanks and hands, Daniel Beeler and hands, Groves Sharp, Warren Mason, and hands, Edward R. Sealy, N. Adkisson, Silas Mitchell, William Shaw, Richard Hill and hands, Robert Scoles, Wm. Hanks, Wm. Connell, John Wisdom, and all other hands within said bounds not alloted to other overseers.

Ordered that Robert Brashears be appointed overseer of the road viewed in a direction to Samuel Cox's in Giles Co., from Lawrenceburg and that he open and keep said road in repair which lies from said Brashears to Phillip Parchman's and that he have the following hands to work under his direction, to-wit, all who live on Moody Fork above said Brashears and all who live on the East prong of said Sugar Creek above Richard Fondas.

Ordered that Walter Brashears be appointed overseer of the road viewed in a direction to Samuel Cos's in Giles Co., from Lawrenceburg and that he open and keep said road in repair from Robert Brashears to the Giles Co. line and that he have all the hands who live the waters of Sugar Creek not under the direction of Robert Brashears within Capt. Sizemore's Company.

Court adjourned til Court in Course. H. Day, Robert Chaffin, Andrew Brown, Jacob Pennycuff, J.P.'s.

MONDAY APRIL 2nd, 1821

At a Court of Pleas and Quarter Sessions holden for the County of Lawrence at the Courthouse in the Town of Lawrenceburg on the 1st Monday in April, 1821, present Court met according to adjournment. Present, Henson Day, Mansil Crisp, Robert Chaffin, Andrew Brown and George Lucas, Esquires, Justices.

It being suggested to this Court that the present road leading from this place to Pulaski was not in such repair as the traveling and intercourse between the two places require, owing to a neglect of Giles Co., on some account unknown to this Co., and as they do believe that it is the duty of County Courts adjourning to each other to act in conjunction relative to roads and in a way to promote public good, and whereas, we have caused the said road through our County to be opened and mile marked and no late attention being paid to the said road through Giles County, it is hereby unanimously agreed that William Davis, Esq., Attorney at law, be requested to make known to the Court of Giles County their wishes on this subject, hoping that some decisive measures may be adopted by said Court so that a direct road may be opened or at least the nearest and best way from this to Pulaski and that the clerk of the County be directed to certify the same to the next County Court for Giles County.

At least five of the acting Justices being present, to-wit, Henson Day, Mansil Crisp, Robert Chaffin, Andrew Brown, John Hillhouse, George Lucas. Rubin Tripp produced in Court 1 wolf scalp over 4 months old which was ordered to be burned and that the clerk certify the same to the State Treasury accordingly.

At least five of the acting justices being present, to-wit, Henson Day, Mansil Crisp, Robert Chaffin, Andrew Brown and John Hillhouse and Geo. Lucas. Gabriel Bumpass produced in court 1 wolf scalp over 4 months old and was ordered to be burned and that the clerk certify the same to the Treasurer of West Tennessee accordingly.

At least five of the acting justices being present, to-wit, (Editors note; Same names copied here as in paragraph above.) John Nelson produced in court 1 wolf scalp over 4 months old and was ordered to be burned and that the clerk certify the same to the Treasurer of West. Tenn., accordingly.

At least five of the acting justices being present, to-wit, (Editors note; Here again was copied same list of J.P.'s as listed in 2nd paragraph above.) William Reynolds produced in court 2 wolf scalps over 4 months old and was ordered to be burned and that the clerk certify the same to the Treasurer of West Tennessee accordingly.

(Editors note; This paragraph same as above EXCEPT James Parchman produced 2 wolf scalps over 4 months old)

113

At least five of the acting Justices being present, to-wit, Henson Day, Mansil Crisp, Robert Chaffin, Andrew Brown, Geo. Lucas and John Hillhouse. Phillip Bryant produced in court one wolf scalp over four months old and was ordered burned and that the clerk certify the same to the Treasurer of West Tennessee accordingly.

Ordered by the court that John McDonald to whom an orphan boy by the name of James McGee was bound by an order of this court at some term passed, the said McDonald having removed out of this County, be released from his bond heretofore given for the education and care of said boy and that the said orphan be rebound.

Ordered by the court that a Tax be layed for the purpose of procuring a standard of weights and measures for this County upon the taxable property therein in the following manner, to-wit, on each white pole 4 cents, on each black poll 8 cents, on each hundred acres of land 4 cents, on each town lot 8 cents, on each stud horse 12½¢, on each bilyard (sic) table five dollars, and that the clerk certify the same to Collector of the State and County taxes for this County for the present year, whose duty it shall be to collect and return the same accordingly.

Wilson Wever having appeared in court a few terms passed in court one wolf scalp over 4 months old and the same being ordered to be burned accordingly which being recollected by the court and not being entered of record and then being at least five justices present it is ordered by the court that an order for the same now for then and that the clerk certify the same accordingly to the Treasurer of West Tennessee accordingly.

Ordered by the court that James Strawn be appointed overseer of that part of the Military Road under the care of John Null, former overseer, and that he have the same hands to work thereon which was under said Null, and all other hands in said bounds and that the said Strawn keep that road in repair which leads by his house.

Ordered that Burwell B. Quimby be appointed overseer of the road to Columbia in the room of James Stricklin, former overseer and that he have the same hands to work thereon which was alloted to said Stricklin.

Ordered by the court that Robt. L. Cobb, Solicitor for this County be allowed the sum of $31 for his ex-officio services for the year passed to be paid out of any monies in the hands of the County Trustee of this County not otherwise appropriated and that the clerk certify the same to said Trustee accordingly.

Ordered by the court that Henry Sharp, Esquire, by consent, be appointed overseer of the Military Road from the upper crossing on Raccoon Branch as far north as the new road to be opened above Col. Josephus Irvine's and that he open the Military Street through the Town of Lawrenceburg and in the direction of said street until it passes through said Irvine's farm and then with a convenient slant until it intersects the present road at a suitable point, and that he have all the hands to work theron which were under the said McDonald and Simon Higgs, former overseer of the Pulaski Road and when the said Sharp shall have this said road opened then the said Old Military Road so far as this is an amendment shall be discontinued.

Ordered by the court that M.H. Buchanan, overseer of the Waterloo Road be directed to open the Waterloo Street and then to extend the road the best way until it unites with the present Waterloo Road at Big Shoal Creek and when the said road shall be opened the said Old road so far as this new addition is an amendment shall be discontinued.

Ordered by the court that Ebenezer Thompson be appointed overseer, of the Waterloo Road in the room of Douglas H. Stockton, removed, and that he have the same hands under his direction which were under the said Stockton with the addition of Daniel Matthews hands and John Matthews and hands, James Kelly and Elet(sic) Lindsey.

Ordered by the court that Abel Hill in Capt. Gresham's Co., John Sellers in Capt. Welch's do., and John Dotan in Capt. Hugh's do., be appointed Constables in and for this County, who gave bond and security according to law and was qualified.

Ordered by the court that the prison bounds of this County contain 12½ Acres in the senter(sic) of which the middle of the Public Square shall be with the addition of the Military Street to Shoal Creek, then four poles in width up the same to the first town spring above.

Jacob Pennycuff and Jeremiah Jackson, Esquires, who were appointed to take a list of taxable property and polls at the last term of this court for this year made return of their said lists, according to order which were received and ordered recorded accordingly.

Ordered that Court be adjourned until tomorrow, 9 o'clock. H. Day, Andrew Brown, Robert Chaffin, John Hillhouse, J.P.'s.

TUESDAY APRIL 3rd, 1821

Tuessday morning 9 o'clock court met according to adjournment, present, Henson Day, John Hillhouse, Robert Chaffin, Andrew Brown, Esquires, Justices.

Robert Chaffin who was appointed to take a list of taxable property and polls as well as Josephus Gist, Esq., made return of their said lists according to the order of this court which was received and ordered to be recorded accordingly.

The sheriff returned into court the Venire Facias returnable to this term containing the following named persons, to-wit, Wm. F. Cunningham, Thomas Howard, Luke Grimes, Solomon Gresham, Willis Lucas, Green Depriest, James Bumpass, Benjamin Morrow,

Edward Higgs, Samuel Woolsey, Willis Hammonds, Walter Brashears, John Inman,Sr., John Inman,Jr., James Moore, Simon Walker, Elijah Melton, Robert Haynes, Groves Sharp, Jacob Blythe, Archibald C. Huston, James E. Hail, Wm. Alton, Annual(sic) Adkisson, John Duckworth, Matthew Swan with the following endorsements made by the Sheriff thereon executed on all the within named except, James Woolsey, Wm. Hammonds, Thomas Blythe, David Adkisson, Walter Brashears, B. Halford Sheriff, and upon calling the venire aforesaid the following named persons appeared to-wit, James Bumpass, Elijah Melton, Robert Haynes, Edward Higgs, Archibald C. Huston, James Moore, Green Depriest, Luke Grimes, John Inman Sr., John Inman Jr., Mathew Swan, Simon Walker, John Duckworth and Solomon Gresham, of whom the following were drawn as Grand Jurors, to inquire for the body of the County of Lawrence,to-wit, all the above named persons except Solomon Gresham, of whom James Bumpass was appointed foreman, who were qualified and after receivingtheir charge withdrew to consider of their presentments under the care of William White, Constable, who was sworn to attend them.

Daniel A. Flanner(sic),Esquire, who was appointed at last court to take a list of taxables and polls returned his said list which was received and ordered to be recorded.

Ordered that Wm. F. Cunningham, Willis Lucas, and Wm. Alton, who were appointed as jurors to this term be exempt from said service.

George W. Barnett
vs
Elijah Melton   An Appeal

This day came the parties by their attornies and thereupon came a jury of good and lawful men, to-wit, Samuel Thomas Nathan McLendon, Stephen Roland, Daniel Pearce, Alexander Miller, George Hanks, Annual Adkisson, Solomon Gresham, Groves Sharp, Lewis Franks, John Foster, Geo. Gresham, who being elected tried and sworn, well and truly to try this issue joined, withdrew to consider of their verdict.

Joseph Gist, Executor of the last will and testament of Joseph Gist, dec'd, made return into court a list of the sale of the property of the estate of the said Joseh Gist,dec'd, which was received and ordered to be recorded accordingly.

William Wisdom, Andrew Brown and Jeremiah Jackson who were appointed to make division and petition of the estate of Joseph Gist,dec'd, made their report which was received in order to be recorded and that the said petitioners be allowed for their services as follows, the said Jackson $3 and the said Wisdom $ 3 and the said Brown $ 4.50 to be paid out of said estate by the executor, the same being estimated at $1.50 per day.

Mary Pennington,Moses Pennington, Abraham Pennington and Isaac Pennington being appointed executors to the last will and testament of Jacob Pennington, dec'd, produced in court the last will and testament of him the said Jacob,dec'd, which was proved by the oaths of Betsy Venable and Jonathon

Morgan two of the subscribing witnesses thereto, which was ordered to be recorded and the asaid executors gave bond and were qualified accordingly.

William Cook who was supoened to appear at this term who lives in Wayne Co., and Peter Swanson in Giles Co., to give evidence in the case now pending wherein Fanny Ozbourn is plaintiff and John Counts is defendant, although solemnly called came not but made default it is therefore ordered by the court that judgement Ni Ci be ehtered up against the said Cook and Swanson according to their supoenas and that a Scire Facias issue returnable to the next term of this court accordingly.

Fanny Ozbourn
vs
John Counce (sic)
This dau came the parties by their attorney and thereupon came a jury of good and lawful men, to-wit, Benjamin Morrow, James Paine, John Smallwood, Charles Cook, John Hamilton, Thomas Holland, Daniel Beeler, John Alsup, Levi Lewis, Wm. Welch, Jr., John McClaren, Thomas Musgrove, who being elected, tried and sworn, well and truly to try this issue joined and the pleading thereon being had withdrew to consider of their verdict.

The Grand Jurors returned into court the following Bills of Indictments & Presentments, The State vs Josiah Tippet-a true bill. The State vs John McCary-a true bill, The State vs Zachnah Inman a true bill.

Ordered that the court be adjourned until tomorrow at 8 o'clock. Henson Day, John Hillhouse, Robert Chaffin, Andrew Brown, and Mansil Crisp, J.P.'s.

WEDNESDAY APRIL 4th , 1821

Wednesday morning nine (sic) o'clock court met according to adjournment, present, Henson Day, John Hillhouse, Mansil Crisp, Andrew Brown, and Robert Chaffin, Esquires, Justices.

Fanny Ozbourn
vs   Travis (sic)
John Counts

This day came the parties by their attorney and thereupon came a jury of good and lawful men, to-wit, Benjamin Morrow, James Paine, John Smallwood, Charles Cook, John Hembleton, Thomas Hollen (sic), Daniel Beeler, John Alsup, Levi Lewis, William Welch, Sr., John McCann, and Thomas Musgrove, who being elected, tried and sworn, well and truly to try this issue joined upon their oaths do say that the defendant is guilty in manner and form as the plaintiff has alleged in his declaration and that they assess the plaintiff damage to $200 besides costs. Whereupon it is considered by the court that the plaintiff recover of the defendant his damages aforesaid assessed in form aforesaid together with his cost by him about his suit in this behalf expended and that the defendant in mercy & c.

117

State
vs
Josiah Tippet

This day came the Solicitor General in behalf of the State as well as the defendant in his proper person and the defendant being charged upon the bill of indictment pleads thereto guilty and thereupon puts himself upon the justice and mercy of the court. It is therefore considered by the court that he be fined with $2 and the cost of this suit, who gave Samuel W. Sullivan as security for the payment of said fine and cost and the defendant in mercy & c.

State
vs   Assault and battery
John McClain

This day came the Solicitor General in behalf of the State as well as the defendant in his proper person and being arraigned upon his arraignment pleads thereto guilty and puts himself upon the justice and mercy of the court whereupon it is considered by the court that he be fined the sum of $2 and the cost of suit and the said defendant in mercy & c.

The State
vs   Assault and Battery
Ezekiel Farmer

This day came as well the Solicitor General for the State as the defendant in his proper person and said defendant being charged on the presentment in this case pleads not guilty and for trial puts himself upon the Country and the Solicitor General for the State, on the part of the State likewise, therefore let a jury come who as well ---to recognize ----- and thereupon came a ury of good and lawful men, to-wit, William Dalton, Wm. Welch, Jr., Jacob Adair, James Edmundson, Ebenezer Thompson, Richard T. Bailey, James McConnel, Asa Elfalvington(sic) John W. Henry, James Kelly, and Patterson Crockett, who being elected tried and sworn well and truly to try this issue of joined between the State and the defendant upon their oaths do say that the defendant is guilty in manner and form as he is charged in the bill of presentment. It is therefore considered by the court that the defendant make his fine with the State to the amount of $5 and that he pay the cost of this prosecution and that he be committed to the custody of the sheriff of this County, there to remain till said fine and costs are paid or made safe by s4curity.

A bill of sale from Obediah Kendrick to Wm. Welch, Jr., for a negro girl named Amelia was produced in court and the execution thereof proven by the oaths of James M. Kendrick and Wm. Henderson the subscribing witnesses thereto and ordered to be certified for registration.

A bill of sale from Obediah Kendrick to James Kendrick for a negro boy named Henry was produced in open court and the execution thereof proven by the oath of Wm. Welch, Jr., the subscribing witness thereto and ordered to be certified for registration.

118

A bill of sale from Obediah Kendrick to Wm. Henderson for a negro boy named John was proven in open court and the execution thereof proven by the oath of "m. Welch,Jr., the subscribing witness thereto and ordered to be certified for registration.

The State
vs
Robert Scoles   Forfeiting a Subpeona

This day came the Solicitor General in behalf of the State and Robert Scoles being solemnly called and coming not he was called out whereupon it is considered by the court that judgement Ni Ci be rendered up against the same Scoles for the amount of the penalty in his subpeona for bot appearing and giving evidence in behalf of the State against Sharck(sic) Oliver and that a Cira Facias issue returnable at the next term of this court.

George W. Barnett
vs
Elijah Melton   An appeal

This day came the parties by their attornies and thereupon came a jury of good and lawful men, to-wit, Samuel Thomas, Nathan McClendon, Stephen Roland, Daniel Pearce, Alexander Miller, George Hanks, Annel Adkison, Solomon Gresham, Groves Sharp, Lewis Franks, John Foster, George Gresham, who being elected tried and sworn well and truly to try this issue joined upon their oaths do say that they can't agree and make a Nul Trial and the parties agree to prefer the case to the court to decide on which court say that the defendant shall pay the plaintiff the sum of $ 5.80 and each pay the cost equa

Shadrack Alvis and Samuel W. Sullivant both acknowledged themselves indebted to the State of Tennessee in sum of $ 100 each for the use of the State to be levied of their goods, chattel lands and tenements to be void on condition that Shadrack Alvis makes his personal appearance at the next County Court to answer the State upon a charge of an Assault and battery.

Ordered by the court that court be adjourned til tomorrow 9 o'clock. H. Day, Robert Chaffin, John Hillhouse, Mancil Crisp and Andrew Brown, J.P.'s.

THURSDAY, APRIL 5th, 1821

Thursday morning, 9 o'clock, court met according to adjournment (Editors note; Minutes do not show names of Justices present.)

James Scott
vs
Groves Sharp   Appeal

This day came the parties by their attorneys and thereupon came a jury of good and lawful men, to-wit, Benjamin Morrow, John Alsup, Solomon Gresham, Thomas Howard, Thomas Keese, Wm. Holland, Richard T. Bailey, Geo. Vandiver, Aaron Anglin, John Foster, Aaron P. Cunningham, and Simon Higgs, who being elected tried and sworn well and truly to try this issue joined, upon their oaths do say that they find for the plaintiff $ 5.50 and that the plaintiff pay to the defendant the sum of the said $ 5 and the cost by him about his suit in this behalf expended and from which judgement the said defendant prayed an appeal which was granted him accordingly who gave bond and security accordingly.

George Beeler
vs
John Welch   Appeal

    Upon motion of the defendant by his attorney and as affadavit of the defendant it is ordered by the court that this cause be continued until the next term of this court.

George Beeler
vs
John Welch

    Upon motion by the defendant by his attorney it is ordered that a commission to issue to take the deposition of Wm. Welch in the State of Alabama to be read for defendant on his giving 20 days notice of time and place also the deposition of John W. Britton of Giles Co., by giving 10 days notice to plaintiff.

Stephen Roland
vs
Charles Cook   Appeal

    This day came the defendant by their attorney and upon motion of the defendant it is ordered by the court that a commission issue to take the deposition of Larkin Baker living in the State of Tenn., Warren County, to be read as evidence in behalf of the defendant by giving the plaintiff 20 days notice of the time and place of taking the same.

Cyrus Powel
vs
George Gresham

    Upon motion of the defendant by his counsil and upon motion of the defendant upon affadavit it is ordered by the court that a cause be continued until the next term of Court.

Elizabeth Stockton
vs
Samuel Thomas   Action of Troon (sic)?

    This day came the parties by their attornies and thereupon came a jury of good and lawful men, to-wit, John Inman, Jr., John Inman, Sr., Edward Higgs, Simon Walker, Matthew Swan, James Moore, Green Depriest, W.C.Huston, Elijah Melton, John Duckworth, Jonathon Jove, Groves Sharp, who being elected tried and sworn well and truly to try this issue joined upon their oaths do say that the defendant is guilty in manner and form as in the plaintiff's declaration mentioned. Whereupon it is the opinion of the jury that the plaintiff recover of the defendant the sum of $8.75 besides cost of this suit and the said defendant in mercy & c.

Cyrus Powel
vs
George Gresham

Upon motion of the defendant by his attorney it is ordered by the court that commission issue to take the deposition of Wm. Higgs living in Alabama State and Marion County to be read as evidence in behalf of the defendant by giving the oposite(sic) party 10 days notice of the time and place of taking the same.

James Broadstreet
vs   An Appeal
Bradley Halford

This day came the defendant by his attorney and the plaintiff although solemnly called came not but made default, it is therefore considered by the court that the defendant recover of the plaintiff the sum of $18.75 the amount of the judgement before the justice together with his Cost by him about his suit in this behalf expended and the defendant in mercy & c.

Richard Hill, Esquire, who was appointed to take the list of taxable property and polls at the last term of this court made return of his said list according to order which was ordered to be recorded accordingly.

John Hillhouse, Esquire, who was appointed to take the list of taxable property and polls at the last term of this court made return of his said list according to order which was ordered to be recorded accordingly.

George Lucus, Esquire, who was appointed to take the list of taxable property and polls at the last term of this Court made return of his said list according to order which was ordered to be recorded accordingly.

State of Tennessee
vs
Solomon Gresham

This day came the Solicitor General in behalf of the State as well as the defendant in his proper person and being arraigned upon his arraignment pleads thereto guilty and puts himself upon the justice and mercy of the court. It is therefore ordered by the court that he be fined the sum of $1 besides cost and c.

Aaron P. Cunningham came into court prayed and obtained a license to keep a House of Ordinary which was granted to him who gave bond and security according to law.

Ordered by the court that John Hillhouse be allowed the sum of $46.50 for building a Temporary Courthouse, to be paid out of any monies in the hands of the County Trustee of this County not otherwise appripriated and that the clerk certifyaccordingly.

STATE OF TENNESSEE, LAWRENCE COUNTY COURT, APRIL TERM, 1821

On this 2nd day of April, 1821, personally appeared in open Court, being a Court of Record created by statute, of unlimited civil jurisdiction on the law side of said Court holden quarterly in and for the aforesaid County, Jeremiah Bentley of the County and State aforesaid, a resident aged sixty-one years on the first day of May 1820, who being first duly sworn according to law doth on his oath declare that he served in the Revolutionary War as

follows, that he, the said Bentley, enlisted for the term of
3 years on the 28th of Aug. 1777 in the State of Virginia, in
the Company of Capt. James Foster, in the 15th Regiment commanded by Col. Ennis in the line of the State of Virginia in
the continental establishment and continued to serve under
the same Captain until his death, when James Mason succeeded
to the command under whom he continued to serve until the
Spring of 1779, when he was enrolled in a Company of Wayne's
Light Infantry, commanded by Capt. Samuel Booker, on Christmas of the same year the infantry was dissolved and he was
placed under the command of Catp. Wm. Mosley of the 1st
regiment commanded by Col. Russell, he was taken prisoner
at the down fall of Charleston, S.C., from which imprisonment
he escaped and was discharged by Col. Davis at Richmond in
the year 1781, that he made his original declaration for a
pension on the 4th of June, 1818, and that he was placed on
the pension list roll of the West Tennessee agency by pention
(sic) Certificate No. 15059, and I do solemnly swear that I
was a resident citizen of the United States on the 18th day
of March, 1818, and that I have not since that time, by gift,
sale or in any manner disposed of my property to bring myself
within the provisions of an Act of Congress entitled an Act
to provide for certain persons engaged in the land and naval
service of the United States in the Revolutionary War, passed
on the 18th of March, 1818, and that I have not nor has any
person in trust for me any property or securities, contracts,
or debts due to me, nor have I any income other than that
which is contained in the schedule hereto annexed and by me
subscribed. I have no trade but farming, my family consists
of myself, aged as aforesaid, and my wife aged 44 years. I
am infirm and unable to work for my living, my left shoulder
is out of place and my arm is withered away, besides when I
attempt to work hard, I am subject to the bloody flux, my
wife is healthy and able to support herself.
      Jeremiah X Bentley
       (his mark)

SCHEDULE OF PROPERTY
One mare, bridle, saddle and saddlebags, five books, one
small chest, 1 old silver watch, 3 brushes, 2 bottles, 1
razor case, shaving glass, 1 handsaw, drawing knife, 1 pair
drawing chains, 2 gimblets, 2 augers, 2 chisels, 1 tin cup,
7 hogs, 6 shoats, four months old, 1 yearling, 2 calves, 1
oven and skillet, 2 pair pot hooks, 2 pots, 1 coffee mill,
compass and rule, coffee pot and 4 cups, 3 cups and saucers,
4 earthen plates, 1 teapot, puter bason, and dish, 4 puter
plates, 1 candlestick, 1 set knives and forks, 6 iron tablespoons, 2 pales and 1 piggin, wash tub, 1 ruler, 1 flax wheel
1 pair cotton cards, big wheel, 3 chairs, 2 ewes, 1 lamb.
I have $ 30 due me in good hands. Daniel Bentley, my son
owes me $ 230 but the said Bentley has left the Country without making any provisions for its payment, 1 umbrella.
      Jeremiah X Bentley
       (his mark)
  Sworn and subscribed to in open court before us, Henson
Day, Mansil Crisp, Robert Chaffin, John Hillhouse and Andrew
Brown, Justices of the Quorum, and said Justices assessed the
value of the said property contained in the schedule to

$177.00 considering the said debt of $230.00 as contained in said schedule as dispute and of no value.

In the case of Elizabeth Stockton against Samuel Thomas, D.H. Stockton who was security for the plaintiff was a material witness for the said plaintiff, on motion of the plaintiff's attorney it is ordered by the court that the said D.H. Stockton be released and that Bradley Halford be given such.

Ordered that court be adjourned until tomorrow at 9 o'clock, John Hillhouse, Robert Chaffin, Andrew Brown and H. Day, J.P.'s.

FRIDAY APRIL 6th, 1821

Friday morning nine o'clock court met according to adjournment, present, John Hillhouse, Robert Chaffin, Andrew Brown and Henson Day, Justices.

James Strawn came into court prayed and obtained a license to keep a House of Ordinary at his own house in said County, which was granted to him, who gave bond and security and was qualified.

Ordered by the court that Abel Hill and John Dalton be appointed to attend at the next County court as Constables to wait on the Court.

Ordered by the court that court be adjourned until court in course. John Hillhouse, Robert Chaffin, Andrew Brown, H. Day, J.P.'s.

MONDAY JULY TERM, 1821 (July 3rd)

At a court of Pleas and Quarter Sessions holden for the County of Lawrence at the Courthouse in the Town of Lawrenceburg on the 1st Monday in July, 1821, present court met according to adjournment, present, Henson Day, Mancil Crisp, Robert Chaffin, Andrew Brown and John Hillhouse, Esquires, Justices.

At least five acting justices being present, to-wit, H. Day, John Hillhouse, Robert Chaffin, Andrew Brown and Mancil Crisp. Edward Higgs produced in open court 1 wolf scalp over 4 months old which was ordered to be burnt and the clerk certify accordingly.

At least five acting justices being present, to-wit, H. Day, John Hillhouse, Robert Chaffin, Andrew Brown and Mancil Crisp. James McConnel produced in open court 4 wolf scalps over 4 months old which was ordered to be burned and that the clerk certify accordingly.

Ordered by the court that Jesse Anglin be appointed overseer of the Military Road in the room of Shadrick Alvis and that he have the same hands to work under his direction that were under said Alvis and that he keep the same in repair.

Ordered by the court that each person who have or shall make application to this court to be exempt from the payment of double tax be exempt therefrom upon the conditions of them entering in due term a true return of their property and therewith paying a single tax thereon.

Ordered by the court that Shadrack Alvis pay to the County Trustee all monies collected by him as overseer of the Military Road, which was seventy-five cents.

Ordered by the court that Levi Lewis be appointed overseer of the road leading from James Strawn's to Lamb's Ferry on the Tennessee River from said Strawn's to Johnston's Mill on Blue Water and that he have all the hands to work under his direction who live on Blue Water between said Strawn's and to said Johnston's Mill.

Ordered by the court that Thomas Allsup be appointed overseer of the road leading from James Strawn's to Lamb's Ferry on the Tennessee River from Johnston's Mill to the State line and that he have all the hands to work under his direction who live on Blue Water between Johnston's Mill so low down as John McClary, Sr., including said McClary and hands and all who live on Second Creek from the head to the State line.

Ordered by the court that James Terrell be appointed overseer of the Military Road in the room of Henry Sharp, Esquire and that he have the same hands under his direction, except those attached to Geo. Hanks and that he keep the same in repair.

Ordered by the court that George Hanks be appointed overseer of the Pulaski Road from the Public Square in the Town of Lawrenceburg to the County line and that he have all the hands as low down as Daniel Boeler and all the hands on Weakley's Creek from the head to the mouth of Reynolds Branch to work under his direction and that he keep same in repairs.

Ordered by the court that the Scite on which Colonel Josephus Irvine has built a gris mill on Shoal Creek be condemned so as to prevent others from building mills or daming up the streams in such a distance above or below so as to injure his mill in any respects whatever.

Ordered by the court that the Military Road by betwixt Alexander Sossums and Daniel McClareys be changed so far as is necessary to avoid some low marsh ground over which the same runs and agreeable to a new way marked out and that the present overseer thereof work and open said new way.

At least five of the acting justices being present, to-wit, Mancil Crisp, Andrew Brown, Thomas Welch, Robert Chaffin. George Archer produced in court 2 wolf scalps over 4 months old which was ordered to be burned and that the clerk certify the same to the State Treasurer accordingly.

At least five of the acting Justices being present, to-wit, H. Day, Mancil Crisp, Robert Chaffin, Thomas Welch, George Lucas, John Hillhouse. Thomas Steele produced in court 2 wolf scalps over 4 months old which was ordered to be burned and that the clerk certify the same to the State Treasurer, accordingly.

At least five of the acting justices being present, to-wit, H. Day, Robert Chaffin, Andrew Brown, Richard Hill, George Lucus, and John Hillhouse. Elijah Pope produced in court 1 wolf scalp over 4 months old which was ordered to be burned and that the clerk certify the same to the State Treasurer accordingly.

Ordered by the Court that Robert Btashears, overseer be allowed the following hands to work under his direction, to-wit, Burrell Gambrell, Thomas Gambrell, Wm. R. Swaford, Thomas Kese and son, Thomas Sharp, John Holoway, Samuel Moore, Joseph Moody, Harmon Calp and John Wankins(sic) and that he keep same in repairs.

Ordered by the court that Walter Brashears, overseer of the road leading from Lawrenceburg to Athens be allowed the following hands, to-wit, James Patterson, James Bassham, Elot(sic) W.Campbell, John Oxford, Calvy Lindsey, Peter Waggoner, James Parker, Nathan Bassham, John Miller, Henry Moody.

Ordered by the court that James Appleton former overseer on the road leading from Pulaski to Florence be allowed the following hands to work, to-wit, Bradley Fifer(sic), Elijah Cooper, Michael Kinesly, Wm. Snodgrass, Jonah Nipper, Alexander Campbell, and that he keep the same in repair.

Ordered by the court that John McClaren, Sr., in Capt. McClarens Company and Hugh C. Withers in Capt. Hammonds Company be appointed Constables in and for the County of Lawrence, who gave bond and security according to law and were qualified.

Ordered by the court that Robert Chaffin, Mancil Crisp, Richar Hill be appointed Judges to superintend the election in the Town of Lawrenceburg on the 1st Thursday and Friday in August, next, and that D.A.Flanary, George Isom and David Steel be appointed to superntend the Election at Pennington on the days aforesaid, and that Alexander Cossums, Thomas Alsup and Jeremiah Jackson,Sr., be appointed to superintend the Election at John Null's on the day above mentioned.

William T. Cunningham, James Bumpass and Martin Prewitt, commissioners ordered to settle with the sheriff and trustee of this County made report of the same which was received and ordered to be certified and the legal number of Justices being present it is ordered that the said Commissioners each be allowed the sum of $6.58 for their services.

Ordered by the court that James Bumpass, Martin Prewitt and Wm. T. Cunningham, Commissioners appointed to settle with the sheriff and Trustee of this be allowed to draw on the County Trustee for monies to purchase a record book out of any monies in the said Trustee's hands not otherwise apporpriated.

Ordered by the court that William Sizemore be exempt from half the appraised value of a certain stray mare by him appraised to $ 16.00.

Ordered by the court that Coleman Nichols an orphan boy be bound unto Lemuel Blythe until he shall arrive at the age of 21 years and that the said Blythe be bound to clothe and feed said orphan and to educate him to read, write and cypher as far as the rule of three and when he arrives of age to give him a good suit of clothes and a horse and bridle and saddle worth eighty dollars.

Ordered that court be adjourned til tomorrow, 9 o'clock. H. Day, Mansil Crisp, and John Hillhouse, J.P.'s.

TUESDAY JULY 4th, 1821

Tuesday morning, July 4th, 1821 court met according to adjournment, at 9 o'clock, present, Mancil Crisp, John Hillhouse, Henson Day, Esquires, Justices.

The Sheriff returned into Court the following venire facias returnable to this term containing the following named persons, to-wit, Asa Yelvington, Samuel W. Sullivant, Stephen Roland Melch Duncan, Nathan Jobe, Solomon Asbell, John Wisdom, Michael Hinesly, Wm. Phillips, Willis Hammons, Anderson Fisher, Robert Newton, Enoch Bennurm, Bennett Wallace, Stephen Early, Eli Kenday, Josiah Herley, Thomas Steele, Josiah Tirpet, James Paine, Aaron Choat,Jr., Wm. Welch,Jr., Nathan Clifton, Hickman Williams and John McCann, with the following endorsements made thereon by the sheriff, executed on all but Michael Hinesly, Bradley Halford, and upon calling the venire facias, the following named persons appeared, to-wit, Asa Yelvington, Samuel W. Sullivan, Stephen Roland, Melcher Duncan, Nathan Jobe, Solomon Asbel, John Wisdom, Michael Hinesly, William Phillips, Willis Hammons, Anderson Fisher, Robert Newton, Enoch Bennam (sic), Bennet Wallis, Stephen Early, Eli Canada, Josia Herley, Thomas Steel, James Paine, Aaron Choat,Jr., William Welch,Sr., Nathan Clifton, Hickman Williams and John McCann, of whom the following named persons were drawn as Jurors to enquire for the body of the County of Lawrence, aforesaid, to-wit, Robert Newton, foreman, Hickman Williams, Nathan Jobe, Aron Choat,Jr., Samuel W. Sullivant, James Paine, Wm. Phillips, Wm. Welch,Sr., Nathan Clifton, Bennett Walker, Thomas Steele, Willis Hammons, and Eli Kenday (sic), who after receiving the charge and were qualified withdrew to enquire of their presentments under the care of John Dalton, constable, who was sworn to attend them.

George Beeler
vs   Appeal
John Welch

This day came the party by their attornies and thereupon came a jury of good and lawful men, to-wit, Asa Yelvington, Anderson Fisher, Solomon Asbel, Enoch Bynum, Josiah Herly, Melcher Duncan, Simon Higgs, Mathew Swan, Lazarous Stewart, Warren Mason, George Archer and Nathan McClendon, who being elected, tried and sworn, well and truly to try this issue joined, upon their oaths do say that the defendant doth owe the plaintiff the sum of $ 41.12½ the amount of the judgement before the justices with the addition of interest thereon, whereupon it is considered by the court that the plaintiff recover of the defendant his debt aforesaid together with his cost by him about his suit in this behalf expended and the defendant in mercy & c, from which judgement the defendant prayed an appeal to the Circuit Court to be holden for this County.

Charles Cook
vs   Certiorari
Stephen Roland

This day came the plaintiff in this case comes into Court by his attorney and withdraws his plea heretofore pleaded, whereupon it is considered by the court that the defendant recover of the plaintiff his cost by him about his defense in this behalf expended and the plaintiff in mercy & c.

Sirus Powell
vs   Trespass on the case
George Gresham

This day came the parties by their attorneys and thereupon came a jury of good and lawful men, to-wit, John Wisdom, Anderson Fisher, Asa Yelington(sic), Solomon Asbell, Enoch Bynum, Josiah Herly, George Rogers, John A. Haile, Elijah Melton, Austin Kendrick, Luke Grimes, Annuel Atkison, who being elected, tried and sworn well and truly to try this issue of traverse upon their oaths do say, that the defendant is not guilty in manner and form as in the plaintiff's declaration mentioned, whereupon it is considered by the court that the defendant go hence without day and recover of the plaintiff his costs by him about his defense in this behalf expended and the defendant in mercy & c.

Nathan McClendon
vs   Trespass
William White

The defendant in this case by his attorney moved the Court that one of the plaintiff's securities in this case was removed without the limits of the State and that the security was insufficient. It is therefore considered by the court that plaintiff be compeled to come into court and give additional security, otherwise that his suit would be dismissed from the docket, otherwise he would be no-suited.

Ordered that court be adjourned till tomorrow, 9 o'clock. H. Day, Mansil Crisp, Robert Chaffin, John Hillhouse and H. Day, J.P.'s. (Editors note; H. Day signed minutes twice.)

WEDNESDAY JULY 5th, 1821

Court met Wednesday morning, 9 o'clock according to adjournment, present, Henson Day, Mancil Crisp, Robert Chaffin, Andrew Brown and John Hillhouse, Esquires, Justices.

State
vs
John Allsup

This day came the Solicitor General in behalf of the State as well as the defendant in his proper person and the defendant being charged upon the bill of indictment and pleads thereto guilty puts himself upon the justice and mercy of the court whereupon it is considered by the court that the defendant make his fine with the State the sum of $ 5 and that he pay the cost of this presentment, who gave David Crockett and John McCann as security and that the defendant be taken &c.

The State
vs
Hartwell Wester

This day came the Solicitor General in behalf of the State as well as the defendant in his proper person and the defendant being charged upon the bill of indictment and pleads thereto guilty and puts himself upon the justice and mercy of the court, whereupon it is considered by the court that the defendant make his fine with the State the sum of $ 5 besides the cost of this indictment, who gave James Strawn as security and that the defendant be taken &c.

Thomas Howard
vs
John Allsup

Upon motion of the plaintiff by his attorney and on affadavit of the plaintiff it is ordered by the court that this case be continued until the next term of this court.

William Voss, Justice of the peace in and for this County came into court as the law directs and made resignation of his Commission aforesaid, which was received and ordered to be entered of record.

The State
vs   Assault and battery
Shadrack Alvis

This day came the Solicitor General in behalf of the State as well as the defendant in his proper person and the defendant being charged upon the bill of Presentment pleads thereto not guilty and for his trial puts himself upon the Country and the Solicitor General for the State likewise, whereupon came a jury of good and lawful men, to-wit, Daniel Pevyhouse, Asa Yelvington, Anderson Fisher, Solomon Asbell, Enoch Eynum, Josiah Herly, Melcher Duncan, Daniel Beeler, Annuel Atkison, John Sandusky, George Archer, and George Hanks, who being elected, tried and sworn well and truly to try this issue of traverse upon their oaths do say that the defendant is not guilty in manner and form as he is charged upon the bill of Presentment, whereupon it is considered by the court that the defendent in all respects be acquitted from the charge aforesaid and that a judgement be entered up against the County in favor of all those entitled to costs in behalf of the State.

William Jackson
vs
John McClaren   Appeal

    This day came the parties by their attorneys and thereupon came the plaintiff in his proper person who withdrew his plea heretofore pleaded and assumes upon himself the payment of all costs except the defendants witnesses and the summoning of the same which the defendant assumes thereupon it is considered by the court that judgement be entered against plaintiff and defendant accordingly.

Nathan McClendon
vs
William White   Trespass on the case

    The plaintiff in this case came into court and agreeable to an order of this court gives additional security for the prosecution of his suit in consequence of the removal of James Forbes who has removed from this State, this cause is also continued until the next term of this court upon affadavit of the plaintiff.

The State
vs
Ebenezer Thompson   Assault and battery

    This day came the Solicitor General in behalf of the State as well as the defendant in his proper person and the defendant being charged upon the bill of Indictment pleads thereto guilty and for his trial puts himself upon the justice and mercy of the court whereupon it is considered by the court that the defendant make his fine with the State to the sum of $1 besides cost of this indictment who gave Bradley Halford as security and that the defendant be taken &c.

The State
vs
William Edmundson

    This day came the Solicitor General in behalf of the State as well as the defendant in his proper person and the defendant being charged upon the bill of Indictment pleads thereto guilty and for his trial puts himself upon the mercy and justice of the Court, whereupon it is considered by the court that the defendant make his fine with the State to the sum of $7.50 besides cost of this indictment and that the defendant be taken &c.

    Ordered by the court that court be adjourned until tomorrow, 9 o'clock, Andw. Brown, Mansel Crisp, and John Hillhouse, J.P.'s.

THURSDAY, JULY 6th, 1821

    Thursday morning July 6th, 1821, court met according to adjournment, 9 o'clock, present, Henson Day, Mancil Crisp, Andrew Brown, John Hillhouse and Robert Chaffin, Esquires, Justices.

The State
vs
Josiah Green   Assault and battery

    This day came the Solicitor General in behalf of the State

as well as the defendant in his proper person and the defendant being charged upon the bill of presentment pleads thereto not guilty and for his trial puts himself upon the Country and the Solicitor General for the State likewise, thereupon came a jury of good and lawful men, to-wit, Asa Yelington, Andrew Fisher, Solomon Asbel, Enoch Bynum, Josiah Herly, Melcher Duncan, John Wisdom, Thomas Keese, Thomas Howard, Willison Hawkins, Nathan McClendon, Samuel Dods, who being elected, tried and sworn well and truly to try this issue of traverse upon their oaths do say, that the defendant is guilty in manner and form as he is charged in the bill of presentment and that defendant be fined the sum of $6 besides costs and that the defendant be taken in custody & c.

The State
vs
Silas Rackley   An affray

This day came the Solicitor General in behalf of the State as well as the defendant in his proper person and the defendant being charged upon the bill of Indictment pleads thereto guilty and puts himself upon the justice and mercy of the court, whereupon it is considered by the court that the defendant make his fine with the State to the sum of $3 besides the cost of this indictment who gave R.T. Bailey as security and that the defendant be taken & c.

The State
vs
Berry Archer   An affray

This day came the parties by their attornies and there upon came a jury of good and lawful men, to-wit, Warren Mason, James Barlow, Baily Alford, Richard T. Baily, Luke Grimes, Wm. McCann, John Foster, Thomas Holland, Simon Higgs, Joseph Barlow, and John Wisdom, who being elected tried and sworn well and truly to try this issue of Traverse upon their oaths do say that the defendant is not guilty in manner and form as he is charged in the bill of Indictment. Whereupon it is considered by the court that the defendant go hence without day and that in all respects he be acquitted from the charge aforesaid and that judgement be entered up against the County in favor of those entitled to cost in behalf of the State.

The State
vs   Indictment for an Assault & Battery
Josephus Irvine

This day came the Solicitor General in behalf of the State as well as the defendant in his proper person and the defendant being charged upon the Bill of Indictment pleads thereto guilty and for his trial puts himself upon the justice and mercy of the court, whereupon it is considered by the court that the defendant make his fine with the State to the sum of $7.40 and that he pay the cost of this indictment and that he be taken & c.

Wm. Gilchrist and Andrew Hays
vs   Debt
Bradley Halford and John Edmundson

This day came the parties by their attornies and upon argument of their counsels and mature deliberations thereon being had upon the defendants plea in abatement and upon the record of the court and the return of the writ being examined it is considered by the court that there is such record and that the plaintiff's writ was executed within five days before Court whereupon it is considered by the court that the plaintiff's suit be abated and quashed and that the defendant go hence without day and recover of the plaintiff's his cost by him about his defense in this behalf expended from which judgement the plaintiff's prayed an appeal to the Honorable the Circuit Court to be holden for this County which was granted him who gave bond and security according to law.

The State
vs
William Welch   Indictment for assault and battery

William Welch and John Wisdom acknowledged themselves to be severally indebted to the State of Tennessee in the sum of $ 50 each to be levyed of their goods chattel lands and tenements to the use of the State to be void on condition that Wm. Welch make his appearance before the Justices of our Court of Pleas and Quarter Sessions to be holden for this County on the 1st Monday in Oct., next, and on the 3rd day of said term then and there to prosecute and give evidence in behalf of the State against Adam Ross for an Assault and Battery and not depart therefrom without leave of the court.

McKree & Lanear
vs
John McClis(sic)   Debt

The defendant by his agent comes into court and sayeth that he cannot deny but that he doth owe the plaintiff the amount in the Plaintiff's writing obligatory, whereupon it is considered by the court and with the consent of the defendant's agent, that judgement be entered against the defendant in favor of the plaintiff against the defendant for the sum of $ 315.75 debt, and interest, together with his costs by him about his suit in this behalf expended, and the defendant be in mercy & c.

On this third day of July 1821 personally appeared in open Court, being a Court of Record, for said County of Lawrence and State of Tennessee, Erastus Tippett.
DISTRICT OF WEST TENNESSEE, STATE OF TENNESSEE, LAWRENCE COUNTY, COURT OF PLEAS AND QUARTER SESSIONS--JULY TERM, 1821.

Erastus Tippett, aged sixty-(60) years on the 1st day of Aug., 1820, resident of Lawrence County and State of Tennessee, who being first duly sworn according to law doth on his oath declare that he served in the Revolutionary War and was as follows, to-wit, that he enlisted in the service in Halifax County, North Carolina, where he was attached to Capt. Mumford's Co., in the 3rd North Carolina Regiment and served nine months as a drummer, that afterwards he served 18 months in Capt. Issac B. Cates Co., belonging to the same Regiment commanded by Curnel(sic) Archibald Little, that all the property he owns in the world are 2 cows, and calves, 3 sows, and 10 piggs(sic), ---1 feather bed of small value, 1

small pot and kettle, one large and 1 small spinning wheel, both old and of little value and that he is indebted for the necessaries of life about $ 50.00, that his occupation is farming and that he is very infirm and is lame in his right arm and is not able to make a support by his own labors as _____. That the remaining part of his family now living with him are as follows, viz, Judah Tippet, his wife, aged about 51 years who is decrepid and unable to labor, James Tippet, his son, about 16 years old, John Tippet, about 14 years old and Nancy Tippet, his daughter about 10 years old, that he has heretofore received a pension and that the number of his pension claim was 13788 and I do solemnly swear that I was a resident citizen of the United States on the 18th day of March, 1818, and that I have not since that time by goft, sale or in any manner disposed of my property or any part thereof with intent thereby to deminish it as to bring myself within the provisions of the Act of Congress, entitled An Act to provide for certain persons engaged in the land and naval service of the United States in the Revolutionary War passed on the 18th day of March 1818 and that I have not nor has any person in trust for me any property or securities, contracts or debts due to me nor have I any income other than what is contained in the schedule hereto annexed and by me subscribed. Erastus Tippet
Sworn and subscribed to in open Court before Henson Day, Chairman, Mancil Crisp, Andrew Brown, John Hillhouse and Robert Chaffin, Esquires, Justices of said Court.
M.H. Buchanan, Clerk
and that the court asessed the value of the property of said Erastus Tippet as set forth in the above application for a pension to $44.50.

Ordered that Court be adjourned till tomorrow, 9 o'clock. Mancil Crisp, John Hillhouse, and H. Day, J.P.'s.

FRIDAY JULY 7th, 1821

Friday morning July 7th, 1821, court met at 9 o'clock, according to adjournment, present, Mancil Crisp, John Hillhouse and Henson Day, Justices, Esquires.

M.H. Buchanan & Co.
vs   On motion
Bradley Halford, Sheriff

This day came the parties by their attornies and the motion being fully argued and well understood by the Court it is ordered that the plaintiff's motion shall not be sustained for want of notice, whereupon it is considered by the Court that the defendant go hence and recover of the plaintiff his costs by him about his defense in this behalf expended and the plaintiff in mercy & c.

Ordered that the application to this Court which is made by Josephus Irvine that he be allowed to enter on single tax his property and polls for this year.

Presly Ward
vs
David Crockett   On motion to dismiss on certiorari

This day came the parties by their attornies and this cause being fully argued and well understood by the Court, it is ordered that the plaintiff's motion be over rooled(sic), and that the defendant recover of the plaintiff his costs by him about his defense in this behalf expended, and from which judgement the defendant by his attorney prayed an appeal to the Honorable Circuit Court to be holden for this County, who gave bond and security according to law, the plaintiff's counsel farther takes an exception to the opinion of the Court, and having preserved his bill, the same is granted him which is made a part of the record in this case

Ordered that the Sheriff be directed to summon the following named persons to attend as Jurors at the next term of this Court, to-wit, Daniel Wolsey, John Farmer, John Bird, Walter Brashears, Annuel Atkison, Wm. Counce, Thomas Howard, Wm. Heifly, Wm. Smith, Wm. Altum, Moses Pennington, Henry Pulock, Hardin Paine, John Foster, Levi Blackard, James Edmundson, Johnathon Jobe, John Wasson, Archibald C. Huston, Martin Gaither, Jesse Williams, Aaron Anglin, Elijah Melton, John Anderson and John Merchant.

This Court now being in session agreeable to an adjournment of County business, it is ordered that Henry Sharp, John Hillhouse and Thomas Welch be apppointed to purchase and procure a lot of ground in the Town of Lawrenceburg on which they shall cause to be lett to the lowest bidder after forming Plans for the same, the building of a stray pen and the removal of the old Jail, and have the same in repair by the next term of this Court.

Ordered that the Sheriff be directed to take possession of and bring into the next County Court on the 1st day of the term, certain minor children hereafter to be named, to-wit, 1 girl child of the widdow Cooper now living with Robert Johnson, also two girls children the offspring of Judith Hunter and also one female child at Ezekiel Farmers.

John Edmundson
vs
Richard T. Bailey   Case

The defendant by his attorney comes into court prays and obtains an order that a commission issue to take the deposition of John McDonald in Limestone County in the State of Allabamma(sic) State by giving the adverse party 20 days notice of the time and place of taking the same.

Warren Mason came into Court and proved in due form that he had served 7 days as Constable. It is therefore ordered that a certificate issue accordingly by the clerk.

At least five acting Justices being present, to-wit, Robert Chaffin, John Hillhouse, Andrew Brown, Mansil Crisp, and Thomas Welch. John Strickland produced in open court 1 wolf scalp over 4 months old which was ordered to be burned and that the clerk certify accordingly.

James Strawn
vs   Certiorari
George Michie

On motion of the clerk it is ordered that Judgement be entered for the costs in this case against the defendant for the cost now for then, the same having been omitted to be spread on the minutes at the rendition of the judgement.

William S. Dalton
vs   Trespass on the case
Daniel Hughs

The plaintiff at the last term of this court having come in and dismissed his suit and the same being not spread on the minutes of said court that judgement now for then be rendered against the plaintiff for the cost of said suit.

Joseph Smith
vs   Trespass
Thomas Spencer

The plaintiff in this case having failed to come into Court and enter his pleas according to Act of Assembly, it is therefore considered by the court that judgement be rendered against the said plaintiff for the cost in this case according to law.

Ordered by the court that John Dalton and Abel Hill, Constables, be appointed to attend at the next Circuit Court as such.

Ordered by the Court that William White and John McClary, Constables, be appointed to attend at the next County Court.

Ordered by the Court that James McGee, a minor boy, be bound unto Thomas Howard, shoe and Boot Maker, and to work for him until he arrives at the age of 21 yrs., and that the said Howard be bound to feed, lodge and clothe said boy during the said term of service and to cause him to be educated to spell, read, write and cypher as far as the rule of three, inclusive, and to learn him the Art of Shoe and Boot-making and furnish him with a reasonable set of Shoe Tools at the end of his service, and to furnish him with two common neat suits of homespun cloaths(sic) and that he give bond and security according to law, which was done accordingly.

Ordered that Court be adjourned until Court in Course, Mancil Crisp, Andw. Brown, H. Day and John Hillhouse and Robert Chaffin, J.P.'s.

MONDAY OCTOBER 1st, 1821

At a Court of Pleas and Quarter Sessions holden for the County of Lawrence at the Courthouse in the ?Town of Lawrenceburg on the 1st Monday in Oct., 1821, and on the 1st day of the month, present Court met according to adjourment, present, Henson Day, Mansel Crisp, Robert Chaffin, Andw. Brown and John Hillhouse, Esquires, Justices.

Ordered by the Court that Willmi Carmi Jones, an orphan girl, be bound to Adam Chronister until she shall arrive at the age of 18 years and that the said Chronister be bound to lodge, clothe and feed said orphan and to educate her to read in the Bible, distinctly, and when of age to give her two good suits of cloth(sic) and a bed to weigh 35 pounds and good furniture, also a good wheel and cards.

At least five acting justices being present, to-wit, Henson Day, Mancil Crisp, Andrew Brown, John Killhouse and Robert Chaffin. James Hail produced in open Court 1 wolf scalp over 4 months old which was ordered to be burned and that the clerk certify accordingly.

Ordered by the Court that George Rogers be appointed overseer in the room of Daniel Kilburn, and that he have the same hands to work under his direction and that he keep the same in repairs.

Ordered by the Court that Margru9Sic) Sutton be allowed until the next term, of this court to give the Court satisfactory proof that she will maintain and educate her children.

Ordered by the Court that Samuel Jineans be exempt from the payment of half the valuation of certain stray sheep by him posted.

Ordered by the Court that Alexander Robertson be appointed overseer in the room of Samuel McKinsey and that he have same hands to work under his direction and that he kkep same in repair.

Ordered by the Court that the securities of Thomas Howard to whom James McGee, an orphan was bound to learn the shoe and bootmaking business, be exempted from their former obligations, & c.

Ordered that Moses Pennington be appointed overseer on the Road leading from Maury County toward Colbert Ferry from the Murry(sic) Co. line as low down as Ezekiel Farmers and that he have all the hands to work under his directions which live on the waters of Buffalow Creek which are not attached to the Military Road, including the said Farmer's that is all above Seahorns.

Ordered by the Court that Wm. McAnaly be appointed overseer of the road leading from Murry County towards Colberts Ferry, beginning at Ezekiel Farmer's and on to the western boundary line of this County and that he have all the hands to work under his direction, who live on Big Buffalow and Little Buffalow within this County below Scorns and that he keep the same in repairs.

Ordered by the Court that Martin Gaither be appointed overseer of the Military road in the room of John Crossthwaite and that he keep the part of said road in repairs which was under the direction of said Crossthwaite, and that he have the same hands to work under his direction which were under the direction of the said Crossthwaite.

Ordered by the Court that Arter Burk an orphan boy be bound unto Charles Cook uhtil he arrives to fulll age and that the said Cook be bound to feed lodge and clothe the said orphan, to educate the said orphan to read and write as far as the rool(sic) of three inclusive and when he arrives at full age to give him a horse worth $50 and a saddle and bridle worth $20 and to give the said orphan two suits of good clothes and that the said Cook enter into bond and security according to law which was done accordingly.

Ordered by the court that Wm. F. Cunningham be appointed administrator to the estate of Thomas Howard, dec'd, who entered into bond and security and was qualified according to law.

Ordered by the court that Thomas Holland, Melcher Duncan, Robert Hayes, Daniel Beeler, Hardin Paine, James Paine, Wm. Lucus and Martin Prewitt, or any five of them be appointed Commissioners to view that part of the Military Road which lies between Henry Phenix and the top of the dividing ground near Phillip Parchman's, the nearest and best way and that they make report to next court.

Ordered by the Court that Millie Sisemon, widow of Sesemon, deceased, have until Wednesday of this term to give bond and security and to be qualified according to law and in case she fails that _____ Sisemon(sic) be allowed to administer said estate.

Ordered by the Court that Archelaous Hogg be allowed to turn the new Florence Road so as not to so injure the said Hogg, provided the said Hogg opens the same to the satisfaction of the present overseer of that part of said road.

Ordered by the Court that George Lucus, John Wasson, Wm. Welch, Sr., Archer Fail, John Vorus, Enoch Binum and Geo, Rogers, or any five of them, be appointed a jury of view to view and mark out a road the nearest and best way to begin on the Giles County line on the ridge between the Big Creek and Weaklie's (Sic) Creek, thence to the west boundary line of this County in a direction to Benjamin Hardin's and that they make report to next Court.

M. H. Buchanan came into court and produced a bill of sale from George Hanks to the said Buchanan for a certain negro man named Samuel which was acknowledged by the said Hanks to be his act and deed for the purpose aforesaid which was ordered to be certified for registration accordingly.

M.H. Buchanan came into Court and produced a bill of sale from Gabriel Bumpass to the said Buchanan for a certain negro or Mulatto boy by the name of Phillip, which was proven to be the Act and deed of the said Bumpass and by the oath of Wm. F. Cunningham a subscribing witness thereto which was ordered to be certified for registration accordingly.

Ordered by the court that Hardin Paine be appointed overseer of that part of the Waterloo Road which was under the direction of M.H. Buchanan in the room of the said Buchanan former overseer and that he have the same hands to work under his direction which were under the said Buchanan and that he keep the same in repair.

Ordered by the Court that an orphan boy by the name of Caswell Lensdy be bound unto Douglas H. Stockton until he arrives to full age and that the said Stockton be bound to lodge, feed and clothe the said orphan and to learn him to read, write and cypher as far as the rool of three, inclusive, and when he becomes of age to give him a horse worth $ 50 and a saddle and bridle worth $30 and that said Stockton be bound to give said orphan two full suits of cloth(sic) of decent clothing and enter into bond and security which was done accordingly.

Ordered by the court that Hugh Weathers and John Sellars, Constables, of this County be appointed to attend as such at the next County Court to be holden for this County.

Nathan McClendon
vs
William White
Trespass

This say came the parties by their attorneys and thereupon came a jury of good and lawful men, to-wit, A.C.Huston, Jonathon Jobe, Wm. Smith, Elijah Cooper, James Payne, Geo. Jones, Daniel Fevyhous, Thomas Spencer, Samuel Price, Geo. Archer, John Henry, Thomas J. Matthews, who being elected, tried and sworn well and truly to try this issue joined upon their oaths do say that the defendant is not guilty in manner and form as in the plaintiff's declaration mentioned whereupon it is considered by the court that the defendant go hence without day and recover of the plaintiff his costs by him about his defense in this behalf expended and the defendant in mercy & c.'

Ordered that court be adjourned till tomorrow, 9 o'clock.
H. Day, Andw. Brown, Robert Chaffin, John Hillhouse, J.P.'s.

TUESDAY, OCTOBER 2nd, 1821

Court met Tuesday morning Oct.2, 1821 at 9 o'clock, according to adjournment. Present, Henson Day, Mancil Crisp, Andrew Brown, John Hillhouse and Robert Chaffin, Justices, Esquires.

The sheriff returned at this Court the venire facias returnable at this Court term containing the following named persons, to-wit, Daniel Woolsey, John Farmer, John Bird, Walter Brashears, Annuel Atkison, Wm. Counce, Thomas Howard, Wm. Agfley, Wm. Smith, Wm. Altum, Moses Pennington, Henry Pollock, Hardin Payne, John Foster, Levi Blackard, James Edmundson, Jonathon Jobe, John Wasson, Archibald C. Houston, Martin Gaither, Jesse Williams, Aaron Anglin, Elijah Melton, John Anderson, John Merchant, with the following endorsement made on the back-executed on all but Daniel Woolsey, John Byrd, Wm. Altum, Henry Pollock, by me, Bradley Halford, sheriff, and upon calling the venire aforesaid the following named jurors appeared, to-wit, Hardin Paine, Martin Gaither, Wm. Hefley, John Foster, Levi Blackard, Moses Pennington, Wm. Counce, John Farmer, Aaron Anglin, Elijah Melton, Annuel Atkison, John Anderson, George Archer, Jonathon Jobe, of whom on balloting the following were drawn as Grand Jurors, to-wit, Hardin Paine, foreman, John Merchant, Martin Gaither, Wm.Hefley, John Foster, Levi Blackard, Moses Pennington, Wm. Counce, John Farmer, Aaron Anglin, Elijah Melton, John Anderson, and Annuel Atkisson, who after receiving their charge and were qualified withdrew to consider of their presentments under the care of William White, a constable, who was sworn to attend them.

John Allsup
vs   Appeal
Thomas Howard

    It being suggested to this Court that the defendant was deceased. It is ordered that for the revival of this suit that a cire facias issue against Wm. F. Cunningham, Adm. to the estate of the said Howard, deceased, returnble to the next term of this Court agreeable to Act of Assembly in such case made and provided.

    Ordered that the Sheriff be directed to summon the following named persons to attend as jurors at the next Circuit Court to be holden for this County on the 4th Monday of Feb., next, to-wit, John Mitchell, Alexander Miller, James Argo, Wm. F. Cunningham, Aaron Choat, Sr., Green Depriest, George Lucus, Willis Lucus, John Crossthwait, Angus McDuffie, Pollard Wisdom, Mansil Crisp, Andrew Brown, George Archer, Wm. Dalton, George Wolf, Wm. Googe(s9c), John Hamilton, Joshua Wharton, Aaron Anderson, Jr., Daniel A. Flannery, Wm. Voss, John Ray, Wm. Welch, Jr., and Joseph Gist, and that they do not depart therefrom without leave of the Court.

    Ordered by the Court that the Sheriff be directed to summon the following named persons to appear as Jurors at the next County Court to be holden for this County on the 1st Monday in January, next, to-wit, Daniel Becler, Jesse Helton, Melcher Duncan, Solomon Gresham, James Paine, Jesse McAnnally, John Gill, Thomas Choate, Nathan Clifton, Austin Kendrick, John Wisdom, Jr., Warren Mason, Jasper Smith, John Smith, Joseph Smith, Sr., Silas Rackley, Isaac Swafford, Julius Brewer, Daniel Pearce, Hynum Cook, Thomas Keese, Thomas Holland, John Voss, Robert Brashears, Wm. Michie, Andrew Fugate and that they do not depart without leave of the Court.

    Ordered that Court be adjourned until tomorrow, 9 o'clock. Mancil Crisp, H. Day, Robert Chaffin, Andw. Brown, J.P.'s.

WEDNESDAY OCTOBER 3rd, 1821

    Wednesday morning nine o'clock, Court met according to adjournment, present, Henson Day, Mancil Crisp, Robert Chaffin and Andrew Brown, Esquires, Justices.

State
vs   Presentment Affray
Aaron Anderson

    This day came the Solicitor General in behalf of the State as well as the defendant in his proper person and the defendant being charged upon the Bill of Indictment pleads thereto guilty and puts himself upon the justice and mercy of the Court. It is therefore considered by the Court that he be fined in the sum of 75 cents and the cost of this said suit who gave Aaron Anderson, Sr., as security for the payment of the fine and costs and the defendant be taken & c.

Wm. F. Cunningham, to the estate of Thomas Howard, deceased, returned into Court an inventory of the property of said estate which was read and ordered to be recorded according to alw and that an order of sale issue accordingly.

The State
vs Assault and Battery
Adam Ross

This day came the Solicitor General in behalf of the State as well as the defendant in his proper person and the defendant being charged upon the Bill of Presentment pleads thereto not guilty and ofr his trial puts himself upon his Country and the Solicitor General for the State, likewise, whereupon came a jury of good and lawful men, to-wit, Jonathon Jobe, Wm. Smith, Andrew Lafferty, Phillip Null, James Moore, Aaron Anderson, Wm.M. Crisp, A.C.Huston, James Burns, Robert Hightower, G.W.Jones, and John Marcum, who being elected, tried and sworn well and truly to try this issue of traverse, upon their oaths do say that the defendant is guilty in manner and form as he is charged in the Bill of Presentment. Whereupon it is considered by the court that the defendant make his fine with the State to the sum of one cent and that he pay the cost of this prosecution and that he be taken & c.

The State
vs Affray
Zachariah Inman

This day came the Solicitor General in behalf of the State as well as the defendant in his proper person and the defendant being charged upon the Bill of Presentment pleads thereto guilty and for his trial puts himself upon the justice and mercy of the Court, whereupon it is considered by the Court that the defendant make his fine with the State to the sum of $3.10 and tht he pay the cost of this prosecution and that he be takn & c. For the payment of said fine and costs John Inman acknowledges himself bound accordingly.

The State
vs Affray
Edward Merchant

This day came the Solicitor General in behalf of the State as well as the defendant in his proper person and the defendant being charged upon the Bill of Presentment pleads thereto guilty and for his trial puts himself upon the Justice and mercy of the Court, whereupon it is considered by the Court that the defendant make his fine with the State to the sum of $3.10 and that he pay the cost of this prosecution and that he be in custody of the Sheriff until the same be paid, but because John Marchant comes into Court and lends himself as security, judgement is hereby rendered against both the defendant and security and the defendant hereby is released from said custody but may be taken & c.

139

The State
vs   Affray
James Burns

    This day came the Solicitor General in behalf of the State as well as the defendant in his proper person and the defendant being charged upon the Bill of Presentment pleads thereto guilty and puts himself upon the justice and mercy of the Court. Whereupon it is considered by the court that the defendant make his fine with the State to the amount of $7.50 and that he pay the cost of this prosecution and that he remain in custody of the Sheriff until the same be paid.

    Henry Sharp, John Hillhouse and Thomas Welch, who were appointed Commissioners to let the rebuilding of the Old Jail made report that the same was done which was received by the Court as the Jail of this County. Whereupon it is ordered by the Court that Andrew Lafferty be allowed the sum of $14.50 for removing and rebuilding the same, to be paid out of any monies in the hands of the County Trustee of this County not otherwise appropriated and that the Clerk certify the same accordingly.

    The Sheriff of this County comes into Court and entered a protest against the sufficiency of the Jail, which was ordered to be recorded.

The State
vs   Indictment
Solomon Gresham

    This day came the Solicitor General in behalf of the State as well as the defendant in his proper person and the defendant being charged upon the Bill of Indictment pleads thereto guilty and puts himself on the Justice and mercy of the Court. Whereupon it is considered by the Court that the defendant make his fine with the State to the sum of $6 and that he pay the cost of this prosecution and that he remain in the custody of the Sheriff until the same be paid.

    Isaac Ficcle comes into Court and acknowledges himself to be indebted to the State of Tennessee in the sum of $100.00, to be levyed of his goods, chattel lands and tenements, respectively to the use of the State to be void on condition that he appear here from day to day to prosecute and give evidence in behalf of the State against Jim. Welch upon an indictment for an Assault and battery and that he do not depart therefrom without leave of the Court.

The State
vs   Affray
William McAnally

    This day came the Solicitor General in behalf of the State as well as the defendant in his proper person and the defendant being charged upon the bill of presentment pleads not guilty and for his trial puts himself upon the Country as well as the Solicitor General for the State likewise, whereupon came a jury of good and lawful men, to-wit, John Edmundson, Daniel Beeler, James Wise, Francis V. Drennan, Alexander Miller,

Groves Sharp, Samuel Perry, Gabriel Bumpass, John A. Haile, Bryant McClendon, Wm. Burnes, John Gill, who being elected, tried and sworn well and truly to try this issue of traverse upon their oaths do say that the defendant is not guilty in manner and form as he is charged in the Bill of Presentment, whereupon it is considered by the Court that the defendant go hence without day and in all respects be acquitted from the charge aforesaid and that judgement be entered up against the County in favor of all those entitled to cost in behalf of the State and that the clerk certify accordingly.

The State
vs
John Jobe   Upon a recognenance

John Jobe who was bound to appear at this term and answer the State upon a charge for an affray altho solemnly called came not but made default, it is considered by the Court that judgement be rendered against the said John Jobe for the sum of____dollars, the amount of his recognenance, unless he show cause at the next term of this court why judgement should not be confirmed against him and that Sci refacias issue accordingly.

The State
vs
John Lockard   Upon a Recognenance

The defendant in this case who was bound in a recognenance for the appearance of John Jobe at this term to answer the State for an affray having failed to appear and to bring into Court the said John Jobe, although solemnly called came not but made default. It is therefore considered by the court that the State recover of the said John Lockard the sum of_____the amount of his said recognenance unless he appear at the next term of this Court and show cause why judgement should not be confirmed against him and that Sci refacias issue accordingly.

The State
vs
Joseph Renolds   Upon a Recognenance

The defendant in this case who was bound in a recognenance for the appearance of John Jobe at this term to answer the State upon a charge of an affray although solemnly called to come into Court and bring with him the body of the said John Jobe came not but made default. It is therefore considered by the Court that the State recover of the said Joseph Renalds(sic)_____dollars the amount of his said recognenance unless, her appear at the next term of this Court and shew cause why judgement should not be confirmed against him and that Scirefacias issue accordingly.

Eleanor Bryant and Luke Grimes came into Court and acknow= ledged themselves to be indebted to the State of Tennessee each in the sum of $100.00 to be severally levied of their goods, chattel lands and tenements for the use of the State to be void on condition that Eleanor Bryant appear here on the first Wednesday after the first Monday in January next to give evidence in behalf of the State against George Archer, Berry Archer, John McClarine and Thomas Mathews on an indictment and that they do not depart therefrom without leave of the Court.

Ordered that Court be adjourned till tomorrow, 9 o'clock. John Hillhouse, Mancil Crisp, Robert Chaffin and Henson Day, J.P.'s.

THURSDAY, OCTOBER 4th, 1821

Thursday morning, 9 o'clock, court met according to adjournment, present, Henson Day, Mansel Crisp, John Hillhouse, Robert Chaffin, Esquires, Justices.

William Wells
vs
Matthews and Others   Debt

This day came the parties by their attornies and thereupon came a jury of good and lawful men, to-wit, William Smith, A.C. Huston, Wm. M. Crisp, Samuel W. Sullivant, Groves Sharp, John C. Spillars, Wm. McCann, James Wise, Daniel Beeler, Nathan McClendon, Bryant McClendon and Thomas Holland, who being elected, tried and sworn the truth to speak upon the issue joined, upon their oaths do say that the defendant hath not payed the debt in the writing obligatory in the plaintiff's declaration mentioned as in pleadings he hath alleged and they do assess the plaintiff damage by reason of the detention thereof to $9.00 besides costs. It is therefore considered by the Court here that the plaintiff recover of the defendant the sum of $399.50 the debt aforesaid in form aforesaid assessed and their costs by them about their suit in this behalf expended and the defendant & c.

John Voss
vs
William Burress   Certiorari

The plaintiff in this case although solemnly called came not but made default it is considered by the Court that the defendant go hence without day and recover of the plaintiff his costs by him about his defense in this behalf expended and the plaintiff in mercy & c.

State
vs
E.W.Tipton

This day came the Solicitor General in behalf of the State as well as the defendant in his proper person and whereupon came a jury of good and lawful men, to-wit, Wm. Smith, A.C. Huston, Wm. M. Crisp, Samuel W. Sullivant, Groves Sharp, John C. Sellars, Wm. McCann, James Wise, Daniel Beeler, Nathan McClendon, Bryan McClendon, and Thomas Holland, who being elected tried and sworn the truth to speak and after argument fully had upon this case they withdrew to consider of their verdict, who having reported to this Court that they could not agree, it is ordered that the Jury in this case be dismissed and that this cause be set for trial at next Court and that the defendant and prosecuter make recogny for their appearance to next Court.

Court was adjourned until tomorrow, morning, 9 o'clock. John Hillhouse, Robert Chaffin, Andw. Brown, Mancil Crisp, H. Day, J.P.'s.

FRIDAY, OCTOBER 5th, 1821

Friday morning, 9 o'clock, Court met according to adjournment, present, Henson Day, Mansel Crisp, Robert Chaffin, John Hillhouse, and Andrew Brown, Esquires, Justices.

Ordered by the Court that judgement Ni Ci be rendered against John Jobe as defendant at the suit of the State and Joseph Reynolds and John Lockard as his security be sett9sic) aside upon there(sic) paying the cost thereby incurred.

The State
vs   For an affray
John Jobe

The defendant who was bound in a Recognenance for his appearance at this term comes into Court and pleads guilty to the Bill of Presentment and agrees to put himself upon the Justice and mercy of the Court. Whereupon it is considered by the Court that the defendant make his fine with the State to the sum of sixty-five cents. As well judgement is also rendered against Johathon Jobe who came into Court and acknowledged himself as security of the said defendant and that the defendant pay the cost of this prosecution and that he be taken.

Presley Ward
vs   Certiorari
David Crockett

This day comes the parties by their attorneys and thereupon came a jury of good and lawful men, to-wit, Wm. Smith, A.C.Huston, Wm. M. Crisp, Samuel W. Sullivant, Groves Sharp, John C. Spillers, Wm. McCann, James Wise, Daniel Bealor(sic), Nathan McClendon, Bryan Mc lendon, and Thomas Holland, who being elected, tried and sworn well and truly to try this issue of traverse upon their oaths do say that the defendant is guilty in manner and form as in the plaintiff's declaration mentioned. It is therefore considered by the Court that the plaintiff recover of the defendant the sum of $71.70, the amount of the judgement before the justices with the sum of $1.43 interest from the rendition of said judgement up to this time, together with his costs by him about his suit in this behalf expended, and the defendant in mercy &c.

John R. Crisp
vs   Certiorari
David Crockett

This day came the parties by their attornies and the plaintiff by his attorney moved to have this suit Quashed, and this cause being fully argued and well understood by the Court, it is ordered by the court that the plaintiff's motion be sustained, and that the plaintiff recover of the defendant the sum of $55.00 the amount of the judgement rendered before the justices together with six per cent, on the amount of said judgement up to this time, together with his cost by him about his suit in this behalf expendedfrom which judgement the defendant prayed an appeal to the Honorable Circuit Court to be holden for this County who gave bond and security accordingly.

Burwell B. Quimby
vs
David Crockett   Certiorari on motion to dismiss

This day came the parties by their attorneys and the defendants attorney moved to have this suit dismissed, and the case being fully argued and well understood by the Court, it is ordered that the plaintiff's motion be sustained, and that the plaintiff recover of the defendant the sum of $50.00, the amount of the judgement rendered before the justice, with the addition of six per cent from the rendering of said judgement until this time, together with his cost by him about his suit in this behalf expended, from which judgement the defendant prayed an appeal to the Honorable the Circuit Court to be holden for this County, who gave bond and security according to law.

John Kenday
vs
James Robertson   Appeal-Motion to dismiss

This day came the parties by their attornies. This cause being fully argued and well understood by the Court, it is ordered that this suit be dismissed and that the defendant recover of the plaintiff and his security, James Argo, for the prosecution of this appeal his costs by him about his defense in this behalf expended and the plaintiff in mercy & c.

Ordered by the Court that Court be adjourned until tomorrow, 9 o'clock. Mancil Crisp, Andw. Brown, Robert Chaffin, John Hillhouse and H. Day, J.P.'s.

SATURDAY, OCTOBER 6th, 1821

Saturday morning, 9 o'clock, Court met according to adjournment, present, Mancil Crisp, Robert Chaffin, John Hillhouse and Andrew Brown, Esquires, Justices.

John Edmundson
vs
R.T. Bailey   Trespass

This day came the parties by their attornies and thereupon came a jury of good and lawful men, to-wit, Wm. Michie, James Parchman, James Bumpass, Isaac Whorton, John Wisdom, Alexander Murphy, John Allsup, Francis Drennam, Andrew Lafferty, Solomon Gresham, John Anglin, and A.P. Cunningham, who being elected, tried and sworn, and one of the jurors who being sick this is made a mistrial and continued until next Court.

M.H. Buchanan
vs
Bradley Halford   Motion against the Sheriff

This day came the parties by their attorney's and upon solemn argument the motion is overruled. Thereupon it is considered by the Court that the defendant go hence and recover of the plaintiff his costs about his defense in this behalf expended & c and from this judgement the defendant prays an appeal & c.

State
vs
E.W.Tipton   October Term, 1821

Be it remembered that on the trial of this cause, the Jury hung from Thursday until Saturday morning, when the Solicitor made a motion to dishcarge the Jury contrary to the consent of the defendant, the defendant objected to the motion, but the Court sustained the motion and dismissed the jury an hour before the Court closed, to which opinion of the Court the defendant excepts and prays this bill of exceptions to be signed, sealed and entered and it is granted him & c. Andrew Brown, J.P., Robert Chaffin, J.P., and John Hillhouse, J.P.

Edmund W. Tipton comes into court and acknowledges himself truly indebted to the State of Tennessee in the sum of $100.00 to be severally levied of his goods, chattel lands and tenements to the use of the State to be void on conditions that he make his personal appearance here at the next term of this court on the 3rd day of the term, then and there to answer the State in a charge of assault and battery committed on the body of Bradley Halford, Sheriff, and that he depart therefrom not without leave of the Court.

James Mabery
vs   Case
John Smith

In this case the plaintiff being taxed with the cost and it appearing that judgement was confirmed against the plaintiff's security it is ordered that judgement be confirmed against JohnInman,Sr., and Mershack Inman, in as full and ample a manner as it is run against the plaintiff.

Bradley Halford came into court and acknowledged himself severally indebted to the State of Tennessee in the sum of $50.00 to be severally levied of his goods, chattel lands and tenements for the use of the State to be void on condition that he make his personal appearance here at the next term to prosecute and give evidence in behalf of the State and against E.W.Tipton and he depart therenot without leave of the Court.

E.W.Tipton who was bound to appear at this term and answer the State upon the charge of an assault and battery, although solemnly called came not but made default. It is therefore considered by the court that judgement be rendered against the said E.W.Tipton for the sum of $100.00 the amount of his recognenance, unless, he shall come at the next term of this Court why judgement should not be confined against him and that a Sci Facias issue accordingly.

State
vs
William White

The defendant in this case who was bound in a recocnenance for the appearance of E.W.Tipton at this term to answer the State for an assault and battery having failed to appear and bring into court the said E.W.Tipton although solemnly called came not but made default. It is therefore considered by the Court that judgement be rendered against the said Tipton and White for the sum of $100.00 the amount of their Recognenance, unless, they appear here at the next term of this Court and shew causewhy judgement should not be confirmed against him and that a Sci facias issue accordingly.

State
vs
John H. Anglin

The defendant in this case who was bound to a Recognenance for the appearance of E.W.Tipton at this term to answer the State for an assault and battery having failed to appear and bring into Court the said E.W. Tipton although solemnly called came not but made default. It is therefore considered by the Court that judgement be rendered against the said Tipton and Anglin for the sum of $100.00 the amount of their Recognenance, unless they appear here at the next term of this Court and shew cause why judgement should not be confirmed against him and that a Sci facias issue accordingly.

Ordered that Court be adjourned until Court in Course.
Andw. Brown, H. Day, John Hillhouse, Robert Chaffin, Mancil Crisp, J.P.'s.

JANUARY TERM, 1822 (Jan.7th, 1822)

At a Court of Pleas and quarter sessions holden for the County of Lawrence at the courthouse in the town of Lawrenceburg, present, Henson Day, Mansel Crisp, Robert Chaffin, Thomas Welch, Richard Hill, and George Lucas, Esquires, Justices.

At least five of the acting Justices being present, to-wit, Henson Day, Mansel Crisp, Robert Chaffin, Thomas Welch, and Richard Hill. Wm. Williams produced in open court 1 wolf scalp over 4 months old which was ordered to be burned and that the clerk certify accordingly.

At least five of the acting justices being present, to-wit, (Editors note; Same J.P.'s as listed in paragraph above). Stephen Rowland produced in open court 1 wolf scalp over 4 months old which was ordered burned and that the clerk certify accordingly.

At least five of the acting justices being present, to-wit, (Editors note; Same J.P.'s as above). John Nelson produced in open court 1 wolf scalp over 4 months old which was ordered burned and that the clerk certify to the State Treasurer accordingly.

At least five of the acting justices being present, to-wit, (Editors note; Same list of J.P.'s as listed above). William Lockard produced in open court 1 wolf scalp over 4 months old which was ordered burned and that the clerk certify the same to the State Treasurer accordingly.

At least five of the acting justices being present, to-wit (Editors note; Same list of J.P.'s as listed in above paragraphs). Thomas Mitchell produced in open court 1 wolf scalp over 4 months old which was ordered burned and that the clerk certify the same to the State Treasurer.

Ordered by the court that Henry Brewer be appointed overseer in the room of Meshack Inman, of the Florence Road and that he have the same hands to work under his direction that was under said Inman, and that he keep same in repairs.

Ordered by the Court that Stephen Roland be exempt from paying the taxes for 160 Acres of land and that he pay for 50 Acres only.

Wm. F. Cunningham, Adm., of Thomas Howard, dec'd, made return to the court a list of the property of the estate of the said Thomas Howard, dec'd, which was received and ordered to be recorded accordingly.

Daniel Lindsey came into court and was exempt from paying his poll tax for the year 1821.

Ordered by the court that Levi Lewis have a certificate issued to him by the Clerk of said Court in lieu of one issued to him for $1.50 for his serving as a juror.

Ordered by the Court that Daniel Archer be allowed to keep a house of Ordinary at his own house in this County, who took the oath to suppress gambling and gave bond and security accordingly.

Ordered by the Court that David Steel be appointed overseer of the Natchez Road and that he have all the hands from Capt. Seahorn's to the West boundary of this County, including said Seahorn and that he keep same in good repair.

Ordered by the Court that Willis Lucas, Martin Prewitt, George Isom, Henry Sharp, David Steel, James Bumpass and Harden Payne, or any five of them be appointed a Jury of View and mark out a road to begin where the Waterloo Road crosses Crowson's Fork, thence the nearest and best way to Steel's Iron Works, and that they make report to next Court.

Ordered by the Court that Benjamin Morrow, Green Depriest, Eliott Lindsey, James Kelly, Wm. Lucas, Abner Bergan, and Willis Lucas, or any five of them be appointed a Jury of View to view and mark out a road the nearest and best way to begin at the foard on Crowson's Fork between Willis Lucas and Capt. Prewitt's, thence in a western direction to intersect to Old Natchez Trace, and that they report to the next term of this Court.

Ordered by the court that Thomas Welch and Cornelius Goforth be appointed a Jury of View to view and report to next Court whether that part of the Military Road to be cut out by John Crosswhaite is perferable to the old part and that they report to next Court.

Elihu Crisp at the request of Bradley Halford, Sheriff,

by and with the consent of the Court, came into Court and was qualified as a Deputy Sheriff of this County.

Ordered by the Court that James Kanady be appointed Constable for Capt., Flanery's Company, who gave bond and ssecurity and was qualified according to law.

Ordered by the Court that James Appleton, overseer of Lambs Ferry Road have all the hands on Sugar Creek from Alexander Campbell's as low down as the widow Duncan's Old Place, and that he keep the same in repairs.

STATE OF TENNESSEE
LAWRENCE COUNTY
    Agreeable to an order of Court in appointing Andrew Brown, Daniel Kilburn, and John Burns to make an allowance to Clizabeth Moore, wife of Stephen H. Moore, deceased, for her maintance for one year and that they make report at next term of this court.

The following persons who were appointed by the last Legislator of this State justices of the Peace in and for this County, to-wit, Lazarous Stewart, Phillip Chronister and George Archer came into Court and were qualified as such according to law.

Ordered by the Court that the last will and testament of Thomas Springer, dec'd, be recorded, that Willis Hammons and Peter P. Allsup, subscribing witnesses to said will be qualified which was done accordingly, and that letters testamentary issue. Thomas Allsup who was qualified and gave bond as Executor to said estate.

Ordered by the Court that John A. Hail be appointed Adm., to the estate of John Baddgett, deceased, who entered into bond and security and was qualified according to law and ordered that letters of administration issue accordingly.

John Jones, David Steel and Thomas Steele, who have in operation Iron Works in this County came into Court and presented their petition praying a jury of twelve men to be appointed to lay off 3000 Acres of land for said works, which was granted them and ordered that George Isom, John McFalls, John Kenady, Eli Kenday, Nathaniel Christian, Moses Pennington, Abraham Pennington, William Pennington, Isaac Pennington, Wm. Seahorn, Jm. Johnson and John McAnally, Sr., be appointed a Jury for that purpose and ordered that they make their report to next Court.

_____ Young came into Court, prayed and obtained a license for a House of Ordinary in the Town of Lawrenceburg, who gave bond and security according to law.

Ordered by the Court that Caswell Lindsy, an orphan boy of this County who at the last term of this court was bound to D.H. Stockton be _____ from said bondage and that the said Stockton and securities altogether released from their obligation given consequence of said bondage.

Ordered by the Court that next Friday be set apart for County business according to Act of Assembly in such case made and provided for.

Whereas William Porter and son, assignee of J. Bowdy obtained an execution issued on the 19th day of Oct. 1821, against the goods, chattel lands and tenements of George Gresham and Solomon Gresham directing to any lawful office(sic) of said County for the sum of $38.18 3/4 debt with the further sum of Seventy-five cents cost before Henry Sharp, a justice of this County. Whereupon the officer into whose hands said excution was put returned said execution to Court with the following endorsement thereon, to-wit, leived on 100 Acres of land this the 22nd day of Dec. 1821 on which said Gresham now lives and no other property found.

J. Halford, Constable

Whereupon it is ordered by the Court that a venditions exponas issue to the Sheriff of this County commanding him to sell said land to satisfy said judgement and make return according to law.

The Court proceeded to the classification of the Justices of the Peace for this County for the purpose of holding the Court of Pleas and Quarter Sessions of this County, agreeable to the Act of Assembly in that case made and provided, in the following manner, to-wit, Pollard Wisdom, George Archer, John Hillhouse, Andrew Brown, and Henry Sharp, Esquires, shall compose the first class to hold the present term, Mancin Crisp, George Lucas, Jeremiah Jackson, Samuel D. Poteet and Phillip Chronister, Esquires, shall compose the Second Class to hold the Court at the next term, Henson Day, Richard Hill, Robert Chaffin, Thomas Welch and Lazarus Stewart, Esquires, shall compose the Third Class to hold court at July term. Daniel A. Flannery, Jacob Pennicuff, Mansel Crisp, Henson Day, and Henry Sharp shall compose the Fourth Class and to hold Court at October Term.

Ordered by the Court that Josiah Wallis be appointed Administrator to the estate of Stephen H. Moore, deceased, who entered into bond and security and was qualified according to law and that letters of Administration issue accordingly.

~~Ordered by the Court that Willis Lucas, Martin Prewitt, George Isom, Henry Sharp, David Steel, Gabriel Bumpass and Hardin Paine, or any five of them, be appointed a jury of view to view and mark out a road to begin where the Waterloo Road crosses Crowsons fork and then in a direction to Steel's Iron Works and that they make report to next term of this Court.~~
(Editors note; The words in this paragraph were similarly struck through in original record book.)

Ordered that Court be adjourned until tomorrow, 9 o'clock. Henry Sharp, John Hillhouse, and George Archer, J.P.'s

TUESDAY, JANUARY TERM 1822 (Jan. 8th)

Tuesday morning 9 o'clock, Court met according to adjournment, present, Henry Sharp, John Hillhouse, and George Archer, Esquires, Justices.

The Sheriff returned the following venure Facias returnable to this term, to-wit, Daniel Beeler, Jesse Helton, Melcher Duncan, Solomon Gresham, James Payne, Jesse McCannaly, John Gill, Thomas Choat, Nathan Clifton, Austin Kendrick, John Wisdom,Jr., Warren Mason, Jasper Smith, John Smith, Joseph Smith,Sr., Silas Rackley, Isaac Swafford, Julius Brewer, Daniel Pearce, Hynum Cook, Thomas Keese, Thomas Holland, John Voss, Robert Brashears, Wm. Michie, and Andrew Fugate with the following endorsement on the back."executed on all but Austin Kendrick, Isaac Swafford, Hynum Cook, and Robert Brashears, by me, E.C.Crisp,Deputy Sheriff", and upon calling the venire aforesaid, the following named persons appeared, to-wit, Thomas Keese, Daniel Beeler, Jesse Helton, Melcher Duncan, Solomon Gresham, James Payne, Jesse McAnnaly, John Gill, Nathan Clifton, Julius Brewer, Thomas Holland, Wm.Michie, Andy Fugate, and Joseph Smith of whom the following named persons were drawn as Grand Jurors, to-wit, Thomas Keese, foreman, Daniel Beeler, Jesse Helton, Melcher Duncan, Solomon Gresham,James Paine, Jesse McAnally, John Gill, Nathan Clifton, Julius Brewer, Thomas Holland, Wm. Michie and Andy Fugate who after having received their charge and were qualified withdrew to consider of their presentments under the care of Wm. White, Constable who was sworn to attend them.

E.W.Tipton
vs
Henry Brashears   Debt

This day came the parties by their attorney and this case being well understood by the Court here it is agreed by the parties that judgement be entered against the defendant for $55.00 and all costs who gave Wm. Michie as security for the payment of debt and cost and the defendant in mercy &c.

John Edmundson
vs
Richard T. Bailey   In case

This day came the parties by their attorney and thereupon came a jury of good and lawful men, to-wit, Joseph Smith, Jacob Blythe, Thomas Spencer, Elijah Melton, Groves Sharp, John Burns, Daniel Hughs, Annuel Adkinson, John Nelson, James McConnel,Samuel McConnel, and Angus McDuffy who being elected tried and sworn well and truly to try this issue of traverse upon their oaths do say that the defendant is guilty in manner and form as in the plaintiff's declaration mentioned and they do assess the plaintiff damage to the sum of $200.00 besides cost. It is therefore considered by the Court that the plaintiff recover of the defendant his damages aforesaid by the jury aforesaid in form aforesaid assessed, together with his costs by him about his suit in this behalf expended and the defendant prayed an appeal which was granted who gave bond and security according to law.

Ordered that Court be adjourned until tomorrow, 9 o'clock.
Henry Sharp, John Hillhouse and George Archer, J.P.'s.

WEDNESDAY JANUARY 9, 1822

Wednesday morning 9 o'clock, Court met according to adjournment. Present, Henry Sharp, John Hillhouse, George Archer, Esquires, Justices.

State
vs
E.W.Tipton   Assault and battery

This day came the Solicitor General in behalf of the State as well as the defendant in his proper person and the Solicitor General prays leave to enter a Nol prosequ whereupon it is ordered by the Court a Nol pros be entered in this case and the prosecutor, Bradley Halford, assumes upon himself one half of the cost of the indictment and the defendant the other half of said cost and the said defendant in mercy & c.

Joseph Lemenster
vs   Case
Andrew Lafferty

By consent of the parties it is ordered by the Court that a commission issue to take the deposition of George Colbern in the State of Alabama to be used as evidence for the plaintiff by giving 10 days previous notice of time and place also Asiam Duly, Augustine Brown and Wm. Vincent of Maury Co., to be read in favor of the defendant by giving 10 days notice of time and place.

Ordered by the court that Wm. Venable be fined in the sum of five dollars for contempt to the Court.

Zacheriah Stricklin came into Court and produced a power of attorney which was executed to Wm. F. Cunningham and was acknowledged by him to be his act and deed and ordered that the clerk certify the same accordingly.

Ordered by the court that court be adjourned til tomorrow, 9 o'clock. Henry Sharp, John Hillhouse, Geo. Archer,J.P.'s.

THURSDAY , JANUARY 10th, 1822

Thursday morning, 9 o'clock, Court met according to adjournment, present, Henry Sharp, John Hillhouse, Geo. Archer, Esquires, Justices.

Hamilton Reynolds
vs
Patterson Crockett

This day came into Court John Nelson, who was special bail for the defendant and produced him the said defendant to the Court and surrendered him up in discharge of himself, whereupon the plaintiff by his attorney prayed the defendant into the custody of the sheriff and by order of the court the defendant was taken into the custody of the Sheriff to be safely kept agreeable to the law in such case made and provided.

State
vs   Upon a Scri Facias
John Anglin

The defendant in this case who was bound in a recognenance of $100.00 for the appearance of E.W. Tipton at last Court to answer to a charge of Assault and battery committed on the body of Bradley Halford, Sheriff, although solemnly calledto come into Court and bring with him the said Tipton, came not, but made default. Whereupon judgement Ni Ci was entered up against the said defeendant and Scrifacias having been issued and served on the said Anglin returnable to this term and the said Tipton having come into court and surrendered himself agreeable to his Recognenance to answer to the above charge and a Noli Prosequi therein by consent of the court be entered by the said Tipton assuming part of said cost the said judgement Ni Ci is sett(sic) aside and that judgement be rendered against the said Tipton for the cost of accuring in this suit and that the defendant go hence without day.

State
vs   Upon a Sciro facias
(Editor note, name not given)

The defendant in this case who was bound in a recognenance of $100.00 for the appearance of Edmund W. Tipton at the last term of this court to answer the State upon a charge of an Assault and Battery committed upon the body of Bradley Halford, Sheriff, Although solemnly called to come into court and bring with him the body of the said E.W.Tipton, came not but made default, whereupon judgement Ni Si was rendered up against the said defendant and sciro facias having been issued and served on the said ____ ____ returnable to the next term having come into court and submitted himself agreeable to his recognemance to answer the above charge and nol prosequi being entered in said case by consent of the court and the said Tipton assumes upon himself to pay the cost in this behalf expended it is ordered that the said judgement Ni Si be sett aside and that judgement be entered up against the said Tipton for all costs accuring in this case.

State
vs   Presentment of Assault and battery
Aaron Choate, Jr.

This day came the Solicitor General in behalf of the State as well as the defendant in his proper person and the defendant being charged upon theBill of Presentment pleads not guilty and agrees to put himself upon his Country and the Solicitor General for the State, likewise, whereupon came a jury of good and lawful men to-wit, Joseph Smith, Nathan McClendon, Austin Kendrick, Patterson Crockett, Daniel Hill, Daniel Hughs, A.C.Huston, John A. Haile, Stephen Busby, James B. Haile, George Rogers, and David Pennington, who being elected, tried and sworn well and truly to try this issue of traverse upon their oaths do say that the defendant is not guilty in manner and form as he is charged in the Bill of Presentment mentioned. Whereupon it is considered by the Court that the defendant go hence without day and in all respects be acquitted from the charge aforewaid and that judgement be entered in favor of all those entitled to cost in behalf of the State.

State
vs
Josiah Tipet   Presentment of Assault and battery

This day came the Solicitor General in behalf of the State as well as the defendant in his proper person and the defendant being charged upon the bill of presentment pleads thereto guil=ty and puts himself upon the justice and mercy of the Court. It is therefore considered by the court that he be fined in the sum of $2.00 and that he pay the cost of this prosecution and that he be taken & c. For the payment of said fine and cost George Rogers acknowledges himself as security.

State
vs
Hartwell Bumpass   Presentment Assault and Battery

This day came the Solicitor General in behalf of the State as well as the defendant in his proper person and the defendant being charged upon the Bill of Presentment pleads thereto gilty (sic) and puts himself upon the justice and mercy of the Court. It is therefore considered by the Court that he be fined in the sum of $2.00 and that he pay the cost of this prosecution and that he be taken & c. For the payment of said fine and cost Aaron Choat acknowledges himself as security.

State
vs
Aaron Anglin   Indictment for an affray

This day came the Solicitor General in behalf of the State as well as the defendant in his proper person and the defendant being charged upon the bill of Indictment pleads thereto gilty and puts himself upon the justice and mercy of the Court. It is therefore considered by the court that the defendant make his fine with the State to the sum of $5.00 and that he pay the cost of this prosecution and that he be taken ¢ c. For the payment of said fine and cost George Michie acknowledges himself as security.

William Welch and Bradley Halford come into Court and acknowledged themselves severally indebted to the State of Tennessee each in the sum of $100.00 to be severly levied of their goods, chattel lands and tenements for the use of the State to be void on the condition that Wm. Welch make his personal appearance at the courthouse in the Town of Lawrence-burg on the First Wednesday after the first Monday in April, next, then and there to answer the State in a charge for an assault and battery committed by him on the body of Issac Fickle and that he depart not without leave of the Court.

Isaac Fickle and Wm. Burris acknowledges themselves severally indebted to the State of Tennessee each in the sum of $100.00 to be severally levied of their goods, chattel lands and tenements to the use of the State to be void on condition that Isaac Fickle make his personal appearance at the Courthouse in the Town of Lawrenceburg on the First Wednesday after the First Monday in April, next, then and there to prosecute and give evidence in behalf of the State against Wm.

Welch and that he depart not without leave of the court.

William Burris and John Foster acknowledges themselves severly indebted to the State of Tennessee each in the sum of $100.00 to be severly levied of their goods, chattel lands and tenements to the use of the State to be void on condition that Wm. Burris make his appearance at the courthouse in the Town of Lawrenceburg on the First Wednesday after the First Monday in April, next, then and there to give evidence against Wm. White and Lewis_____ and that he depart therefrom not without leave of the Court.

State
vs   Presentment for Assault and Battery
George Rodgers

George Rodgers and John Edmundson comes into Court and acknowledges themselves to be severly indebted to the State of Tennessee each in the sum of $100.00 to be severly levied of their goods, chattel lands and tenements for the use of the State to be void on condition that Geo. Rodgers make his personal appearance at the Courthouse in the Town of Lawrenceburg on the First Wednesday after the First Monday in April, next, then and there to answer the State upon a charge of Assault and Battery committed upon the body of Wm. White and that he depart not without leave of Court.

Jonathon Ramsey
vs   Debt
Phillip Parchman

This day came the parties by their attorney's and thereupon came a jury of good and lawful men, to-wit, Joseph Smith, Nathan McClendon, Austin Kendrick, Patterson Crockett, Daniel Hill, Daniel Hughs, A.C. Huston, John A. Mail, Stephen Busby, James E. Mail, George Rogers, David Pennington, who being elected, tried and sworn well and truly to try this issue joined upon their oaths do say that the defendant is gilty in manner and form as in the plaintiff's declaration mentioned and they do assess the plaintiff damage by reason thereof to the sum of $5.75 besides cost. Thereupon it is considered by the court that the plaintiff recover of the defendant the sum of $100.00 debt aforesaid together with his damages aforesaid by the jury aforesaid in form aforesaid assessed together with his cost by him about his suit in this behalf expended and the defendant in mercy &c.

David Pennington
vs   Appeal
Nathaniel Christian

This day came the parties and it being suggested to the Court that the plaintiff in this case has withdrawn his plea heretofore pleaded and having failed to prosecute. It is therefore commanded by the Court that this suit be dismissed and that the defendant recover of the plaintiff his cost by him about his defense in this behalf expended and the plaintiff in mercy & c.

M.H. Buchanan
vs   Debt
George Rodgers

This day came the defendant George Rodgers in his proper person and says that he cannot gainsay but that he owes the plaintiff $89.93 3/4 this being what is due on the note mentioned in the plaintiff's declaration after deducting all credits and the plaintiff agrees that this is correct. It is agreed by the parties that this judgement be stayed three months. It is therefore considered by the court that the plaintiff recover of the defendant aforesaid sum of $89.93 and 3/4th cents debt together with his cost by him about his suit in this behalf expended and the defendant in mercy & c.

Jesse Evans
vs
Duchley Donalson & Others

This day came the parties by their attorneys and the plaintiff withdrew his pleas heretofore plead and assumes upon himself all costs. It is therefore considered by the court that this case be dismissed and that the defendant recover of the plaintiff his costs by him about his defense in this behalf expended and the plaintiff in mercy & c.

Charles Cook
vs
William Kanada

This day came the plaintiff into Court and withdraws his suit heretofore pleaded and the plaintiff assumes upon himself all costs. It is therefore considered by the Court that the defendant recover of the plaintiff his costs by him about his defense in this behalf expended and the plaintiff in mercy & c.

State
vs   Peace Recognenance
William Melton

The defendant in this case comes into court and assumes the payment of all costs whereupon it is ordered by the Court with the assent of the Solicitor that the case be dismissed and that judgement be entered against the defendant and Elijah Melton, security for all costs.

This day came into Court Joseph Spears and James Curtis, pensioners, and filed their affadavits and schedules according to Act of Congress, which was received and ordered to be certified accordingly.

James Jones
vs   Case
James Terrell

This day came the plaintiff by his attorney as well as the defendant in his proper person and the defendant saith that he cannot gainsay but that he doth owe the plaintiff the sum of $100.00 and one dollar damages as in the plaintiff's declaration mentioned. Whereupon it is considered by the Court that the plaintiff recover of the defendant the sum of $101.00 his damage aforesaid together with his costs by him about his suit in this behalf expended and it is agreed that the execution be stayed nine months.

155

James Jones
vs   Case
James Terrell

    This day came the plaintiff by his attorney as well as the defendant in his proper person and the defendant saith that he cannot gainsay but that he doth owe the plaintiff the sum of $100.00 and $50.00 damages as in the plaintiff's declaration mentioned. Whereupon it is considered by the court that the plaintiff recover of the defendant the sum of $150.00 his damages aforesaid together with his costs by him about his suit in this behalf expended and it is agreed that the execution be stayed for nine months.

Wm. M. Berryhill & Alexander McRee
vs   Motion
Richard T. Bailey

    Ordered that his cause be continued until to-morrow. (Editors note; The next page contained the case copied on last page, re-James Terrel and James Jones case of $101 and the record pertaining to Spears and Curtis pensions. This page was either copied twice by micro-filmer or the Clerk of the Court copied it twice. We are NOT recopying here.)

    Court was adjourned until tomorrow. Henry Sharp, John Hillhouse and George Archer, J.P.'s.

FRIDAY JANUARY 11th 1822

    Friday morning court met according to adjournment. Present, Henry Sharp, John Hillhouse and George Archer, Esquires, Justices

    A majority of the acting Justices being present, it is ordered that the following named magistrates be appointed to take a list of taxable property and poles(sic) in the following Captains Company's, to-wit, Thomas Welch in Capt. Welch;s Co., Henson Day in Capt. Gresham's Co., Phillip Cronister in Capt. Flanery's Do., Andrew Brown in Capt. Melton's Do., Mansel Crisp in Capt. Prewitt's Do., George Archer in Capt. Hugh's do, Lazarous Stewart in Capt. McClaren's Do., Samuel Poteete in Capt. Hammon's do., and that they make report to next Court.

    Ordered that the sheriff be directed to summon the following named persons to attend as jurors at the next County Court to be holden for this County at the Courthouse in the Town of Lawrenceburg on the first Tuesday after the first Monday in April next, to-wit, John Wisdom, Henry Brashears, Joseph Gosnal, Wm. Smith, Jacob Blythe, Elijah Melton, James Argo, John Mitchell, Samuel McClain, Robert Haynes, Edward Mobley, Stephen Roland, Andrew Johnston, Meagy Lewis, Thomas Allsup, Green Depriest, William Lucas, Isaac P. Willson, Burrell Quimby, Wm. Henderson, Simeon Edwards, Adam Chronister, John Anthony, Ebenezer Kanada and John Ray.

    A majority of the acting Justices being present, it is ordered by the court that Bradley Halford, Sheriff, be allowed the sum of $50 for his ex-officio services for the year 1821, to be paid by the County Trustee of any money not otherwise appropriated and that the clerk certify accordingly.

Ordered by the Court that Francis Wisdom be appointed overseer of the Florence road in the room of Henry Brashears, the former overseer and that he have the same hands to work under his direction that were under the said Brashears and that he keep the same in repairs.

Ordered by the Court that Wm. McAnally, overseer of the road leading from Maury County towards Colbert's Ferry, beginning at Ezekiel Farmers and on to the West boundary of this County, and that he have all the hands on little Buffalow and on the head of Chisms Fork including the Reynolds and that he keep same in repair.

Ordered by the Court that Joseph Halford and John Sellars be appointed Constables to attend at the next County Court as such.

A majority of the acting justices being present, it is ordered by the court that the Tavern rates of this County be as follows, for each ½ pint whiskey or peach Brandy sold 12½ cents, for each ½ pint of Furen Sperits 25 cents, for each meals victuals 25 cents, for each horse feed 12½ cents, for lodging a person per night 12½ cents, for each horse per night 37½ cents.

State
vs
John McClaren

This day came the Solicitor General in behalf of the State as well as the defendant in his proper person and the defendant being charged upon the bill of indictment pleads thereto not guilty and for his trial puts himself upon his Country and the Solicitor for the State, likewise. Whereupon came a jury of good and lawful men to-wit, Joseph Smith, Henry Brashears, John A. Hail, James Crawford, Daniel Hughs, Robert Chaffin, Jr., James Welch, John Mitchel, Samuel McClain, Nathan McClendon, Samuel Askew, John L. Hinson, who being elected, tried and sworn well and truly to try this issue of traverse upon their oaths do say that the defendnat is not gilty(sic) as charged in the bill of indictment. Whereupon it is considered by the Court that the defendant go hence without day and in all respects be acquitted from his charge aforesaid, and that judgement be entered up against the County in favor of all those entitled to cost on behalf of the State.

Ordered by the Court that the County Tax of this County be lade(sic) at the rate of 100 per cent on the State Tax, and that the Clerk render a list of the same to the Collector who (sic) duty it shall be to collect the same accordingly.

Ordered that Bradley Halford, Sheriff and Collector, of the Public and County Tax of this County be allowed as a credit of five dollars and 31 cents for insolvencies, to be deducted out of the State Tax agreeable to his return to us made agreeable to law, and that the clerk certify the same to the State Treasurer.

Ordered that Bradley Halford, SSheriff (Editors note; this paragraph same as one above--copied twice.)

There was produced in Court a bill of sale of Obediah Kendrick to Wm. Henderson for a certain negro boy named John which was prved to be the act of the said Obediah Kendrick by Wm. Welch, a subscribing witness thereto in order to be certified for registration.

There was produced in Court a bill of sale of Obediah Kendrick to Wm. Welch for a negro girl named Emerly which was proven to be the act of the said Kendrick by James M. Kendrick, a subscribing witness thereto in order to be certified for registration.

There was produced in Court a bill of sale of Obediah Kendrick to James M. Kendrick for a negro boy named Henry about two years old, which was proven to be the act of the said Obediah Kendrick by the oath of Wm. Welch, a subscribing witness thereto in order to be certified for registration.

M.H. Buchanan, Clerk, produced his receipt from Thomas Crutcher, Treasurer of West Tennessee certifying that the said clerk had paid over to the Treasurer the State Tax on lawsuits and on licenses to merchants, peddlers, keepers of Houses of Ordinary, shows & c which receipt was acknowledged satisfactory and ordered that the same be entered as record.

Ordered by the Court that M.H. Buchanan be allowed the sum of $25.00 for making out a Tax list for the year 1821, out of any monies in the hands of the County Trustee not already appropriated and these the Clerk certify accordingly.

Ordered by the Court that M.H. Buchanan be allowed the sum of $12.00 for furnishing a stray pen for the year 1821, to be payed out of any money in the hands of the County Trustee not already appropriated and that the Clerk certify accordingly.

Ordered by the Court that Andrew Lafferty be allowed the sum of $1.75 for furnishing a Lock for the Jail door of this County to be paid by the County Trustee of any money in his hands not otherwise appropriated and that he certify according.

Ordered by the Court that Henson Day, Esquire, be allowed to turn the Pulaski road so as not so materially to injure the said Day, provided the said Day open the same to the satisfaction of the present overseer of that part of said road.

Ordered by the Court that Wm. Welch, Sr., be allowed the sum of $4.00 for holding an inquest over the body of Thomas Howard, deceased, to be paid by the County Trustee of any monies in his hands not already appropriated, and that the clerk certify accordingly.

Ordered that Court be adjourned until tomorrow, 9 o'clock. Henry Sharp, John Hillhouse and George Archer, J.P.'s.

SATURDAY, JANUARY 12, 1822

Saturday morning, 9 o'clock, court met according to adjournment. Present, John Millhouse, Henry Sharp, and George Archer, Esquires, Justices.

George Archer, Lazarous Stewart and Elijah Melton came into court and acknowledged themselves severally to be indebted to the State of Tennessee in the sum of $100.00 each to be levied of their goods, chattel lands and tenements to the use of the State to be void on conditions that George Archer make his personal appearance at the Courthouse in the Town of Lawrenceburgh on the first Wednesday after the first Monday in April next, then and there to answer the State upon a charge of Vi Qt Armis, and not depart without leave of the Court.

John McClaren
vs
Elijah Melton   An apeal

This cause is continued on an affadavit of the plaintiff and it is ordered that a commission issue to take the deposition of James Bogard in the Mississippi State in Marion County by giving the adverse party 20 days notice.

The case of Jesse Melton, plaintiff and Stephen Busby, defendant, this cause is continued on affadavit of the plaintiff until the next term of this Court.

George J. Shall
vs   In debt
The Commissioners of the Town of Lawrenceburg

This day came the parties by their attorneys and thereupon came a jury of good and lawful men, to-wit, Joseph Smith, Daniel Hugs, George Rogers, Joel Phillips, James Melton, Richard Freeman, Shadrack Alvis, Wm. Burns, and Stephen Busby, we being elected, tried and sworn well and truly to try this isssueof traverse, upon their oaths do say that the defendant is gilty in manner and form as in the plaintiff's declaration mentioned and they do assess the plaintiff's damage to $36.00 besides costs, whereupon it is considered by the Court that the plaintiff's recover of the defends(sic) the sum of $1,280.00 in the plaintiff's declaration mentioned, together with their costs by them about their suit in this behalf expended, together with his damages aforesaid, by the jurors aforesaid in form aforesaid assessed, and the defendant in mercy & c.

James R. Bennett
vs   Certiorari
Burwell B. Quimby

This day came the parties by their attorneys and the defendant withdraws his plea heretofore pleaded whereupon it is considered by the court that the plaintiff recover of the defendant the sum of $17.00 debt the amount of the judgement rendered before the Justices with the deduction of 50¢ together with the plaintiff's cost by him about his suit in this behalf expended and the defendant in mercy & c.

Eleanor Bryant and Etheldred Thomas came into court and acknowledged themselves each to be indebted to the State of Tennessee in the sum of $100.00 to be levied severaly of their goods, chattel lands and tenements to the use of the State to be void on conditions that Elenor Bryan (sic) appear here on the first Wednesday after the First Monday in April, next, then and there to prosecute and give evidence in behalf of the State against George Archer for an offense of Violamas and that she depart not without leave of the court.

Charles Cook
vs
Charles Woods   Appeal

This day came the parties by their attornesy and the plantiff although solemnly called came not but made default, Whereupon it is considered by the court that the plaintiff recover of the defendant the sum of $10.12 the amount rendered before the justice together with his cost by him about his suit in this behalf expended and the defendant in mercy & c.

Wm. F. Cunningham
vs
David Crockett   Appeal

This day came the parties by their attornies and thereupon came a jury of good and lawful men, to-wit, Thomas Keese, Daniel Bealor, Jesse Helton, Melcher Duncan, Solomon Gresham, James Paine, Jesse McAnally, John Gill, Nathan Clifton, Julius Brewer, Wm. Michie, and Andrew Fugate, who being elected, tried and were sworn well and truly to try this issue of traverse, upon their oaths do sya that the defendant is guilty in manner and form as in the plaintiff's declaration mentioned, whereupon it is considered by the court that the plaintiff recover against the defendant and John Edmundson and John Foster the defendant's surety the sum of $70 debt together with the sum of $1.40 damages, toge___ with his costs by him about his suit in this behalf expended and the defendant in mercy & c.

William Berryhill & Alexander McRae
vs
Richard T. Bailey, Constable

On motion for money collected and his securities, Henry Sharp and Bradley Halford.

This day came Richard T. Bailey who says he cannot gainsay the justice of this motion and by his consent on motion of the plaintiff it is ordered that the plaintiff recover of the said Richard T. Bailey, Constable and his securites the sum of $61.25 this being the amount of an execution in favor of the plaintiff by the said Richard T. Bailey collected of Phillip Parchman including interest and that they recover also the cost of this motion in this behalf expended and the defendant in mercy & c.

Josiah Bowdery
vs
Joseph Halford, Constable   On motion against said Halford

This day came the parties by their attornies and on motion of the plaintiff by his attorney and it appearing to the satisfaction that the two executions in favor of the plaintiff, one for $44.30, the other for $44.06¼, against Thomas Musgrove, (con't.)

was on the 26th day of March 1821 delivered to the defendant and and that the said monies appearing not have been made through the neglect of the defendant except $39.75 which has been paid over to the plaintiff, it is considered by the Court that the plaintiff recover of the defendant and his securities David Crockett and Bradley Halford the sum of $50.69¢ the balance of said execution including interest together with all costs as well before the justices as in this Court and the defendant be in mercy & c.

Daniel Cutbirth
vs
Daniel Hughs   An Appeal

This day came the defendant by his attorney and the plaintiff although solemnly called to come into Court and prosecute his said appeal came not but made default. It is therefore considered by the Court that the defendant recover his cost by him about his defense in this behalf expended, and the plaintiff in mercy & c.

Court was adjourned until Court in Course. John Hillhouse, George Archer, and Henry Sharp, J.P.'s.

MONDAY APRIL 1st, 1822

At a Court of Pleas and Quarter Sessions holden for the County of Lawrence at the Courthouse in the Town of Lawrenceburg on the first Monday in April, 1822, and on the first day of the month, Court met according to adjournment, present, Henson Day, Robert Chaffin, Henry Sharp, Pollard Wisdom, Richard Hill, George Lucas and Lazarous Stewart, Esquires, Justices.

There was produced in open court a bill of sale from Josephus Irvine to James Kendrick for fifty acres of land and acknowledged to be his Act and deed and ordered to be certified for registration.

Ordered by the court that an orphan girl by the name of Betsey Dicus be bound unto Daniel Matthews, to live with him until she arrives at the age of eighteen and that the said Matthews be bound to feed, loge(sic) and cloth said orphan during the term of eight years and cause said orphan to read distinctly in the Bible and Testement and at the end of said eight years to give said orphan a good bed and furniture and spinning wheel and cards, and that he give bond and security which was done accordingly.

At least five of the acting justices being present, to-wit, Henson Day, Henry Sharp, Robert Chaffin, Phillip Chronister, and George Lucas. Berry Hill produced in open court a wolf scalp over four months old which was ordered to be burned and that the clerk certify the same to the State Treasurer accordingly.

Ordered by the Court that Eramus Tracy be allowed to turn the road so as not so materially to injury the said Tracey(sic).

Ordered by the Court that John Hillhouse be allowed to turn the Waterloo Road so as not so materially to injure the said Hillhouse.

Ordered by the Court that Jesse Anglin overseer of the Military Road be directed to work on the new part of the Military road that leads by Peter Winn's and that he keep the same in repairs.

Ordered by the Court that Aaron Choat, Jr., be appointed overseer of the Waterloo Road in the room of Ebenezer Thompson and that he have the same hands to work under his direction and that he keep the same in repair.

Peter Winn came into Court and prayed and obtained a license to keep a House of Ordinary at his own dwelling house, who gave bond and security according to law and took the oath to suppress gaming.

Ordered by the Court that George Vandiver be appointed overseer of the Waterloo Road in the room of John Burns and that he have the same hands to work under his direction and that he keep the same in repairs.

Ordered by the Court that George Rogers, overseer of the Waterloo Road have Enoch Tucker and hands to work under his direction.

Ordered by the Court that Ruthie Burk be allowed to take the child that was bound to Charles Cook and that the said Cook and securities be released from any further obligation.

State
vs
Willson Brown

Samuel McKinney and James Robertson came into Court and acknowledged themselves to be indebted to the State of Tennessee each in the sum of $100.00 to be severaly levied of their goods, chattel lands and tenements to be void on condition that Samuel McKinney make his personal appearance at the Courthouse in the Town of Lawrenceburg on the First Wednesday after the first Monday of this term then and there to give evidence and prosecute in behalf of the State against Willson Brown for an Assault and Battery and that he depart therefrom not without leave of the Court.

Ordered by the Court that D.H. Stockton in Capt. Gresham's Company, that Absalom B. Bailey in Capt. Melton's Co., and John G. Sharp in Capt. Prewitt's Co., be appointed Constables in and for the County of Lawrence who gave bond and security according to law and was qualified.

Ordered by the Court that Peter Winn be appointed overseer of the Military Road in the room of James Strawn and that he have the same hands to work under his direction and that he keep the same in repairs.

Ordered by the Court that Daniel Beeler, John Mitchel, Robert Scoles, Simon Higgs, Edward Higgs, Burrell Gambrell, John Garner or any five of them be appointed a jury of view to view and mark out a road from Lawrenceburg down Smallwood's fork of Sugar Creek and on in a direction toward Elkton and that they make report to next Court.

Ordered by the court that H.J.Bumpass be allowed the sum of two dollars for furnishing a house to hold Court in at last term to be paid by the County Trustee out of any money in his hands not already appropriated and that the Clerk certify the same accordinly

Ordered by the Court that next Saturday be set apart for County business agreeable to an Act of Assembly in such cases made and provided for.

Ordered by the Court that John Bird, Robert Nuton, Wm. Futon, John Holt, Samuel Woolsey be appointed a jury of view to view and mark out a road to turn off at Hurricane Creek and then in a direction to Lambs Ferry and that they make report to next Court.

Ordered by the Court that Willis Lucus be appointed overseer of the road leading from the Giles County line to Wayne County line to commence at Crowson's Fork and work to the Wayne County line and that he have all the hands to work under his direction on the waters of Crowson's Fork and on the West all the hands within 8 miles of said road until said road be cut out.

Ordered by the Court that John Worden be appointed overseer of the road from the Ford of Crowson's Fork to the Giles County line and that he have all the hands within 8 miles of said road except those attached to Lucus, to work under his direction until said road be cut out.

There was produced in open Court two deeds of gift from Shadrack Alvis to his brother John A. Hail for certain property therein mentioned and the said Shadrack Alvis came into Court and acknowledged the execution of the same. Whereupon it is ordered by the Court that it be certified for registration.

There was produced in open Court a deed of gift from David Crockett to Nancy and Ann Musgrave for certain property therein mentioned and which was proven by Wm. M. Crisp, a subscribing witness thereto, which was ordered by the Court to be certified for registration.

There was produced in open Court a deed of gift from Benet Musgrave to his sisters Nan and Ann for certain property therein mentioned and the said Benet Musgrave came into Court and acknowledged the execution of the same, whereupon it is ordered by the Court to be certified for registration.

Thomas Alsup executor of the estate of Thomas Springer, ded'd, came into Court and returned a bill of sale which was read and ordered to be recorded.

State of Tennessee
Lawrence County

Agreeable to an order of the Court in appointing Andrew Brown,

John Burns, Daniel Kilburn to make an allowance to the wife of
Stepehn H. Moore, deceased, for her maintanance for one year.
We have allowed her Seventy-five dollars to-wit, reducting(sic)
nine dollars for 300 weight of pork already laid in which leaves
Sixty-six dollars to be paid to the said widow and is the allowance made to the said widow. Given under our hands and seals
the 22nd Jan.1822, which was received and ordered to be made a
part of record which report was assingned by the said Andrew
Brown, John Burns and Daniel Kilburn.

    Ordered by the Court that Andrew Brown be allowed the sum
of $3.00 and John Burns and Daniel Kilburn be allowed the sum
of $1.00 each and Gilbert McMillain be allowed the sum of $2.00
for their services as commissioners and clerk at the sale of
Stephen H. Moore, deceased, to be paid by the County Trustee out
of any money in his hands not already appropriated and that
the clerk certify accordingly.

    Ordered that Court be adjourned until tomorrow, 9 o'clock.
Mansel Crisp, Jeremiah Jackson, Phillip Chronister, Andrew
Brown, and Samuel Poteet, J.P.'s.

TUESDAY APRIL 2nd, 1822

    Tuesday morning 9 O'clock court met according to adjourn-
ment, present, Mansel Crisp, Jeremiah Jackson, Phillip Chronister, Andrew Brown and Samuel Poteete, Esquires, Justices.

    The Sheriff returned into Court the venore facias return-
able to this term, containing the following named persons, to-
wit, John Wisdom, Henry Sharp, Joseph Gosnal, Wm. Smith, Jacob
Blythe, Elijah Melton, James Argo, John Mitchell, Samuel Mc-
Clain, Robert Haynes, Edward Mobly, Stephen Roland, Andrew
Johnston, Micagy Lewis, Thomas Allsup, Green Depriest, William
Lucus, Isaac P. Willson, Burel B. Quimby, Wm. Henderson, Simon
Edwards, Adam Chronister, John Anthony, Ebenezer Kanada, John
Ray, with the following endorsement,"Executed on all but Thomas
Allsup, Wm. Henderson and Ebenezer Kanada, by me E.C.Crisp,
D. Shff", and upon calling the venire aforesaid the following
named persons appeared, to-wit, Samuel McClain, Henry Brashears,
I.P.Willson, Robert Haynes, Elijah Melton, Micagy Lewis, John
Ray, John Mitchel, Adam Chronister, John Wisdom, John Anthony,
Wm. Lucus, Stephen Roland, Green DePriest, simon Edwards,
Joseph Gosnal, of whom the following named persons were drawn
as grand jurors, to enquire for the body of the County of Law-
rence, to-wit, Samuel McClain, who was appointed foreman,
Henry Brashears, I.P.Willson, Robert Haynes, Elijah Melton,
Micagy Lewis, John Ray, John Mitchel, Adam Chronister, John
Wisdom, John Anthony, Wm. Lucas, and Stephen Roland, who were
qualified and after having received their charge withdrew to
consider of their presentments under the care of John Sellars,
a Constable, sworn to attend them.

    The Court having advertised on the First day of this term
that they should proceed on this day to the election of County
Trustee and Coroner for this County, and proceeded to the election of the same, whereupon it was found that Thomas Welch was

duly elected County Trustee, and Wm. H. Crisp, Coroner, who gave bond and security and was qualified.

Jesse Helton
vs
Stephen Busby   Trespass on Case

This day came the parties by their attorneys and therefore came a jury of good and lawful men, to-wit, Green Depriest, Joseph Gosnal, Annuel Adkisson, Wm. Hefly, John Edmundson, Samuel Askew, Daniel Hill, Wm. Cook, James McConnell, Nathan McClendon, Lewis, and Wm. Welch, who being elected, tried and sworn, well and truly to speak the truth upon this issue joined upon their oaths do say that the defendant is not guilty as in plaintiff's declaration mentioned. It is therefore considered by the Court that the defendant recover of the plaintiff his cost by him about his defence in this behalf expended and the defendant in mercy & c.

Hamilton Reynolds
vs
Patterson Crockett

On motion of the defendant by his attorney and as on affadavit of the defendant, whereupon it is ordered by the Court that this cause be continued until the next term of this Court.

Aaron Anglin
vs
Samuel Askew

On motion of the defendant by his attorney and as on affadavit of the defendant whereupon it is ordered by the Court that this cause be continued until the next term of this Court.

John McClain
vs
Elishar Helton   Appeal

This day came the parties by their attorneys and thereupon came a jury of good and lawful men, to-wit, Joseph Gosnal, Green Depriest, Stephen Busby, Jesse Helton, Eliott Lindsey, Alexander Miller, James Payne, Wm. McCann, Josiah Tippet, Joel Phillips, A.C. Houston, John A. Hail, who being elected, tried and sworn well and truly to try this matter in dispute between the parties upon their oaths do say that they find in favor of the defendant. It is therefore considered by the Court that the defendant recover of the plaintiff his cost by him about his suit in this behalf expended and the plaintiff in mercy & c.

John McClain
vs
William Null   An Appeal

This day came the plaintiff by his attorney and the defendant although solemnly called came not but made default. It is therefore consdiered by the Court that the plaintiff recover of the defendant his cost by him about his suit in this behalf expended and the defendant in mercy & c.

165

Andrew Brown
vs
John Hamilton   An Original Attachment

This day came the plaintiff by his attorney and the defendant although solemnly called came not but made default. It is therefore considered by the Court that the plaintiff recover of the defendant the sum of $00.00 the debt in the declaration mentioned with the sum of $5.05 interest thereon together with his costs by him about his suit in this behalf expended and the defendant in mercy & c.

Joseph Lemaster
vs
Andrew Lafferty   Case

Ordered that this cause be continued by consent until the next term of this Court and that the parties have commission to take the depositions generally by their giving the adverse party 20 days notice for depositions taken out of this State and 10 days notice in the State, of the time and place of taking the same.

Andrew Brown
vs
Reynols(sic) May   Attachment-Garnisee

This day came the plaintiff by his attorney and Elishuh Melton after having been duly qualified to declare what of property debts or effects he hath in his hands belonging to John Hambleton or knows of in the hands of any other person, agreeable to Act of Assembly. The said Melton declareth that he has a promissary note of $100.00 given by Reynolds Mayto said Hambleton due the 25th day of December last and dated the 20th of November, 1821. Whereupon it is considered by the Court that the said Melton deliver over said note to said plaintiff and that the plaintiff have judgement for the same which note was handed over in open Court accordingly.

Mansel Crisp who was appointed at the last term to take a list of taxable property and poles for the year made return according to order which was ordered to be recorded accordingly.

Henson Day who was appointed at the last term to take a list of taxable property and poles for the year made return according to order which was ordered to be recorded accordingly.

Thomas Welch who was appointed at the last term to take a list of taxable property and poles for the ear made return according to order which was ordered to be recorded accordingly.

Jacob Pennycuff who was appointed atht eh last term to take a list of taxable property and poles for the year made return according to order which was ordered to be recorded accordingly.

Court adjourned until tomorrow, 9 o'clock. Mancel Crisp, Jeremiah Jackson, George Lucus, Phillip Chronister and Samuel Poteet, J.P.'s.

WEDNESDAY APRIL 3rd, 1822

Wednesday morning, 9 o'clock, Court met according to adjournment, present, Mansil Crisp, Jeremiah Jackson, George Lucas, Philip Chronister and Samuel Poteet, Esquires, Justices.(Editors note, the Clerk had first written the name "Andrew Jackson" but had run a line through the word Andrew and inserted above it the name Jeremiah.)

State
vs
William Welch   Assault and battery

Thiss day came the Solicitor General in behalf of the State as well as the defendant in his proper person and the defendant being charged upon the Bill of Indictment pleads thereto not gilty and for his trial puts himself upon his Country and the Solicitor General for the State, likewise, whereupon came a jury of good and lawful men to-wit, Joseph Gosnal, Green Depriest, Erastus Tipet, Josiah Tipet, George Rogers, Solomon Asbel, Samuel McKinney, Warren Mason, Thomas Spencer, Nathan Jobe, Yarnel Reece, Levi Lewis, who being elected tried and sworn well and truly to try this issue of travis(sic) upon their oaths do say that the defendant is gilty(sic) in manner and form as in the bill of indictment is charged against him. It is therefore considered by the Court that hemake his fine with the State to $6.00 and that he pay the cost of this prosecution and that he be committed to the custody of the Sheriff until said fine and costs are paid or made safe by security.

State
vs
Jacob Turnbow   Assault and battery

This day came the Solicitor General in behalf of the State as well as the defendant in his proper person and the defendant being charged upon the bill of presentment pleads therefore not gilty and for his trial puts himself upon his Country and the Solicitor General for the State, likewise, whereupon came a jury of good and lawful men, to-wit, George Hanks, Nathaniel Mason, Simon Edwards, Michael Sherley, Joseph Gosnal, Michael Speck, Wm. White, Wm. Poter, Silas Rackley, Lewis Franks, Green Depriest, and Philip Jones, who being elected tried and sworn, well and truly to try this issue of travis(sic) upon their oaths do say that the defendant is gilty(sic) of an assault as in the bill of present(sic) he is charged. It is therefore considered by the Court that he make his fine with the State to the sum of $1.50 and that he pay the cost of this prosecution and that he be taken & c.

Yarnel Reece and William Hefley came into Court and acknowledgedthemselves to be indebted to the State of Tennessee each in the sum of $100.00 to be severly levied of their goods, chattel land and tenements to be void on condition that Yarnel Reece make his personal appearance at the Courthouse in the Town of Lawrenceburg on the first Wednesday after the first Monday in July next, then and there to answer the State in a charge for an assault and battery committed by him on the body of Thomas Howard and further to be delt with as the law directs and that he depart therefrom not with(sic) leave of the Court.

167

State
vs
Daniel McIntire   Assault

This day came the Solicitor General in behalf of the State as well as the defendant in his proper person and the defendant being charged upon the bill of presentment pleads thereto not gilty and for his trial puts himself upon the Country and the Solicitor General for the State likewise. Whereupon came a jury of good and lawful men, to-wit, Wm. Hofley, Joseph Gosnal, Richard Freemon, Samuel Thomas, John L. Henson, Philip Jones, Wm. Cook, John Vorus, Aaron Anglin, Green Depriest, Warren Mason, and John McClendon, who being elected, tried and sworn well and truly to try this issue of Travis upon their oaths do say that the defendant is gilty of an assault as in the bill of presentment as he is charged. It is therefore considered by the Court that he make his fine with the State the sum of $5.20 and that he pay the cost of this prosecution and that he be taken & c.

Samuel McKinney, Jonathon Jones, Erastus Tipet came into Court and acknowledged themselves indebted to the State each in the sum of $100.00 to be severly levied of their goods, chattel lands and tenements to be void on condition that Samuel McKinney make his personal appearance at the Courthouse in the Town of Lawrenceburg on the First Wednesday after the First Monday in July, next, then and there to prosecute and give evidence in behalf of the State and that he depart therefrom not without leave of the Court.

State
vs
Hartwell J. Bumpass   Affray

This day came the Solicitor General in behlaf of the State as well as the defendant in his proper person and the defendant being charged upon the bill of indictment pleads thereto gilty and for his trial puts himself upon the justice and mercy of the Court. Whereupon it is considered by the Court that he make his fine with the State to the sum of $1.20 and that he pay the cost of this prosecution and that he be taken & c, who gave Jonathon Jobe as security for the payment of fine and cost.

State   Affray
vs
Lewis Yarnel(Could mean Gosnel, editors)

This day came the Solicitor General in behalf of the State as well as the defendant in his proper person and the defendant being charged upon the bill ofpresentment pleads thereto not gilty and for his trial puts himself upon his Country and the Solicitor for the State likewsie. Whereupon came a jury of good and lawful men,to-wit, Joseph Gosnal, Green Depriest, Erastus Tipet, Josiah Tipet, George Rogers, Solomon Asbel, Samuel McKinney, Warren Mason, <u>Thomas Spencer</u>, Nathan Jobe, Yarnel Reece, and Bryan McClondon, who being elected, tried and sworn well and truly to try this issue of traverse upon their oaths do say that the defendant is gilty in manner and form as in the bill of presentment is charged against him. It is therefore considered by the Court that he make his fine with the State to the sum of $7.00 and that he pay the cost of this prosecution and that he remain in the custody of the Sheriff until said debt and costs are paid or made safe by security.

Patrick McGuire
vs
John McClish   Attachment

The defendant failing to appear and the attachment awarded against the defendant's estate being returned executed on 480 Acres of land more or less whereon John McClish formerly lived, lying on Big Buffalow Creek, supposed to be the property of the said John McClish, B. Halford, Sheriff. And the defendant although solemnly called came not but made default and on motion of the plaintiff by his attorney it is consdered by the Court that the plaintiff recover of the defendant the sum of $182.55½ debt and damages $9.93½ in the declaration mentioned and his costs by him about this behalf expended and the defendant in mercy and it is ordered that the Sheriff make sale of the land by him attached according to law and out of the money arising from said sale pay and satisfy this judgement unto the plaintiff and return the overpay if any unto the defendant and that he also return an accounting of the sale to Court.

State
vs
George Rodgers   Assault and battery

This day came the Solicitor General in behalf of the State as well as the defendant in his proper person and by consent of the Court it is ordered that a Nol Prosequi be entered against the County and the defendant assumes upon himself all costs and that the defendant be taken & c, who gave Erastus Tipet as security.

State
vs
Miles Birdson   An Affray

This day came the Solicitor General in behalf of the State as well as the defendant in his proper person and by consent of the Court it is ordered that a Nol Prosequi be entered against the County and the defendant assumes upon himself all costs and that the defendant be taken & c., who gave George Rogers as security.

State
vs
William Craig   An Affray

This day came the Solicitor General in behalf of the State who moved the Court that a Noli Prosequi be entered up against the County for costs. It is therefore considered by the Court that the same be done and that the County pay all those entitled to cost in behalf of the State and out of any monies in the hands of the County Trustee not otherwise appropriated.

E.W.Tipton
vs   Debt
Gabriel Bumpass

This day came the plaintiff by his attorney and the defendant being solemnly called came not but made default. Therefore it is considered by the Court that the plaintiff recover of the defendant the sum of $100.00 the debt in the declaration mentioned together with $9.00 interest thereon up to the rendition of the judgement together with his costs by him about his suit in this behalf expended and the defendant in mercy & c.

Patrick McGuire
vs
John McClish   Orignial Attachment

This day came the plaintiff by his attorney and the defendent being solemnly called came not but made default, therefore it is consdered by the Court that the plaintiff recover against the defendant the sum of $180.55½ the debt in the declaration mentioned, together with $9.93 and 3/4 cents interest, thereon up to the time of the rendition of this judgement, together with his costs by him about his suit in this behalf expended, and the defendant in mercy & c., whereupon upon motion of the plaintiff by his attorney, it is ordered that the Sheriff expose to sale the estate of the said defendant attached by the plaintiff to satisfy the plaintiff, his debt, interest and costs aforesaid.

Lemuel Phillips
vs
John McClish   Attachment

This day came the plaintiff by his attorney and the defendant being solemnly called came not but made default. Therefore it is considered by the Court that the defendant recover of the plaintiff the sum of $100.00 debt in the declaration mentioned, together with $6.66 and 3/4 cents interest thereon up to the rendition of judgement, together with his cost by him about his suit in this behalf expended, and the defendant in mercy & c., whereupon motion of the plaintiff by his attorney it is ordered by the Court that the sheriff expose to sale the estate of the said defendant attached by the plaintiff to satisfy the plaintiff his debt, interest and costs aforesaid.

Groves & Smith
vs
John McClish   Attachment

This day came the plaintiff by their attorney and the defendant although solemnly called came not but made default, it is therefore considered by the Court that the plaintiff recover of the defendant the sum of $463.06½ debt in the declaration mentioned , together with the sum of $29.00 interest thereon up to the rendition of the judgement, together with their costs by them about their suit in this bhalf expended, and the defendant in mercy & c., whereupon, upon motion of the plaintiff by their attorney, it is ordered that the Sheriff expose to sale the estate of the defendant attached by the plaintiff's to satisfy the debt, interest and costs aforesaid.

(Editors note; The following is not a part of records from this book, but research shows that these judgements involve 480 Acres a tract of land which had been reserved to John McClish/McLish, by the Treaty of the Chickasaw Council House, Sept. 20, 1815 and confirmed by treaty of "Old Town", Oct. 19, 1818. McClish/McLish -name found spelt both ways- was an Indian and at one time kept a stand on the old Natchez Trace. This land was "secured" to him-on the north side of Buffalo River-.Part of this land was

170

as mentioned above sold by the sheriff and purchased by Patrick McGuire of Maury Co. Tenn., to whom Thomas J. Matthews, as sheriff made a deed, as shown by the records in the Register of Deeds office at Lawrenceburg. This land was at that time in Lawrence County, but as a result of changes in the County lines, is now located in Lewis County. At the time of this sherriff sale the said John Mc Clish had removed to the " Chickasaw Nation."

Court was adjourned until tomorrow 9 o'clock. Jeremiah Jackson Mansil Crisp, Phillip Cronister and George Lucas, J.P.'s.

THURSDAY APRIL 4th 1822

Thursday morning 9 o'clock court met according to adjournment, present, Mansil Crisp, Jeremiah Jackson, George Lucas, Phillip Cronister(sic) and Samuel Poteet, Esquires, Justices.

The State
vs   Judgement Tiplers house
Wm. Burns & Michael Speck

This day came the Solicitor General in behalf of the State as well as the defendants in their proper persons and the defendant being charged upon the bill of Indictment pleads thereto gilty, and for trial puts themselves upon the justice and mercy of the Court whereupon it is considered by the Court that they make their fine with the State to the sum of $2.00 and that they pay the costs of this prosection and that the defendants be taken & c.

The Grand Jurors of the County of Lawrence returned the following Bills of Indictments to the State. Etheldred Thomas for pety(si larceny, State vs H.J.Bumpass for an affray, State vs James McHughs for an affray, Simon McClain, foreman of the Grand Jury.

State
vs   (Editors note; Nothing was recorded for this case.
Solomon Gresham

James Moody
vs   Appeal
Charles Cook

It appearing from the record and recollection of this Court fully to the Noli Facias of said Court that the Clerk did not at last term enter the judgement correctly in this cause and it being ordered by the Court that a judgement now for then be entered. It is therefore considered by the Court that the Defendant recover of the plaintiff his cost about his defense in this behalf expended and the plaintiff in mercy & c.

Presley Ward
vs   Certiorari
David Crockett

It appearing to the satisfaction of the Court by the record of this cause that no judgement was rendered in this cause against Bradley Halford and John King, the securities as should have been done, wherefore, upon motion of the ptff., by his attorney it is ordered by the Court that judgement now for then be entered up against the said Crockett and his said securities . It is therefore considered by the Court that the plaintiff recover of the said David Crockett and the said Bradley Halford and John King, his securities the sum of $70.7o debt, together with the sum of $1.43 interest, the amount of said judgement and his costs about his suit in this behalf expended, and the defendant in mercy & c.

Hartwell J. Bumpass
vs   Certiorari
Hugh H. Withers

    This day came the parties by their attornies as well as the defendant in his proper person and plaintiff releases his debt to the saidDefendant and the said Defendant asumes the payment of the costs except the attornies tax for which is not charged. It is therefore considered by the Court that said defendant be discharged of his debt and that the plaintiff recover of the defendant and Thomas D.Martin his security the sum of $5.65 his cost in this behalf expended & c.

State
vs   Judgement for Petty Larceny
Etheldred Thomas

    This day came the Solicitor General in behalf of the State as well as the defendant in his proper person and the defendant being charged upon the bill of Indictment pleads thereto not gilty and for his trial puts himself upon the Country and the Solicitor General for the State likewise. Whereupon came a jury of good and lawful men, to-wit, Joseph Gosnal, Green Depriest, Wm. Poter, John L. Henson, James Payne, Michael Waldrup, Austin Kendrick, Wm. Welch,Sr., George Rodgers, Nathan Jobe, Solomon Asbel, Erastus Tipet, who being elected, tried and sworn well and truly to try this issue of Travis and a true verdict to render agreeable to evidence upon their oaths do say that the defendant is gilty in manner and form as charged in the Bill of Indictment and they do say the value of the corn stolen as charged in the Bill is 25 cents. Whereupon the defendant by leave of court enters a rule(sic) to show cause why a new trial should be granted.

    Whereas John Edmundson obtained an execution against David Crockett on the 31st day of Jan., 1822 against the goods and chattels lands and tenements of David Crockett directed to any lawful officer of said County for the sum of $90.00 debt and the further sum of 25 cents cost before Mansil Crisp, a Justice in and for said County and the officer whose hands the execution was first returned said execution with the following endorsement thereon, to-wit, Feb. 4th 1822, levied on 160 Acres ofland lying on the head of Shoal Creek about 3 miles East of Lawrenceburg where Reuben Tripp and Thomas Pryor now live, supposed to be the property of David Crockett,E.E Crisp, D. Sheriff. Whereupon it is ordered by the Court that a Venetito Exponas issue to the Sheriff commanding him to sell said land to satisfy said judgment and make return according to law.

    Whereas, John Brumly obtained a judgement against David Crockett on the 2nd day of Feb., 1822, against the goods, chattels lands and tenements of David Crockett directed to any lawful officer of said County, Greetings, for the sum of $10 and ¼ cent debt, and 75 cents cost before Mansil Crisp, a Justice of the Peace in and for Said County, and the officer who hands said execution was put maze the following endorsement, to-wit, Feby 4th, 1822, levied on 160 Acres of land on the head of Shoal Creek, about 3 miles East of Lawrenceburg where Thomas Prier(sic) and Reuben Tripp now live, supposed to be the property of David Crockett. Whereupon it is ordered that a Venetitio Exponas issue to the Sheriff commanding him to sell said land to satisy said judgement and make return agreeable to law. E.C.(sic) Crisp, ͞. Shff.

Whereas Presley Ward received a judgment against David Crockett on the 4th Oct., 1821, against the goods, chattels lands and tenements of David Crockett, directed to the Shff. of said County the sum of $73.13 debt, and costs, $10.44 and the shff returned said execution with the following endorsements, to-wit, Came to hand same day issued, Feby. 19th, 1822, levied on 160 Acres of land lying on the head of Shoal Creek about 3 miles East of Lawrenceburg where Rueben Tripp and Thomas Pryor now lives, supposed to be the property of David Crockett, E.C. Crisp, Shff. Whereupon it is considered by the Court that a Venetitio Exp9nas issue to the Shff. commanding him to sell said land to satisfy said judgment and make return according to law.

Jesse Melton
vs
Stephen Busby

The plaintiff prays an appeal to the next Circuit Court of this County from the Judgment of this Court and having given bond and security it is granted accordingly.

Elisha Melton
vs
John McClaren, Sr.   Appeal

The plaintiff in this case came being dissatisfied with the judgment of the Court prays therefrom an appeal in the nature of a writ of error to the next Circuit Court of this County and having given bond and security agreeable to law it is granted according

George Archer and George Michie came into Court and acknowledged themselves to be indebted to the State of Tennessee each in the sum of $100.00 to be severally levied of their goods, chattels lands and tenements to be paid on condition that George Archer make his appearance at the courthouse in the town of Lawrenceburg on the first Wednesday after the first Monday in July, next, then and there to answer the State upon a charge and further to be delt with as the law directs and that he depart not without leave of the Court.

Ealenor(sic) Bryant came into Court and acknowledged herself indebted to the State of Tennessee in the sum of $100.00 to be severally levied of her goods, chattels lands and tenements to be void on condition that Eleanor Bryant make her personal appearance at the courthouse in the town of Lawrenceburg on the first Wednesday after the first Monday in July , next, then and there to prosecute and give evidence in behalf of the State and that she depart not without leave of the Court.

State
vs   An Affray
Solomon Gresham

  This day came the Solicitor General in behalf of the State as well as the defendant in his proper person and by consent of the Court it is ordered that a Noli Prosequi be entered against the County and the defendant assumes to pay the costs of this prosecution and that the defendant be taken & c.

  Ordered that Court be adjourned until tomorrow, 9 o'clock. Mancil Crisp, Samuel D. Poteet and Pollard Wisdom, J.P.'s/

FRIDAY APRIL 5, 1822

  Friday morning nine o'clock, court met according to adjournment, present, Mansel Crisp, Jeremiah Jackson, George Lucus, Philip Chronister and Samuel D. Poteet, Esquires, Justices.

  There was produced in open Court a power of Attorney from David Crockett to Mansil Crisp, which was proven by the oath of Wm. Lucus and Green Depriest, subscribing witnesses thereto, and ordered to be certified for registration accordingly.

State
vs   Judgment Assault and Battery
James McHughs

  This day came the Solicitor General in behalf of the State as well as the defendant in his proper person and the defendant being charged upon the Bill of Indictment pleads thereto not gilty and for his trial puts himself upon the Country and the Solicitor General for the State, likewise, whereupon came a jury of good and lawful men, to-wit, Issac W. Brown, Warren Mason, Wm. Welch, John McClendon, Austin Kendrick, James Payne, Wm. Poter, Nathan McClendon, Green Depriest, Joseph Gosnal, James Forgy and Nathan Jobe, who being elected tried and sworn well and truly to try this issue of travis upon their oaths do say that the defendant is gilty in manner and form as in the Bill of Indictment. It is therefore ordered by the Court that he make his fine with the State to the sum of $13.00 and that he pay the costs of this prosecution and that the defendant be taken & c., who gave Joseph Halford and Stephen Roland as securities for the payment of said fine and cost.

Martial D. Spain
vs   Judgment for debt
Richard T. Bailey & Josephus Irvine

  This day came the parties by their attorneys and thereupon came a jury of good and lawful men, to-wit, Samuel McClaren, Henry Brashears, I.P. Willson, Robert Haynes, Elijah Melton, Micagy Lewis, John Ray, John Mitchel, Adam Chronister, John Wisdom, John Anthony, Wm. Lucus, who being elected, tried and sworn well and truly to try this issue joined, upon their oaths do say that the defendant is gilty in manner and form as in the plaintiff's declaration mentioned and they do assess the plaintiff damage by reason thereof to the sum of $11.20 besides cost. Whereupon it is considered by the Court that the plaintiff recover of the defendant the sum of $226.75 together with his damages aforesaid by the jury aoforesaid, in form aforesaid assessed together with his costs by him about his suit in this behalf expended and from which judgmentthe defendant prayed an appeal to the Circuit Court of this County who having given bond and security it is granted him accordingly.

John Davis
vs
Ezekiel Mobly   Judgment for debt

This day came the parties by their attorneys and thereupon came a jury of good and lawful men, to-wit(editors note: here are listed same jurors as in case of Spain AS LISTED ON LAST PAGE) who being elected, tried and sworn well and truly to try this issue of traverse joined upon their oaths do say that the defendant is gilty in manner and form as the plaintiff's declaration mentioned and they do asess the plaintiff's damage by reason thereof to $51.00. Whereupon it is considered by the court that the plaintiff recover of the defendant the sum of $155.40 together with his damages aforesaid, by the jury aforesaid in form aforesaid asessed together with his costs by him about his suit in this behalf expended and from which judgment the defendant prayed an appeal to the Circuit Court of this County who having given bond and security it is granted accordingly.

Henry Sharp, Ranger of Lawrence County
vs
Solomon Asbel

This day came the parties by their attorneys and thereupon came a jury of good and lawful men, to-wit, Samuel McClaren, Henry Brashea5s, Isaac P. Willison, Robert Haynes, Elijah Melton, John Ray, Micagy Lewis, John Mitchel, Adam Chronister, John Wisdom, John Anthony, Wm. Lucus, who being elected tried and sworn well and truly to try this matter in dispute between the parties and a true verdict given agreeably to evidence having heard the evidence, retired to consider of their verdict and return into Court and say that they are not agreed. Whereupon by consent of the parties, Samuel McLean one of the said jurors is withdrawn and it is considered by the Court that this cause stand for trial at next term.

Nathan McLendon
vs   Judgment
John Hillhouse & Bradley Halford

This day came the parties by their attorneys and the defendants withdraw their plea heretofore pleaded and assumes upon themselves the cost of this suit. It is therefore considered by the Court that the plaintiff recover of the defendants his cost by him about his suit in this behalf expended and the defendant in mercy&c

Ordered that Court be adjourned until tomorrow at nine o'clock
Mansel Crisp, Samuel D. Poteet, and Pollard Wisdom, J.P.'s

SATURDAY APRIL 6th, 1822

Saturday morning April 6th 1822 Court met according to adjournment, present, Mansil Crisp, Samuel D. Poteet, and Pollard Wisdom, Esquires, Justices.

Aaron P. Cunningham
vs
William Hanks   Case

This day the defendant was solemnly called to come into Court and plead to the declaration filed by the plaintiff but came not and made default. Whereupon it is considered by the Court that the plaintiff recover of the defendant his costs by him about his suit in this behalf expended but because the Court are not informed what is the amount of damage which plaintiff has in this case sustained from the defendant it is ordered by the Court that a writ of inquiry issue and that thereupon the Sheriff have here before this Court at next term a jury of good and lawful men to inquire upon doth say what damages the plaintiff hath sustained.

Joshua Bowdry
vs
Phillip Parchman   Case

This day the defendant though solemnly called to come into Court and plead to the declaration of the plaintiff came not but made default. Whereupon it is considered by the Court that the plaintiff recover of the defendant his cost by him about his suit in this behalf expended but because the Court are not informed what is the amount of the damages which plaintiff has sustained from the defendant it is ordered by the Court that a writ of inquiry issue and that thereupon the sheriff have before the court at next term a jury of good and lawful men to inquire and upon oath say what damages the plaintiff hath sustained.

State
vs
Etheldred Thomas   Indictment P. Larceny

The defendant who was recognized in the sum of_____dollars appear at this court and anser the State on a charge of petit larceny and not depart hence without leave of the Court is this day solemnly called to come into Court and comes not but makes default, whereupon it is considered by the Court that the State recover of him_____dollars the amount of his said Recognizance unless he appear at the next term of this Court and shew cause to the contrary and it is ordered that a scri facias issue accordingly.

State
vs
Etheldred Thomas

Samuel Thomas who was bound in a Recognizance in the sum of_____dollars to be void on condition that Etheldred Thomas would appear at this term before this Court and anser the State on a charge of petit larceny and not depart hence without leave of the Court was solemnly called to come into Court this day and bring with him the said Etheldred Thomas but came not nor brought said Etheldred, but made default, whereupon it is considered by the Court that the State recover of him ____dollars the amount of his recignenance aforesaid unless he appear at the next term of this Court and shew cause to the contrary and it is ordered that a scri facias issue accordingly.

State
vs
Etheldred Thomas
    Solomon Grishan who was bound in a Recognizance in the sum of _____dollars to be void on condition that Etheldred Thomas make his personal appearance at this term before this Court to answer the State upon a charge of petty larceny but made default, although solemnly called to come into Court and bring the body of Etheldred Thomas came not but made default. It is therefore considered by the Court that the State recover of him the sum of_____ dollars the amount of his Recognizance aforesaid, unless he appears at next term and shew cause if any he has and it is ordered that a Scri facias issue accordingly.

State
vs   Indictment Petit Larceny
Etheldred Thomas
    The Jury having returned a verdict of gulity against defendant and he having by leave of Court entered a Nile to shew cause for a new trial and now when the Court are ready to proceed thereon and consider of the saem and defendant though solemnly called coming not but made default, and the Court not being well advised what in this behalf should be done upon said rule and said verdict considered order that the business be continued to next term of this Court to be then finally adjudged and acted upon and that a Capious issue commanding the sheriff to take him said defendant and and him keep and secure without bond, or bail, or monie prize and produce him before this Court at next term.

    Ordered that George Lucas, Esquire, be appointed overseer of the Crowson Fork road and that he have M.H.Buchanan and hands, Wm. Lucas and hands, Green Depriest and hands, and James Bumpass and hands to work under his direction, and that he keep the same in repairs.

    John A. Haile who was appointed Administrator to the estate of John Badgett returned a list of the sale which was received and ordered to be recorded.

    Ordered that Wm. Reynolds be appointed overseer of the Shelbaville (sic) road from the pole bridge west to the County line, and that he have all the hands to work under his direction that live on Granddday(sic) Creek, Piney and Chisems(sic) Fork as low down so as to include John Burns and that he kkeep the same in repair.

    Ordered that John Wasen be appointed overseer of the Shelbavile road from Crowson's Fork to the Military Road and that he have all hands west of McKnights and on the creek below said McKnights northwardly so as to leave Nathan Clifton on the upper end and so continue, and that he keep the same in repair.

Ordered that the justices who was appointed to take a list of taxable property and polls at the last term of this Court who having not made return of the same be reappointed and that they make return without delay and recorded by the clerk accordingly.

Ordered that the Sheriff be directed to summon the following named persons to attend at the next Circuit Court as Jurors, to-wit, Wm. M. Crisp, Henry Sharp, George Lucas, Wm. Burlston, Phillip Chronister, George Isom, Jacob Pennington, Robert Brashears, Henry Moody, Robert Chaffin, Thomas Welch, James McMillian, James McConnell, Samuel McConnell, Alexander Robertson, Andrew Brown, Wm. Tucker, Enoch Tucker, John A. Hail, Henson Day, Richard Hill, Thomas Allsup, Henry Phenix, and Alexander Cessims.

Ordered that D.H. Stockton and I. J. Sharp be appointed Constables to attend at the next Circuit as such.

Ordered that the Sheriff be directed to summon the following named persons to attend at the next County Court as jurors, to-wit, James Bumpass, Hartwell J. Bumpass, John Buchanan, Wm. Seahorn, Wm. Voss, John Vorters, Abraham Pennington, Samuel Woolsey, Simon Higgs, Wm. Newton, Warren Mason, Gilbert F. Simonton, Nathan Jobe, Sterling Lindsey, Francis Wisdom, James Smith, Joseph Smith, James Moore, Melcher Duncan, Wm. F. Cunningham, Nathan McLendon, Wm. White, Daniel McClary, Jacob Turnbow and James Brooks.

Ordered that John McClarin and Absolom B. Bailey, Constables be appointed to attend as such at the next County Court.

Ordered by the Court that Richard Hill have till the next term of this Court to find a bond that Jane Gray gave him for the support of her child.

Ordered by the Court that George Isom be appointed overseer of the Crowson Fork Road from the Shelbyville Road to Steels Iron Works, and that he have all the hands on big and little Buffalow in this County as high up as to include the Pennington's and that he keep the same in repair.

Ordered by the Court that Austin Kendrick be appointed overseer of the Shelbaville Road from Esq. Welch's to the Giles County line and that he have all the hands to work under his direction that live East of McKnights and within eight miles of said road and that he keep the same in repair.

Ordered that Wm. Crisp, John McCannelly, Josephus Irvine, Wm. Seahorn, Jesse Helton, Nathan McLendon, Ebenezer Thompson, or any five of them be appointed a jury of view to view and mark out a road the nearest and best way from Lawrenceburg in a direction to Steels Iron Works and that they make report to next Court.

There was produced in open court a deed from Samuel H. Williams to Nathan McLendon which was proven by Wm. Davis and James Terrell subscribing witnesses thereto which was ordered to be certified for registration.

Ordered by the Court that Esquire Holland an orphan boy be bound unto William Poter until he arrives at the age of 21 years he being under 17 at the time, and that the said Potter(sic) be bound to learn said orphan the Hatting business and he is further bound to feed, lodge, and cloth(sic) said orphan during the term he may stay and at the expiration of said term to give said orphan two good suits of clothes and six months scooling(sic), who gave bond and security according to law.

Ordered by the Court that Mary McGee be allowed to keep her two daughters, and the said Mary McGee binds herself to give her daughters a bed and furniture each and school them to read distinctly in the Bible and Testement, who gave bond and security according to law.

Ordered that Court be adjourned until Court in Course.

Mansil Crisp, J.P.
Thomas Welch, J.P.
H. Day, J.P.

(Editors note: The above order of adjournment is the last ORDER in this book, however, below the same and on same page appears the following signature and address;

Chester A. Crockett
Jany, 25th 1936
Okla City, Okla.
GREAT, GREAT GRANDSON OF DAVID CROCKETT.

AND RIGHT ABOVE THIS WAS WRITTEN, Rev. Jas. ?, Norman, Ky.

One more page follows this closing day of Court, Sat. April 6, 1822. Possibly micro-filmer or clerk failed to place it in proper place.)

NINE DAYS OF JURY BUSINESS IN 1818
Wisdom, Forbes, Hillhouse and Rea--Tickets issued.

At least five of the acting Justices being present, to-wit, Henson Day, Mancil Crisp, Andrew Brown, John Hillhouse, Robert Chaffin. James Hail produced in court one wolf scalp over 4 months old which was ordered to be burned and that the clerk certify the same to the State Treasurer accordingly.

I do hereby certify that the above is a true copy of the records of said Court.

TEST: M. H. Buchanan
CLERK OF SAID COURT

INDEX

A

Aaron 95
Abner 56
Adair 9,21,22,45,55,58,59
    109,111,117.
Adams 9,54,57,63,64
    100,107,111
Adkins 21,33,56,109,117
Adkinson (See Adkins)
Adkisson 2,32,45,46,56,57,
    58,59,111,115,
    116,118,136,149,
    164,
Adkison (See Adkisson)
Agfley 136
Alexander 1,6,8,32,45,46
    54,55,58,59
Alford 8,32,46,55,85,92,94,
    99,129
Allford (See Alford)
Alison 1,32,46,54
Allison (See Alison)
Allen 29,85
Alsup (See Allsup)
Allsup 3,5,9,12,14,16,23,
    26,33,35,36,41,43,44,
    47,54,56,57,58,62,64,
67,72,73,76,78,81,82,83,98,
106, 109,116,118,123,124,125,
126,127,137,143,147,155,
163,177
Alton (See Altum)
Altum 46,56,98,106,109
    115,132,136
Alvis (See Allvice)
Allvice 8,10,11,23,47,51,56,
    59,82,83,86,108,118,
    122,123,129,158,162
Anderson 98,132,137,138
Anglin 10,11,34,37,41,42,44,
    47,48,49,52,54,55,72,
84,107,118,122,132,136,143,
145,152,161,164,165,167
Anthony 1,6,8,46,56,155,
    163,173,174
Appleton 46,57,102,124,147
Archer 8,21,33,34,35,37,43,
    54,56,64,122,125,127,
    129,137,140,149,150,
    155,172
Argo 111,137,143,155,163
Armstrong 8,20,54,55,95
Arp 9,16
Asbel (See Asbell)

Asbell 8,9,10,32,46,54,88,96,
    125,129,174,
Asbill (See Asbell)
Asburn 108
Ashmore 8,10,23,45,56,58,
    59,88,93,103
Askew 54,55,156,164
Aswell 11
Atkison (See Atkinson)
Atkinsdon 6,65,127,131,135
Aultom 114
Austin 8

B

Bacy 107
Badgett 147,176
Bailey 9,12,21,22,23,31,33,
    43,54,77,78,90,93,
    102,111,117,129,131,
    132,143,149,155,159,
    161,173,177
Baker 9,54,119
Baldwin 8,33,54,92
Bankhead 14,42,43,44
    47,64,72
Barlar (See Barlow)
Barlow 129
Barnes 8,75
Barnett 79,115,118
Bassham 2,124
Bealer (See Beeler)
Beeler 49,54,69,80,98,111,
    116,119,123,125,127,
    135,137,139,141,149,
    159,161
Bell 54
Bennett 158
Bennurm (See Benum)
Benum 125,134
Bentley 92,121
Bergin 15,30,55
Berryhill 155,159
Billingsly 3
Binum (See Benum)
Bird 5,10,13,17,21,33,44,
    57,86,97,132,136,162
Birdsong 46,56,69,80,84,168
Blackard 8,21,32,33,44,46,
    47,48,49,54,55,88,
    99,132,136
Blackburn 61,65,74
Blassingham 56

Blythe 12,16,21,22,25,32,33,
34,35,36,37,40,42,43,
45,46,52,56,60,61,62,
64,88,109,115,124,
149,155,163
Bocy 106
Bogard 36,41,46,47,48,49,
50,52,56,62,84,
90,158
Boguard (See Bogard)
Boid 9
Bolds 8
Booker 33,59,121
Bowdy 148,158,175
Bowdery (See Bowdy)
Brace 17
Bramlet 46
Brandon 1,21,30
Brashears 8,21,54,57,78,86,
96,98,106,109,111,
115,124,132,137,
149,156,163,173,
174,177
Brewer 2,55,56,80,98,106,
137,146,149,159
Britton 119
Broadstreet 1,6,8,15,18,21,
31,32,45,55,72,
90,94,120
Bromley 21, 56,172
Brumly (See Bromley)
Brooks 2,5,10,12,16,17,18,25,
27,28,34,35,38,39,40,
45,47,48,52,56,59,60,
78,80,89,90,107,177
Brown 8,32,46,54,75,77,81,
86,88,93,103,104,106,
110,111,112,116,117,
122,123,124,126,128,
130,131,132,133,137
141,142,145,148,150;
155,161,163,165,173,
177,178
Bryan 8
Bryant 45,56,58,113,140,
158,159,172
Bryon 75
Buchanan 1,9,22,31,32,50,54,
73,77,78,85,87,95,
101,102,105,107,109,
112,114,131,135,143,
153,157,176,177,178
Bumpass 1,6,9,10,12,14,15,17,
21,22,23,30,46,49,55,
58,60,64,67,71,78,81,
86,96,98,101,107,108,
112,114,124,135,140,
143,146,147,148,152,

Bumpass (cont.) 162,167,
168,171,176,177
Burgin 9,13,15,16,18,109,
146
Burgan (See Burgin)
Burk 134,161
Burleson 46,56,177
Burleston (See Burleson)
Burns 2,8,30,55,56,95,139,
140,147,148,149,158,
161,163,170,176,
Burris 8,46,56,73,76,92,
108,141,153,177

Burress (See Burris)
Burrow 55,89
Busby 56,151,153,157,164,
172,
Bynam 55, 57,125,127,129
Bynum (See Bynam)
Byrd 136
Byrne 8

C

Calp 124
Campbell 17,55,57,78,90,
94,96,124,147
Canada 56,125
(See also Kanada)
Canida (See Canada,Kanada)
Carcothers 43
Carr 56
Carrau 57
Caruthers 7
Casey 21,45,54,58,68
Cash 63,66
Cates 130
Cessims 124,177
(See also Sessums)
Chaffin 1,6,8,21,45,55,
58,77,88,89,93,
94,95,96,97,98,
105,106,107,111,
112,114,116,118,
123,124,125,126,
128,130,131,132,
134,137,141,142,
145,148,156,160,
177,178
Chambers 55
Choat 1,3,5,6,9,10,11,13,
14,15,18,28,45,55,
58,59,71,72,73,76,
108,109,125,137,149,
151,161
Christian 45,56,58,59,
78,147,153

Chronister 21, 33,43,56,
69, 75,80,81,
88,134,148,155,
160,163,165,166,
170,173,174,177
Cisemon 135
Clack 2,4,8,12,17,18
Clacks (See Clack)
Clain 83
Clifton 94,125,137,149,
159,176
Cobb 31,46,77,113
Cobbs (See Cobb)
Coblern 150
Cockburn 53
Cockran 56
Coffee 43
Colbert 134,155
Cole 22
Connell 111
Conner 96
Cooch 13,89
Cook 4,54,59,61,62,64,
68,108,114,116,119,
126,134,137,149,
154,159,164,167,170
Cooper 2,30,57,58,72,
77,86,89,91,124,
132,136,
Cottle 10,11
Counce 29,38,56,59,64,
80,81,85,98,114,
132,136
Counts 8,42,48,108,116,
Cowan 9,34,37,55
Cowen (See Cowan)
Cox 111
Craig 168
Crawford 156
Crisp 8,10,21,23,34,34,
35,45,46,55,58,77,
78,79,81,84,85,88,
89,91,93,96,97,98,
100,104,106,110,
112,113,118,123,
124,125,126,128,
131,134,136,138,
141,143,145,146,
148,149,155,165,
166,170,171,173,
174,175,177,178
Crockett 1,2,3,5,6,21,22,
23,30,32,34,41,
44,45,47,48,49,
50,54,55,61,66,
67,68,69,84,94,

Crockett 105,107,117,127,132,
142,151,153,160,162,164,170,
173,178
Cronister (See Chronister)
Crosswaite 93,134,137,146
Crostwaite (See Crosswaite)
Croswhite 94
Crowson 146,162
Crumley 57
Crutcher 32,157
Cunningham 9,54,56,69,78,82,
83,86,89,91,96,
98,111,115,118,
120,124,135,137,
138,143,146,149,
150,159,175,177
Curnel 129
Curtis 155
Cuthbert 4
Cutbirth 3,7,160

D

Dale 54
Dalton 47,48,49,55,69,86,
117,122,125,133,137
Daughtery 83
Davidson 102
Davis 4,30,54,78,106,111,
112,120,174,178
Day 1,2,3,5,7,20,21,22,23,
26,30,32,34,41,44,45,
46,47,50,54,57,58,61,
66,67,68,71,73,76,77,
78,79,81,84,85,88,89,
91,93,95,96,97,98,100,
104,106,110,111,112,
114,116,118,123,124,
125,126,128,131,132,
134,137,142,145,148,
155,157,160,165,177,178
Denton 56
Depriest 55,69,110,114,119,
137,146,155,164,
167,171,172,173,
176,
Dickson 20,67
Dicus 160
Dillingham 9
Dixon 24,30
Dods 129
Dollams 12
Dollens 48
Donalson 154
Dotan 114
Downs 21,57

Drennan 111, 139, 143,
Duncan 9, 33, 37, 41, 54, 58, 60,
68, 71, 78, 81, 87, 89, 91,
125, 127, 129, 135, 137,
147, 149, 159, 177
Duck 8
Duckworth 21, 33, 56, 109, 115,
119
Duly 150

E

Early 125
Edminston 21, 23
Edmonson 9, 10, 22, 32, 53, 55,
60, 69, 70, 98, 99,
106, 117, 129, 132,
136, 139, 143, 148,
153, 159, 164, 172,
Edmundson (See Edmonson)
Edmundston (See Edmonson)
Edwards 6, 8, 43, 45, 51, 55, 58,
59, 72, 73, 76, 92, 94, 155, 163, 166
Egnew 81
(See also Askew)
Elfalvington 117
(See also Heffington)
Ellison 46
Ennis 119
Ervin 52, 90
Erwin (See Ervin)
Etherage 5, 10, 17, 32, 46, 54,
86, 88
Ethrodge (See Etherage)
Ethridge (See Etherage)
Evans 9, 10, 14, 21, 23, 33, 54, 154

F

Farmer 1, 5, 7, 8, 10, 11, 13, 14,
15, 16, 17, 20, 22, 23, 30,
32, 35, 36, 37, 44, 45, 46,
48, 49, 50, 56, 59, 67, 72,
76, 90, 100, 103, 108, 109,
117, 132, 134, 136, 156
Ferguson 8, 10, 16
Ficcle 139, 152
Fickle (See Ficcle)
Fifer 2, 124
(See also Fisher ?)
Fisher 57, 127, 129,
Flannery 46, 56, 77, 88, 93, 96,
105, 110, 115, 124,
137, 148, 155
Flatt 8, 78
Fondas 110

Fondren 87
Fonland 57
Fonlin 57
Forbes 1, 2, 3, 4, 5, 7, 10, 11,
14, 20, 23, 24, 25, 29,
30, 34, 37, 40, 54, 76,
77, 86, 88, 95, 128, 178
Forgy 173
Foster 8, 56, 69, 75, 80, 84,
115, 119, 129, 132,
136, 151, 159,
Franks 9, 12, 54, 58, 72, 115,
118, 166
Freemon 158, 167
Frigate 17
Fuefason 5 (See Ferguson)
Fugate 34, 43, 69, 80, 81, 92,
137, 149, 159
Futtrell 54, 69, 80, 111

G

Gabels 88
Gable 21
Gabriel 2, 45, 56
Gaither 8, 21, 55, 58, 71, 78,
89, 94, 132, 134, 136
Gambrell 54, 57, 93, 94,
124, 161
Gardner 31, 67
Garner 81, 161
Garrison 56, 69
George 136
Gilchrist 46, 129
Gill 137, 138, 149, 159
Gist 1, 2, 3, 5, 7, 11, 20, 22,
23, 30, 45, 46, 56, 67,
68, 76, 77, 86, 88, 103,
105, 106, 115, 137, 148,
Goff 38
Goforth 9, 25, 56, 88, 146
Gogue 55
Goodman 85, 99
Gorrell 56
Gosnal (See Gosnell)
Gosnell 57, 98, 106, 155, 164,
167, 171, 173
Graham 3, 10, 13, 23, 34, 37, 55
Gray 52, 54, 178
Grayham 8, 12, 36
Green 8, 20, 24, 41, 44, 55, 57,
67, 72, 73, 128
Gresham 9, 10, 23, 25, 26, 27,
31, 33, 35, 38, 40,
Grisham 41, 42, 52, 53, 54, 58,
60, 62, 64, 66, 71,

Grisham, cont, 77,78,82,
87,88,105,107,
109,111,115,
120,126,137,139,
143,149,155,159,
161,170,173,
Grimes 9,22,54,78,99,108,
110,114,126,129,140
Groves 60,168
Guest 1,22,30
Guin 9,52
Guinn (See Guin)

H

Hackney 50
Hail 2,5,7,8,10,17,30,34,
55,66,69,72,73,75,
77,94
Haile 109,115,126,134,
140,147,151,153,
156,161,164,176,
177,178
Hale 23, 43
Halford 9,23,53,55,61,
65,69,77,89,
95,96,98,100,
102,106,110,115,
120,122,125,129,
131,136,144,147,
148,149,152,155,
156,158,168,170,
171,173,174
Hamilton 9,26,37,41,42,
55,69,81,98,
116,137,165
Hammonds (See Hammons)
Hammons 109,115,125,
147,155
Hanks 4,5,7,9,12,21,22,
23,26,30,42,45,54,
57,58,63,65,71,79,
88,111,115,119,123,
127,134,166,175
Hardin 135
Haris 5,8,10
Harris (See Haris)
Harlson 2
Harrison 8,50,54,80,81,
89,91
Hawkins 129
Hayes 5,10,17,21,23,33,35,
36,37,44,84,129,135
Hays (See Hayes)

Haynes 9,54,58,71,73,76,78
105,108,111,115,
155,163,174.
Hearldson 55,56
Hearlson (See Heraldson)
Heffington 56
Heifly 111,132,135,164,167
Helton 1,2,6,8,26,33,39,41,
45,54,58,59,62,64,
72,82,83,94,100,106,
137,149,159,164,
172,177
Hembleton 116,164
Henderson 31,45,58,94,117,
118,155,157,163
Henry 8,45,54,60,61,62,64,
76,82,117,136
Hensley 57,78,89,91,96,98,
124,125
Hinsley (See Hensley)
Henson 54,55,156,167,171
Herly 60,64,125,127,129
Hickman 69
Higgs 9,10,11,13,14,15,18,
22,26,33,34,43,46,54,
58,60,64,71,73,76,78,
81,82,83,84,87,88,90,
98,100,102,107,111,
114,115,117,119,120,
122,124,129,161,177
Hightower 98,138
Hill 52,54,59,69,75,80,88,
93,96,98,103,105,111,
114,120,121,123,124,
133,145,148,151,153,
160,164,177
Hillhouse 1,2,3,4,5,6,10,
14,20,22,23,24,
29,33,46,54,56,
69,76,77,78,81,
84,86,88,89,91,
93,95,96,98,106,
108,111,112,114,
116,118,123,124,
125,126,127,132,
134,136,141,142,
145,148,149,150,
155,158,160,
174,178
Hillis 45
Hinson (See Henson)
Hogan 101
Hogg 45,54,135
Holcomb 33

Holland 5,32,45,56,58,59,73,76,
         89,98,108,129,141,142,
         149,177,178
Hollen   116,118,128,135,137,178
Holloway 16,55,72,73,76,124
Holt   78,162
Horn   94
Horton   77
Houston 136,140,164
         (See also Huston)
Howard   8,56,108,111,114,118,
         127,129,131,133,137,
         138,146,157,166
Hughs   5,8,45,54,55,114,133,149,
         151,153,156,158,160
Hughston 142
Hunt   55,88
Hunter   2,7,50,87,132
Hurley   45,56,58,61,68
Huston   84,94,102,109,115,119,
         132,138,141,151,153
         (See also Houston)
Hutchinson 56

I

Inman   8,55,95,109,116,119,138,
         144,146
Irvine   1,4,7,9,14,17,19,20,24,
         30,43,45,46,47,48,49,50,
         54,57,62,67,68,72,76,84,
         87,88,94,96,101,102,105,
         111,113,114,122,129,131,
         160, 173,177
Irwin   10
Isham   56
Isom   5,32,46,88,99,110,124,
         147,148,177
Issax   8

J

Jack   8,10,23,32,46,54,
Jackson 6,10,11,57,78,82,88,93,
         105,115,124,128,148,
         163,165,166,169,170,
         173
Jenchers 78
Jenkins 66,103,134
Jincans (See Jenkins)
Jernigan 76
Jernak   10,11,12,14
Jobe   15,19,30,31,45,54,56,58,
         77,110,119,125,132,136,
         138,140,141,167,171,173
         177

Johnson 5,56,58,66,69,72,
         98,106,132,147,
Johnston 10,123,155,163
Jones   9,13,21,36,54,55,58,
         71,72,80,86,88,91,
         111,134,136,138,147,
         155,167,

K

Kanada   78,88,125,143,147,
         155,163
Kanday   (See Kanada, Canada
Keese   22,23,35,45,46,47,48
         49,52,54,58,59,63,64
         71,72,73,81,111,118,
         124,129,137,149,159
Kese   (See Keese)
Kelly   114,117,145
Keltner 8,26,36,55,82
Kelton   60
Kemenester 149
Kendrick 8,48,49,56,58,61,
         65,72,74,87,89,94
         103,117,118,125,
         126,137,149,151,
         153,157,160,171,
         173,177
Kenfrich 78
Kennedy 56,125
Kerley   8
Kewis   115 (See Lewis)
Keyes   1,6,9,10,16,32,34
Keys   (See Keyes)
Kilbreath 9 (See Gilbreath
Kilburn 8,54,95,134,147,16
Killen   44
King   9,21,55,99,171
Kirk   74
Kirksey 51,55
Kutch   58,69,89

L

Lafferty 138,139,143,150,
         157,165
Lancaster 56
Langley 83
Lanier   108
Lenear   130
Lemaster 165
Lemenster 150
Lensday (See Lindsey)
Lester   53

Lewis 5,10,17,69,80,87,
       98,116,123,146,155,
       164,166,173,178
Linam 111
Lindsey 8,10,23,30,32,46,
         54,56,58,72,73,
         76,78,90,92,95,
         114,124,135,140,
         147,164,177,178
Linsy (See Lindsey)
Little 130
Lockard 3,7,8,10,17,21,
         23, 32,34,37,46,
         56,60,75,140,142
Lochard (See Lockard)
Long 56
Lucas 5,9,10,11,22,45,
       46,55,58,69,77,
       78,85,86,87,88,
       93,95,96,98,100,
       105,111,112,114,
       120,124,135,137,
       145,146,147,148,
       155,163,165,170,
       173,174,176,177

M

Mabery 5,8,97,107,144
Maberry (See Mabery)
Mackey 42,43,51,53
Macy 29
Maples 23
Marcum 138
Martin 171
Mason 2,3,5,7,8, 12,18,
       25,32,34,35,37,45,
       46,47,48,52,53,55,
       58,60,62,64,65,72,
       84,87,90,92,94,98,
       108,111,121,125,
       129,132,137,149,
       169,173,177
Mathews 1,5,6,9,10,11,
         12,15,18,19,20,
         21,29,30,33, 34,
         35,36,37,39,41,
         46,47,48,49,55,
         69,87,99,105,
         111,114,136,140,
         160,170,
Matthews (See Mathews)
Mathis 3,30
May 7,21,33,43,55,88,98,
     106,108,165

Mayes (See May)
Mayfield 67
Maxy 85
Meardy 74
Melton 21,32,33,42,44,46,56
        79,88,98,109,115,126,
        132,136,149,155,158,
        161,163,165,172,
        173,174
Merchant 132,136,137
Merryman 98,108,
Michie 133,139,143,149,
        151,159,172
Mickey 61,62,68
Miller 1,23,32,35,46,54,
        69,84,88,94,98,106,
        115,118,124,137,
        139,164
Millner 5
Mitchel 5,8,54,55,56,111,
         137,145,156,161,
         163,173,174
Mitchell (See Mitchel)
Mobley 155,163,174
Montgomery 4,6,9,54,102,
            109,111,
Moody 57,72,74,78,96,110,
       124,170,177
Moor 23
Moore 5,8,10,17,109,115,
       119,124,138,147,148,
       163,177
Morgan 56,116
Morphis 65
Morrow 10,23,45,55,56,58,
        59,69,109,114,
        116,118,146
Mosley 22,47,69,121
Mumford 101,129
Murphy 94,143
Musgrave 8,54,69,72,73,84,
          116,158,161

Mc

McAnnally 21,33,43,55,82,
           88,95,134,137,
           139,147,148,
           156,159
McAnala (See McAnnally)
McBride 56
McCan 1,13,15,16,18,26,35,
       41,54,61,80,82,83,84,
       88,98,106,115,125,127
       129,142,164
McCann (See McCan)

McCannally 149,177
  (See also McAnnally)
McCarely 55
McClain 47,116,156,164,170
McClaren 45,57,59,69,77,78,
  116,124,128,140,156
McClarine 155,158,172,173,
  174,177
McClary 105,116,123,133,176
McClendon 9,13,15,16,18,33,
  41,52,54,58,60,71,
  98,107,111,115,118,
  126,129,136,141,142,
  147,151,153,156,164,
  167,173,174,177,178
McClish 45,56,58,59,66,80,83,
  108,167,168,169,130
McLish (See McClish)
McClure 66
McComick 39
McCommac 38
McConnell 1,5,6,8,10,23,32,46,
  54,67,84,86,98,99,
  106,117,122,149,164,
  177
McCory 115
McCue 83,109
McDonald 7,9,22,26,34,54,69,
  78,80,91,98,106,111,
  113,132
McDuffie 92,94,137,149
McDuffy (See McDuffie)
McFalls 57,94,147
McGee 8,22,98,113,134,178
McGuire 168,169,170
McHughs 35,37,43,54,55,170,173
McIntire 1,2,3,4,5,6,7,8,10,11,
  12,14,15,16,18,20,21,
  23,24,25,27,28,30,33,
  34,36,37,38,39,40,41,
  44,45,46,47,48,50,53,
  55,56,57,58,59,60,61,
  66,67,69,71,72,73,76,
  77,78,79,80,88,89,94,
  167
McIntyre (See McIntire)
McKee 129
McKenady 87
McKew 8,36,91
McKinney 55,95,161,167
McKinsey 134
McKnight 176,177
McLaughlin 8
McLean 174
McLowren 80

McMahan 44,65
McMilliam (See McMillian)
McMillian 5,8,10,11,14,15,
  18,43,57,163,177
McRee 155,159
McRely 57
McWhorton 2,57

N

Nail 54,78,89,91,97,107,13
Needham 5,8,77
Nelson 9,21,35,54,58,112,
  145,149,150
Newton 125,162,177
Nichols 124
Ninesly 124(See Hinsly)
Nipper 98,100,124
Norman 179
Null 7,8,23,24,34,37,42,
  46,50,51,57,61,64,
  84,92,113,124,138,164

O

Oliver 118
Ozbourn 116,
Oxford 57,124

P

Page 54
Paine 6,72,98,114,116,
  125,132,135,136,
  137,148,159
  (See also Payne)
Parchman 8,9,16,24,30,35,
  36,37,56,60,65,
  94,98,112,135,
  143,153,159,175
Parchment 14
Parker 65,87,124
Parkes 2,5,8
Pascal 54
Pashel 64
Patterson 124
Patton 49
Payne 55,58,60,78,81,86,
  101,107,136,146,
  147,149,164,171,173
Pearce 6,21,35,36,37,43,
  46,55,57,68,115,11
Pierce 137,149
Pennicuff 2,77,88,105,110
  112,114,148,165
Pennycuff (See Pennicuff)

Pennington 1,6,8,21,26,32,
            45,46,52,56,58,
            60,64,69,74,80,
            82,85,88,94,97,
            110,114,124,
            132,134,136,147,
            151,153,177
Peoples 56
Perkins 56
Perrimore 87
Perry 140
Pevihous 94,127,136
Phenix 9,54,67,69,88,
        105,135,177
Phoanix 21,22,32,33,34,
         43,45
Phillips 5,6,8,10,17,35,
          36,37,43,45,54,
          55,60,62,64,
          125,158,164,169
Pickard 78
Pickens 4,5,22,23,30,33,
         46,57,86
Pierce 21,32,33
        (See Pearce)
Pilburn 27
Pitchford 56
Plumer 62
Poleer 57
Poley 9,13,37,55,89,91
Polly (See Poley)
Pollock 56,131,136
Pope 56,124
Porter 148(See Poter)
Poteet 57,77,78,85,86,87,
        88,94,97,147,148,
        155,163,165,166,
        170,173,174,175
Poter 166,171,173,178
Powel 119,126
Prewitt 9,46,54,55,58,71,
         77,78,86,91,96,
         97,98,105,107,110,
         124,135,146,148,
         155,161
Price 5,8,10,23,43,48,55,
       60,94,136
Prier 57,171
Prince 111
Pritchett 57
Pryor 68,172
Purvard 23

Q

Quilleen 80,92

Quilling 56
Quimby 77,78,99,113,143,
        155,158,163

R

Rackley 8,22,54,58,78,80,
         84,86,89,91,98,
         106,108,129,137,
         149,166
Ragsdale 9
Ramsey 48,153
Ray 10,11,14,20,23,24,25,
     29,30,56,58,93,94,98,
     103,137,155,163,173,
     174
Rea (See Rhea and Ray)
Rhea 4,21,22,24,30,46,178
Reece 167
Renolds 8,37,54,55,58,72,
         76,86,95,103,109,
         112,123,140,142,
         150,164,156,176
Reynolds (See Renolds)
Rice 54
Richardson 45
Richmond 59
Rickman 45, 57
Roberson 109
Robertson 134,143,161,177,
Rodgers 1,2,6,14,30,43,46,
         55,67,68,77,84,94,
         98,106,126,134,
         135,153,154,158,
         161,166,168,171
Rogers (See Rodgers)
Roland 8,21,33,55,58,91,
        98,115,119,126,145.
        155,163
Rollen 89
Rollins 22,86,108
Rose 1
Ross 1,6,8,10,21,22,23,24,
      55,69,75,82,83,92,94,
      98,106,138
Rowland 31,33,41,54,145,146
Rowlins 28
Russell 121

S

Sandusky 127
Santa Anna 67
Scoles 106,111,116,118,161
Scott 54,95,111,118

Seahorn 30,32,46,47,56,74,75,
         87,94,105,110,134,
         147,177
Sealy 54,58,69,81,87,111,
Sellars 56,103,114,136,
         141,156,163
Selly 46
Sessums 123 (See Cessims)
Shadrack 56
Shall 158
Sharp 1,2,5,7,21,22,23,26,30,
       32,34,41,45,46,47,50,
       53,54,57,58,60,61,66,
       69,71,73,75,76,77,78,
       79,80,81,84,85,86,87,
       88,89,90,91,94,95,96,
       97,98,100,104,109,111,
       112,115,117,119,124,
       132,139,142,146,147,
       148,149,150,157,160,
       161,163,177
Shaw 108,111,149,155,158,
Sherly 5,8,9,19,23,26,29,
        33,43,47,48,49,55,
        56,59,68,69,78,81,
        93,94,98,99,108,166
Shirley (See Sherly)
Shipman 56
Shurkley 12
Siesmon 134
Silers 93
Sims 56,76,
Simmons 57
Simonton 2,5,6,8,47,48,49,
          55,56,60,69,87,
          94,177
Simpson 54
Sinclair 5,6,8,10,17,23,41,
          54,59,64,72,73,75
Sinclear 82(See also Sinclair)
Sisemon 135
Sizemore 57,78,88,105,109,
          111,124
Sisemore (See Sizemore)
Smallwood 21,57,58,71,87,93,
           94,96,99,116,162
Smelyer 69
Smith 3,5,8,9,10,17,18,24,27,
       52,54,55,56,57,67,69,
       82,83,88,95,96,97,107,
       133,136,137,138,142,
       144,149,151,153,156,
       158,163,169,177
Snodgrass 98,106,124
Spain 173

Spears 24,54,56,57,69,155
Speck 166,170
Spencer 2,7,10,33,57,58,
         62,94,133,136,149,
         167
Spillars 142
Springer 98,106,147,162
Steel 98, 147,148
Stewart 9,54,57,58,78,79,
         97,125,148,155,
         158,160
Stinson 8,94,102
Stockard 9,10
Stockart (See Stockard)
Stoddert 7
Stockton 95,111,114,119,
          122,135,147,161
Stone 21,26,33,36,39,42,
       43,55
Story 8,54,47,64
Straughn 5,10,46,54
Strawn 6,8,23,31,69,72,84,
        92,97,99,113,123,
        127,133,161
Stribling 73,111
Strickland 8,38,88,132
Stricklin 5,20,56,68,69,
           94,113,149,150
Strickling (See Stricklin)
Sullivan 8,12,21,23,43,
          54,71,98
Sullivant 71,118,125,142
Sutton 134
Swaford 57,87,92,96,98,
         102,124,137,149
Swafford (See Swaford)
Swain 55,86,88
Swan 94,109,115,119,125
Swanson 116

T

Tacker 69,80,88,99
Tally 8,10,23,54,55
Tancerly 67
Tankersly 33,53
Taylor 4,5,15,18,25,28,
        29,94
Tease 32,46,56,
Terrell 123,155,178
Thomas 32,45,46,47,48,49,
        52,54,58,60,62,64,
        108,111,115,119,
        122,159,167,171,
        175,176

Thornton 28,35,38,40,47
Tipet 3,9,13,14,16,95,98,
       101,106,116,117,125,
       130,131,141,151,152,
       164,166,168,171,178
Tippett (See Tipet)
Tipton 140,142,144,145,
       148,149,150,168
Tinsley 90
Tracey 6,21,55,107,108,
       109,160
Trantham 9,49,55,
Tripp 5,32,57,69,112,172
Tucker 8,55,58,72,73,76,
       161,177
Turnbow 21,57,166,177

U

NONE

V

Vance 77,78
Vandiver 1,2,6,7,8,56,94,
       118,161
Vandover 21,32,44,78
Venable 114,150
Vincent 150
Voriss 8,69,116,135,167
Voras, Vorus,Vorous(See
Voriss and Vorees)
Vorees 32,46,55,77,80,98
Vorter 177
Voss 1,2,6,7,8,33,41,47,
       48,49,56,69,81,84,
       85,86,87,88,89,91,
       93,95,96,98,100,103,
       127,137,141,149,177

W

Waggoner 124
Waldrup 171
Walker 55,57,109,115,119,
       125
Wallace 2,8,10,56,57,69,
       80,125
Wallis 125,148
Wankins 124
Ward 57,132,141,170,173
Warren 5,8,14,15,19
Wasen 132,135,136,176
Wayne 121
Weathers 136

Weaver 69,80,97,112
Webb 8,34,36,60
Webster 57
Welch 1,2,3,5,6,7,8,9,10,
       11,12,13,14,15,18,21,
       23,32,37,38,42,44,48,
       50,54,55,58,59,60,64,
       65,66,67,69,72,76,77,
       79,80,82,83,84,85,91,
       92,94,98,99,105,107,
       110,114,116,118,119,
       123,125,130,132,135,
       137,139,146,148,152,
       153,157,166,171,173,
       177,178
Wells 141
Wester 127
Wharton 5,8,30,42,51,52,55,
       58,59,72,88,95,96,
       105,129,137,143
Whorton (See Wharton)
White 3,6,7,9,22,23,45,46,
       58,64,78,80,80,126,
       128,133,136,144,149,
       153,166,177
Whitley 6,13,69,89
Wiley 12
Williams 56,57,80,81,94,100,
       107,125,132,136,
       145,177,178
Willis 47
Willson 155,163,173,174
Winn 161
Wisdom 1,2,3,4,5,8,13,16,
       23,29,30,32,34,35,
       36,37,41,43,45,46,
       47,50,53,54,55,57,
       58,59,60,61,66,67,
       68,69,71,73,76,77,
       80,84,85,86,87,88,
       89,91,93,95,98,99,
       103,105,106,111,115,
       126,130,137,143,148,
       149,156,,60,163,174,
       175,177,178
Wise 55,109,139,142
Withers 124,171
Wolf 54,55,98,109,137,138,
       140,141
Wolfe (See Wolf)
Woodruff 56,66,67
Woods 159
Woolsey 21,57,109,115,
       132,136,162,177
Wolsey (See Woolsey)

Wooten 21,33,41,55,98
Wooton (See Wooten)
Worden 162
Wynn 8,160
Winn (See Wynn)

X

NONE

Y

Yarnel 167
Yelington 127,129
Yelvington (See Yellington)
Yewmans 56
Young 56,147

Z

NONE

www.ingramcontent.com/pod-product-compliance
Lightning Source LLC
Chambersburg PA
CBHW030551080526
44585CB00012B/343